Ethics in Data Science

Preface

In an age where data is hailed as the new oil, the responsibility that comes with handling it has never been more significant. The growing reliance on algorithms, artificial intelligence, and machine learning in critical decision-making processes has placed data science at the heart of societal transformation. While these advances open doors to innovation and efficiency, they also raise profound ethical questions about fairness, transparency, accountability, and privacy.

This book was born out of a desire to explore these pressing concerns. As researchers and practitioners in the field, we have often encountered situations where technical solutions clashed with ethical boundaries. These experiences underscored the need for a deeper, more structured reflection on how data is used, shared, and interpreted in today's interconnected world.

The purpose of this work is not to prescribe a rigid set of rules, but rather to encourage thoughtful dialogue and critical engagement with the ethical dimensions of data science. Whether you are a student beginning your journey in analytics, a professional grappling with real-world dilemmas, or an academic seeking a comprehensive overview, this book aims to provide both clarity and challenge.

Throughout the chapters, we have strived to balance theory with practical insights, and reflection with action. Ethics in data science is not just about avoiding harm—it's about proactively ensuring that our technological progress contributes to a more just and equitable society.

We hope this book serves as a useful guide and a catalyst for further conversations. As the field evolves, so must our understanding of what it means to be responsible stewards of data.

— Dr. Ranjitha M, Ms. Divya M O

Contents

Course Objective

The objectives of the course are to,

1. Understand and critically examine the ethical dimensions and responsibilities inherent in data science.
2. Explore various moral and philosophical frameworks relevant to ethical decision-making in data collection, analysis, and usage.
3. Learn best practices for safeguarding sensitive data, ensuring user privacy, and maintaining security infrastructure.
4. Identify and address bias and unfairness in data and algorithmic systems, promoting equity and inclusivity.
5. Develop the ability to explain and audit AI and machine learning models to ensure transparency and accountability.
6. Examine the ethical implications of automation, autonomous systems, and the potential for displacement of human labor.
7. Understand the legal and regulatory frameworks guiding ethical data science practices at local and global levels.
8. Learn from real-world case studies to foster ethical reflection and apply principles to practical scenarios.
9. Promote a culture of ethical awareness within organizations and teams engaged in data science work.
10. Prepare for future challenges and innovations by building resilient, ethically aligned data-driven systems.

Course Outcomes

After successful completion of this course, students will be able to:

1. Articulate the significance of ethics in data science and its impact on individuals, society, and organizations.
2. Apply moral reasoning and ethical frameworks to real-world dilemmas involving data-driven technologies.
3. Implement responsible data collection methods, ensuring informed consent, transparency, and voluntary participation.

4. Design and maintain secure data systems that protect personal and confidential information in accordance with best practices and legal requirements.
5. Detect, evaluate, and mitigate algorithmic bias, ensuring fairness and avoiding discriminatory outcomes.
6. Improve the explainability and interpretability of AI models, enabling users and stakeholders to understand and trust automated decisions.
7. Recognize the ethical boundaries of automation and AI, including concerns around self-learning systems and human role replacement.
8. Ethically manage and share data in collaborative and open environments, respecting ownership and original context.
9. Reflect on ethical failures in the industry and develop strategies to build more responsible and transparent data systems.
10. Align organizational practices with ethical standards and legal regulations while fostering continuous ethical learning among data professionals.

Chapter 1: Introduction to Ethical Concerns in Data Science

Learning Outcomes

1. Explain why ethics is essential in data science and recognize the impact of data-driven decisions on individuals and society.
2. Describe key ethical principles such as fairness, transparency, accountability, privacy, and beneficence, and apply them to real-world data science scenarios.
3. Do critical evaluation on ethical dilemmas in data projects, understand challenges like bias and lack of transparency, and use ethical decision-making frameworks to guide responsible practices.

Introduction

In an increasingly data-driven world, the practice of data science is no longer a purely technical endeavor. It is a domain deeply entangled with ethical, societal, and human values. The decisions made by data scientists and the systems they build can shape economies, influence public opinion, and affect the lives of millions. As such, engaging critically with the ethical implications of data science is not a luxury—it is a necessity.

This chapter lays the foundation for understanding the ethical concerns that arise in data science. It outlines the key concepts, challenges, and questions that professionals must grapple with, and it highlights why ethical considerations are essential to the practice of responsible data science.

1.1 The Ethical Dimension of Data

Data, in itself, may appear neutral. However, the processes through which it is generated, collected, interpreted, and applied are deeply embedded in human choices and societal structures. Ethics in data science refers to the values and principles guiding these processes, ensuring that they are aligned with social good, justice, and individual rights.

In practical terms, this means evaluating not only what we can do with data, but what we should do. The distinction between these two questions is at the heart of ethical inquiry. When a dataset is available, should we use it? If an algorithm can predict behavior, should it influence decision-making? Ethical concerns arise wherever data is used to make judgments, allocate resources, or shape opportunities.

1.2 Why Ethics Matters More Than Ever

The increasing ubiquity of data science applications magnifies their impact. Algorithms are now used to determine creditworthiness, diagnose diseases, select job candidates, and inform criminal sentencing. These decisions, once made by humans with contextual understanding and moral reasoning, are now influenced by models trained on historical data.

The challenge is that historical data often reflects systemic biases. If not addressed, these biases can become embedded in algorithms, perpetuating inequality rather than reducing it. For example, if loan approval systems are trained on data from a bank that historically denied loans to certain demographics, the resulting model may unjustly continue this trend.

Beyond bias, ethical concerns extend to privacy violations, manipulation of behavior through targeted content, and the opacity of decision-making processes. As systems grow more complex and autonomous, their inner workings become harder to interpret, creating what is often referred to as the "black box" problem.

Furthermore, as data collection becomes more pervasive, the risk of surveillance increases. Many individuals are unaware of how their data is collected, used, and shared. This lack of transparency and control can undermine trust in institutions and technologies.

1.3 Key Ethical Principles in Data Science

Several guiding principles have emerged as foundational to ethical data science:

- **Fairness**: Ensuring that data-driven decisions do not result in discriminatory outcomes. This involves identifying and mitigating bias in both datasets and algorithms.
- **Transparency**: Making systems understandable and decisions explainable to users and stakeholders. This includes being open about data sources, model assumptions, and limitations.

- **Accountability**: Holding developers, organizations, and institutions responsible for the outcomes of their data systems. This requires clear governance structures and the ability to audit and redress harmful impacts.
- **Privacy**: Respecting individuals' rights to control their personal information. Data minimization, informed consent, and secure data handling are central components.
- **Beneficence**: Striving to use data for the benefit of individuals and communities, and actively seeking to prevent harm.

These principles serve as a compass for ethical reflection and action, guiding data scientists as they navigate complex and often ambiguous situations.

1.4 Challenges to Ethical Practices

Despite broad agreement on ethical principles, implementing them in practice presents numerous challenges:

Ambiguity and Trade-offs Ethical dilemmas often involve competing values. For example, increasing transparency might conflict with preserving proprietary algorithms. Enhancing privacy might reduce the utility of a dataset for beneficial research. Navigating these trade-offs requires careful judgment and dialogue with stakeholders.

Bias and Representation Bias in data is often subtle and difficult to detect. It can stem from sampling errors, historical inequalities, or proxy variables that correlate with sensitive attributes like race or gender. Addressing bias requires technical solutions (such as fairness-aware algorithms) and broader reflection on the social context of data.

Lack of Ethical Infrastructure Many organizations lack formal structures to support ethical reflection. Deadlines, resource constraints, and market pressures can push ethical considerations to the sidelines. Integrating ethics into project planning, review processes, and team culture is essential.

Rapid Technological Change The fast pace of innovation often outpaces the development of ethical norms and legal regulations. New technologies emerge before society fully understands their implications. Ethical foresight—anticipating potential harms and designing with them in mind—is crucial.

1.5 The Role of the Data Scientist

Data scientists are not mere technicians; they are stewards of systems that affect real lives. As such, they have a responsibility to understand the ethical landscape of their work and to act with integrity.

This involves:

- Being aware of how their work intersects with social values and human rights.
- Engaging in continuous learning about ethics, law, and the societal impacts of technology.
- Advocating for ethical standards and practices within their organizations.
- Collaborating with ethicists, domain experts, and affected communities.

Empowering data scientists with the tools and support they need to navigate ethical challenges is key to building trustworthy and just technologies.

1.6 Frameworks for Ethical Decision-Making

Several frameworks have been developed to guide ethical decision-making in data science:

- **The Data Ethics Canvas** (Open Data Institute): A collaborative tool to identify potential ethical issues at every stage of a project.
- **FAT Framework**: Emphasizes Fairness, Accountability, and Transparency as core pillars of responsible AI.
- **IEEE Ethically Aligned Design**: Offers a comprehensive set of principles and guidance for designing ethically aligned autonomous systems.
- **Value-Sensitive Design**: An approach that integrates ethical values into technology design through stakeholder engagement and iterative reflection.

These tools help teams to structure conversations, document decisions, and reflect on the ethical dimensions of their work. They also provide mechanisms for accountability and stakeholder participation.

1.7 Embedding Ethics into the Data Lifecycle

Ethical considerations must be integrated into every phase of the data lifecycle:

- **Collection**: Are individuals aware of and consenting to data collection? Is the data necessary and proportionate to the purpose?
- **Processing**: Are steps taken to clean and preprocess data in ways that avoid reinforcing bias or erasing context?
- **Modelling**: Are the chosen models appropriate, fair, and interpretable? Are they tested against multiple fairness criteria?
- **Deployment**: Are systems monitored for unintended consequences? Is there a feedback mechanism for affected users?
- **Evaluation**: Are outcomes assessed not only for accuracy but also for ethical impact and social good?

Embedding ethics into each step ensures that concerns are addressed proactively, rather than as afterthoughts.

1.8 Case Study: Algorithmic Bias in Criminal Justice

A widely cited example of ethical concerns in data science is the use of predictive algorithms in the criminal justice system. Tools like COMPAS (Correctional Offender Management Profiling for Alternative Sanctions) have been used to assess the risk of recidivism among defendants.

Investigations revealed that these algorithms often over-predicted the risk of reoffending for Black defendants and under-predicted it for white defendants. Despite being trained on historical data, these models reinforced racial disparities present in the justice system.

This case underscores several ethical concerns:

- Lack of transparency in how scores are generated
- Absence of recourse for individuals affected by incorrect predictions
- Insufficient scrutiny of the data and modeling assumptions

It highlights the importance of fairness, transparency, and accountability, particularly when algorithms influence life-altering decisions.

1.9 Moving Towards a Culture of Ethical Data Science

Cultivating an ethical culture within data science requires commitment at multiple levels:

- **Individual**: Data scientists must take personal responsibility for ethical reflection and growth.
- **Organizational**: Companies and institutions must embed ethics into policies, practices, and incentives.
- **Societal**: Governments, civil society, and the public must play active roles in shaping the norms and regulations that guide data use.

Creating a culture of ethical data science means fostering open dialogue, encouraging critical thinking, and valuing long-term impact over short-term gains. It also involves recognizing that ethical challenges are not always clear-cut and that disagreement and debate are part of ethical maturity.

As this chapter has shown, ethics is not an optional add-on to the practice of data science—it is a core component of doing responsible, meaningful, and trustworthy work in the field. From the data we collect to the models we deploy, every stage of the data lifecycle carries the potential to impact individuals, communities, and society at large. These impacts can be positive, but without ethical foresight, they can also perpetuate harm, injustice, and inequality.

Understanding and applying ethical principles such as fairness, transparency, accountability, privacy, and beneficence is essential for navigating the complex, real-world dilemmas that arise in data projects. Challenges like bias, lack of transparency, and rapidly evolving technologies require data scientists to think critically, act conscientiously, and engage with diverse perspectives.

Ultimately, ethical data science is about more than just avoiding harm—it's about actively contributing to a more equitable and informed society. This begins with awareness, continues through structured frameworks and practices, and is sustained by a culture that values reflection, responsibility, and integrity. As we move forward, the role of the data scientist must expand to include not only technical expertise but also ethical leadership.

Summary

Ethics is foundational to data science in the 21st century. As data systems become more powerful and pervasive, the need for principled guidance grows stronger. Ethical data science requires more than good intentions—it demands deliberate, informed, and courageous action.

This chapter has explored the ethical landscape of data science, highlighting the key principles, challenges, and responsibilities that define ethical practice. In the chapters that follow, we will delve deeper into specific areas—such as privacy, bias, governance, and transparency—offering both theoretical insights and practical tools for navigating the complex terrain of ethical data work.

As stewards of data, we must strive not only for technical excellence but also for moral clarity. The future of data science depends on our ability to align innovation with justice, and progress with humanity.

Test your Understanding

Fill in the Blanks

1. Data science is deeply entangled with ethical, __________, and human values.
2. Ethical data science is not just a technical issue but also a __________ imperative.
3. Data, in itself, may appear __________, but its use reflects human choices.
4. The distinction between what we can do and what we __________ do is central to ethical inquiry.
5. Historical data can reflect systemic __________ if not carefully examined.
6. A common problem with complex models is the lack of __________ in their decision-making.
7. Respecting individuals' rights to control their information refers to the principle of __________.
8. Ensuring that algorithms do not produce discriminatory results falls under the principle of __________.
9. Making models understandable and decisions explainable reflects the principle of __________.
10. Holding developers and organizations responsible for outcomes demonstrates __________.
11. The ethical principle that seeks to do good and prevent harm is called __________.
12. Ambiguity in ethics often arises due to competing __________.
13. Bias can stem from historical inequalities and poor __________ methods.
14. Many organizations lack formal structures to support ethical __________.
15. Rapid technological change can outpace __________ and social norms.
16. Data scientists must act as __________ of systems that impact real lives.
17. The FAT framework stands for Fairness, Accountability, and __________.
18. The __________ is a tool created by the Open Data Institute to identify ethical issues in data projects.
19. Ethical considerations should be embedded in every phase of the data __________.
20. The COMPAS tool is an example of algorithmic bias in the __________ justice system.

Short Answers

1. What are the five key ethical principles in data science?

2. What does the term “black box” refer to in algorithmic systems?
3. Which tool is used to identify ethical issues throughout a data project?
4. What does the acronym FAT stand for in responsible AI?
5. Name one commonly cited example of algorithmic bias in criminal justice.
6. Who developed the Data Ethics Canvas?
7. What principle is concerned with avoiding harm and promoting well-being?
8. In data science, what does the term “bias” typically refer to?
9. What is meant by data minimization?
10. What ethical principle focuses on giving people control over their personal data?

11. Why is data not considered ethically neutral?
12. How can historical data perpetuate systemic inequality?
13. Explain why transparency is important in data-driven decision-making.
14. How does the lack of ethical infrastructure affect data science practices?
15. Why is stakeholder engagement important in ethical decision-making?
16. Describe how rapid technological change poses ethical challenges.
17. How does accountability differ from transparency in ethical terms?
18. In what ways might increased privacy limit the usefulness of data?
19. What does it mean to embed ethics into the data lifecycle?
20. Why is the role of the data scientist described as a “steward”?

Long Answers

1. Apply the ethical principles outlined in Chapter to evaluate the use of predictive algorithms in hiring. What ethical risks and safeguards would you consider?
2. Given a dataset collected without explicit user consent, how would you apply ethical guidelines to decide whether it should be used in research?
3. Using the Data Ethics Canvas, apply its steps to a real-world scenario such as facial recognition in public surveillance.
4. Imagine you are leading a data science team at a healthcare startup. How would you implement ethical practices during the modeling and deployment phases of your data project?

5. Apply the concept of fairness to a credit scoring algorithm. How would you ensure it treats users from different socioeconomic backgrounds equitably?

6. Analyze the ethical implications of algorithmic opacity ("black box" systems) in high-stakes domains like criminal justice or healthcare.
7. Compare and contrast transparency and accountability in the context of AI ethics. How are they related, and where do they differ?
8. Analyze how bias enters the data lifecycle, and suggest points of intervention to mitigate its impact.
9. Examine the trade-offs between data utility and privacy. Use examples to analyze how these conflicts can be addressed.
10. Critically evaluate the COMPAS case study from Chapter. What ethical principles were violated, and how could a more ethical approach have been designed?

Answers

Fill in the Blanks

1. societal
2. moral
3. neutral
4. should
5. biases
6. transparency
7. privacy
8. fairness
9. transparency
10. accountability
11. beneficence
12. values
13. sampling
14. reflection

15. ethics
16. stewards
17. Transparency
18. Data Ethics Canvas
19. lifecycle
20. criminal

Short Answer Keys

1. Fairness, Transparency, Accountability, Privacy, Beneficence
2. Systems whose inner workings are opaque or not easily understandable
3. The Data Ethics Canvas
4. Fairness, Accountability, and Transparency
5. The COMPAS tool
6. The Open Data Institute
7. Beneficence
8. Systematic unfairness or prejudice in data or algorithms
9. Collecting only the data necessary for a specific purpose
10. Privacy
11. Because data is generated, collected, and used in ways shaped by human and societal choices
12. By encoding past discrimination or imbalances into algorithms
13. It helps users understand and trust decisions, making systems more accountable and fair
14. It can result in overlooking critical ethical considerations during project development
15. It brings diverse perspectives and helps align data practices with societal values
16. It can outpace ethical norms, making it hard to assess risks in time
17. Accountability means being responsible for outcomes; transparency means being open about processes
18. By reducing detail or access to data, limiting potential insights or solutions
19. Considering ethical implications at each phase of data use—from collection to evaluation
20. Because they manage systems with real-life impacts and must ensure responsible use

Long Answers

1. **Ethical risks in predictive hiring algorithms:**
   - Risk of bias in training data
   - Lack of transparency in scoring models
   - Invasion of privacy from scraped data
   - Safeguards: fairness-aware algorithms, transparency tools, regular audits, stakeholder consultation
2. **Use of dataset without consent:**
   - Evaluate legality and ethical acceptability
   - Assess data minimization and necessity
   - Consider anonymization and risk of re-identification
   - Use consent frameworks or ethical review boards
3. **Application of the Data Ethics Canvas to facial recognition:**
   - Map stakeholders (e.g., citizens, government)
   - Identify ethical risks (e.g., surveillance, discrimination)
   - Discuss mitigation steps (e.g., transparency, opt-out mechanisms)
   - Document decisions at each project phase
4. **Implementing ethical practices in healthcare data science:**
   - Ensure informed consent and data protection
   - Embed fairness checks in models (e.g., race or gender bias)
   - Keep models explainable
   - Set up redress and accountability mechanisms
5. **Fairness in credit scoring algorithms:**
   - Evaluate features for proxies of protected attributes
   - Ensure equitable outcomes across groups
   - Use techniques like disparate impact testing
   - Regularly audit and revise model behavior

6. **Ethical implications of black-box systems:**
   - Reduced accountability
   - Erosion of public trust

    - Risk of unfair or unexplainable outcomes
    - Need for explainable AI, stakeholder transparency, oversight
7. **Transparency vs. Accountability:**
    - Transparency: focuses on openness (how decisions are made)
    - Accountability: focuses on responsibility (who is answerable)
    - Analysis of overlap (both reduce harm) and divergence (one reveals, the other enforces)
8. **Bias in the data lifecycle:**
    - Data collection: sampling bias
    - Preprocessing: cleaning that erases context
    - Modeling: unbalanced training data
    - Solutions: diverse datasets, fairness audits, stakeholder review
9. **Trade-offs between privacy and utility:**
    - More privacy (e.g., anonymization) may reduce model accuracy
    - Less privacy may expose individuals to risk
    - Use of synthetic data, federated learning, or privacy-preserving computation as balanced approaches
10. **Ethical analysis of COMPAS case:**

- Violations: fairness (racial bias), transparency (opaque model), accountability (no redress)
- Could be improved with bias audits, public scrutiny, explainability, and legal safeguards

Chapter 2: Moral Frameworks and Their Relevance to Data Science

Learning Outcomes

1. Identify and critically evaluate ethical tensions such as transparency vs. security and fairness vs. accuracy, and articulate their implications in real-world AI and data systems.
2. Apply moral theories—like deontology, utilitarianism, rights-based ethics, care ethics, and virtue ethics—to complex ethical dilemmas in data science practices.
3. Become familiar with tools such as ethics checklists, impact assessments, stakeholder mapping, and deliberative workshops, enabling them to integrate ethics throughout the lifecycle of data science projects.
4. Understand the role and components of an organizational ethics infrastructure, including codes of ethics, internal review boards, training programs, and incentive-aligned policies, and evaluate their importance in fostering a culture of ethical responsibility.

Introduction

As data science continues to shape decisions in healthcare, finance, policing, and social platforms, the ethical responsibilities of data professionals have become increasingly important. Relying solely on technical performance is no longer enough—decisions must also be guided by well-established moral reasoning. This chapter introduces key ethical frameworks that provide structured ways to examine complex dilemmas in data science.

We explore several foundational theories, including **duty-based ethics (deontology)**, which emphasizes obligations such as honesty and respect for privacy; **outcome-based ethics (consequentialism)**, which evaluates actions by their results; and **virtue ethics**, which highlights the importance of moral character. **Care ethics** focuses on relationships and responsibilities to others, especially those who may be vulnerable, while **rights-based approaches** advocate for individual freedoms such as consent and data ownership.

These perspectives offer different, yet often complementary, tools for navigating ethical questions. For example, ensuring fairness in algorithmic outcomes might conflict with achieving maximum predictive accuracy. Balancing such trade-offs requires thoughtful reflection grounded in ethical principles.

To bridge the gap between theory and practice, the chapter also discusses practical methods like stakeholder analysis, ethics checklists, and impact assessments. These tools help integrate ethics into the design and deployment of data systems.

By understanding and applying these moral frameworks, data practitioners can make decisions that are not only technically sound but also socially responsible. Ethics in data science is not an add-on—it's a core part of building trust and accountability in our digital future.

2.1 Guiding Principles for Ethical Decision-Making

Ethical Frameworks in Data Science: Foundations for Responsible Practice

As data science continues to shape critical decisions across sectors—from healthcare and finance to education and criminal justice—the ethical implications of data-driven technologies have come under increasing scrutiny. With algorithms influencing hiring processes, medical diagnoses, social interactions, and even law enforcement, data scientists are expected to think beyond accuracy and performance. They must engage deeply with the ethical dimensions of their work.

To navigate this complex ethical terrain, practitioners can draw upon a range of moral frameworks developed through centuries of philosophical inquiry. These frameworks offer structured approaches to identifying ethical issues, weighing competing values, and guiding principled action. While developed in vastly different contexts, these traditions remain remarkably relevant to the ethical dilemmas posed by modern data technologies.

1. Deontology: Ethics Grounded in Duty

Deontological ethics, also known as duty-based ethics, is concerned with the morality of actions themselves, rather than their consequences. Rooted in the philosophy of Immanuel Kant, this approach emphasizes adherence to rules, duties, and moral principles that are considered universally binding.

In the context of data science, deontological reasoning often leads to clear ethical boundaries. For example, a deontologist might argue that personal data should never be used without explicit consent, regardless of how useful or profitable the data may be. Similarly, they might insist on honesty in model reporting, refusal to manipulate outcomes, and transparency about data sources—because these are obligations that respect human dignity and autonomy.

This framework proves especially useful in areas like data privacy, user consent, and algorithmic transparency. It challenges data professionals to ask: *What are my responsibilities to users, regardless of the results?*

2. Consequentialism: Ethics Based on Outcomes

Consequentialism, particularly its most well-known form—**utilitarianism**—evaluates actions by the extent to which they produce desirable outcomes. From this perspective, the right action is the one that maximizes overall benefit or minimizes harm.

Applied to data science, this framework encourages the use of data and algorithms to promote social good. A consequentialist might support the use of machine learning models in public health to track and predict disease outbreaks, even if the data used includes some privacy compromises. The reasoning is that the overall benefit—saving lives and containing disease—justifies the potential risks.

However, consequentialism can be controversial in data ethics. While it promotes scalable good, it may overlook harms to specific individuals or groups. For instance, a predictive policing algorithm might reduce crime rates citywide, but disproportionately target minority communities, raising questions about fairness and justice.

Thus, this framework requires careful balancing of collective benefit against individual cost. Key questions include: *Who benefits? Who is harmed? Are the outcomes justly distributed?*

3. Virtue Ethics: Ethics of Moral Character

Rather than focusing on rules or outcomes, **virtue ethics** is concerned with the kind of person one should be. Originating with Aristotle, this tradition emphasizes the development of moral character and habits that reflect values such as honesty, courage, fairness, and compassion.

For data scientists, this means striving to be ethical professionals—not just in individual decisions, but in the overall approach to their work. A virtuous data scientist might question whether a model is being built for the right reasons, resist pressure to manipulate results, and advocate for transparency and fairness, even when it's inconvenient.

Virtue ethics promotes long-term thinking and integrity, encouraging data professionals to act not out of obligation or fear of consequences, but from a sincere commitment to doing what is right. It fosters a culture of ethical awareness within teams and organizations, which is essential in high-stakes environments.

4. Care Ethics: Ethics of Relationship and Empathy

Care ethics, developed in response to more abstract and impersonal theories, emphasizes the moral significance of relationships, empathy, and contextual understanding. This approach asks us to consider how our actions affect others—especially those in vulnerable positions—and to respond with compassion and responsibility.

In data science, care ethics becomes especially relevant when working with data from marginalized communities. For example, if a data scientist is developing a tool for social welfare allocation, a care ethicist would urge them to engage directly with the communities affected, understand their specific needs, and design solutions that prioritize human dignity over technical efficiency.

Care ethics challenges the often detached, data-first mindset in tech environments. It asks: *Who is affected by this model? Have their voices been heard? Are we showing care in our design and deployment choices?*

This framework encourages inclusive practices, participatory design, and a deep sense of ethical responsibility toward those most impacted by data technologies.

5. Rights-Based Approaches: Protecting Fundamental Freedoms

A **rights-based ethical framework** prioritizes the protection of individual rights—such as privacy, freedom of expression, autonomy, and control over personal data. It aligns closely with legal and human rights discourses, especially in digital contexts where personal information is constantly collected, analyzed, and monetized.

This approach underscores the need for consent, transparency, and respect for digital agency. For instance, a rights-based ethicist would oppose data harvesting from users without their knowledge, regardless of whether the data is used for beneficial purposes. Similarly, they would challenge mass surveillance or AI systems that limit free expression, even if those systems improve security or efficiency.

This perspective is vital in defending democratic values and preventing abuses of power through data. It raises questions such as: *Does this system respect users' autonomy? Are individuals given meaningful control over their data? Are digital rights being protected?*

6. Integrating Frameworks: Ethical Complexity in Real-World Scenarios

These moral theories are not mutually exclusive. In practice, ethical decision-making in data science often involves drawing from multiple frameworks simultaneously. For instance, while a project may align with consequentialist goals (e.g., maximizing social good), it must also respect deontological duties (e.g., obtaining consent) and uphold individual rights.

Consider the example of facial recognition technology. A utilitarian might highlight its benefits in enhancing public safety, while a deontologist may question its use without consent, and a care ethicist might raise concerns about its impact on marginalized communities. A rights-based advocate would likely challenge its use in public spaces altogether, arguing it infringes on privacy and freedom.

Rather than choosing one framework over others, ethical practice in data science often involves **balancing** these perspectives. This makes ethical reasoning a nuanced, ongoing process rather than a one-time checklist.

7. From Theory to Practice: Operationalizing Ethics

Understanding ethical theory is only the first step. Turning these frameworks into actionable guidance requires tools and structures that support ethical reflection and accountability. Organizations can adopt a range of strategies to put ethics into practice:

- **Ethical checklists** that prompt reflection at different stages of data projects.
- **Impact assessments** that evaluate the societal, legal, and economic consequences of models and algorithms.
- **Stakeholder mapping** to identify who is affected and how.
- **Deliberative workshops** that bring together diverse voices to surface concerns and discuss trade-offs.
- **Internal review boards** and **ethics committees** to evaluate high-risk data projects.
- **Training programs** that develop ethical awareness and reasoning skills among data professionals.

By embedding ethics into design processes, governance structures, and team cultures, organizations can move from abstract principles to meaningful action. Ethics in data science is not just a theoretical exercise—it is a practical necessity in shaping technologies that are fair, accountable, and aligned with human values. Classical moral frameworks like deontology, consequentialism, virtue ethics, care ethics, and rights-based approaches offer powerful tools for navigating today's complex challenges. By understanding and thoughtfully applying these frameworks, data professionals can make better decisions, earn public trust, and contribute to a more just and equitable digital future.

2.2 Balancing Ethical Intent with Practical Application

While moral principles provide essential direction, their implementation often involves tension and compromise. Ethical practice in data science requires navigating a gap between idealistic goals and operational constraints.

2.2.1 Trade-Offs in Ethical Design

In the design and implementation of data systems, especially those driven by artificial intelligence or machine learning, ethical practitioners face significant **trade-offs** between competing priorities. These conflicts aren't easily resolved and require a careful balance to ensure that technology serves society's needs while respecting ethical principles. The following sections examine three major trade-offs in ethical design—**Privacy vs. Utility, Transparency vs. Security,** and **Fairness vs. Accuracy**—along with concrete examples to illustrate their real-world implications.

Privacy vs. Utility

Trade-Off Explanation:

The balance between **privacy** and **utility** arises when the need to protect individuals' personal information conflicts with the desire to use data to its fullest potential. In data science, utility often refers to the ability of a dataset or model to provide accurate, actionable insights or predictions. Privacy, on the other hand, emphasizes the protection of sensitive information from unauthorized access or misuse.

As data-driven systems become more sophisticated, the push for using detailed, high-quality data often runs into the challenge of ensuring privacy. Privacy-preserving techniques such as **anonymization** and **data masking** can reduce the utility of data because important context or details may be lost in the process.

Example: Consider a healthcare model designed to predict patient outcomes. A model that uses fully identifiable data (e.g., names, social security numbers, addresses) would be more accurate, as it can track individual health histories and interventions. However, this violates privacy principles and could expose individuals to data breaches. To preserve privacy, the dataset might be anonymized or aggregated, which would reduce the granularity of the data, making the predictions less specific or reliable for certain cases.

Ethical Challenge:

- How much anonymization is enough to protect privacy without sacrificing predictive accuracy?

- How do you balance the potential public health benefit of accurate predictions against the risk of compromising individuals' privacy?

Solution Approaches:

- **Differential Privacy:** Introduces noise into datasets, making it difficult for anyone to identify an individual's data while still allowing meaningful analysis.
- **Data Minimization:** Collect only the data necessary to meet the desired objectives, reducing the risk of privacy violations.

Transparency vs. Security

Trade-Off Explanation:

The tension between **transparency** and **security** arises when organizations must decide how much information to disclose about their systems. Transparency involves making the decision-making process, model behavior, and underlying data available for scrutiny, which is essential for fostering trust and accountability. On the other hand, full transparency can potentially expose security vulnerabilities, allowing malicious actors to exploit weaknesses in algorithms or data infrastructure.

Example: Imagine a financial institution that uses an AI-powered fraud detection system to prevent fraudulent transactions. If the organization openly shares how the model works, including its specific algorithms, features, and thresholds, it could increase public trust in the system. However, this level of disclosure could also allow cybercriminals to understand and exploit weaknesses in the model, such as using specific patterns that the algorithm is unable to detect.

Ethical Challenge:

- How can transparency be balanced with the need to safeguard proprietary algorithms and protect sensitive information from being exploited?

Solution Approaches:

- **Model Cards & Explainability:** A model card could include high-level information about how an AI model works without disclosing sensitive details. Additionally, **explainability tools** can help decision-makers and affected individuals understand how a model makes predictions without revealing vulnerabilities.
- **Selective Disclosure:** Share enough information to assure stakeholders of fairness, accountability, and correctness, without compromising the model's security or business interests.

Fairness vs. Accuracy

Trade-Off Explanation:

The conflict between **fairness** and **accuracy** emerges when the need to ensure that a model performs equitably across different demographic groups competes with the goal of optimizing overall accuracy. Often, algorithms perform better for the majority group, but fairness considerations demand that the model also works effectively for minority groups, which may require sacrifices in accuracy.

Example: In criminal justice, predictive algorithms are used to assess the risk of recidivism among offenders. The algorithm might be highly accurate in predicting re-offending for certain demographic groups, such as Caucasian individuals, but less accurate for minority groups such as Black or Hispanic individuals. To make the system fairer, adjustments might be made to ensure the model's performance is more even across all groups, but this could reduce its overall accuracy.

Ethical Challenge:

- Should we prioritize the accurate prediction of outcomes for the majority group or ensure the model's performance is equally effective for all demographic groups, even at the cost of overall performance?
- How do we define fairness in a way that is both meaningful and measurable, particularly when different stakeholders may have different expectations of fairness?

Solution Approaches:

- **Fairness Constraints:** Models can be adjusted to minimize disparities in error rates across different groups (e.g., using fairness-aware algorithms). However, these adjustments may slightly reduce overall accuracy.
- **Fairness Metrics:** Define and measure fairness in a way that is acceptable to diverse stakeholders, such as ensuring **demographic parity** (ensuring equal outcomes across groups) or **equalized odds** (equalizing both false positive and false negative rates across groups).

Ethical decision-making in data science is not about finding a one-size-fits-all solution but rather navigating these competing priorities with care and responsibility. It's essential for data practitioners to be transparent about the choices they make, document the reasoning behind decisions, and engage relevant stakeholders to understand their concerns and values.

By identifying and addressing these trade-offs effectively, organizations can design data-driven systems that maximize benefits while minimizing harm, ensuring that ethical considerations are integrated throughout the entire lifecycle of a project—from conceptualization and development to deployment and impact assessment. Ultimately, resolving these trade-offs requires a continuous dialogue about ethical values, technical trade-offs, and the broader societal impact of data-driven technologies. Practitioners must be proactive in acknowledging these ethical challenges and seeking solutions that respect the rights, dignity, and fairness of all individuals affected by their work.

2.2.2 Ethical Frameworks in Action: Practical Tools for Data Science Ethics

Bringing ethical theory into practical application requires structured approaches and tools that help practitioners navigate complex ethical dilemmas. These tools help ensure that ethical principles are not just theoretical but are actively incorporated into the development, deployment, and evaluation of data-driven systems. Below are several key tools that bridge ethical theory and practice, ensuring that ethical considerations are deeply integrated at every stage of a data science project.

1. Ethics Checklists

Ethics checklists are structured lists of questions or prompts that guide practitioners through ethical considerations at key stages of their projects. These checklists help ensure that all relevant ethical issues are considered systematically, reducing the risk of overlooking important concerns.

Application:

- **In Data Collection:** Before starting a data collection process, a checklist might include questions like:
  - Is informed consent being obtained from all individuals providing data?
  - Are there mechanisms in place to anonymize sensitive data?
  - Have potential biases in the sample been identified and addressed?
- **During Model Development:** A checklist for model development may ask:
  - Does the model minimize bias, especially against vulnerable groups?
  - Is the data being used fairly and without discrimination?
  - Are model outcomes transparent and explainable to stakeholders?
- **At Deployment:** At deployment, the checklist could consider:
  - Are there mechanisms in place to continuously monitor the model's fairness and accuracy over time?
  - Is there a feedback loop for users to report unintended consequences or harms?

Example: An ethics checklist for a machine learning-based hiring tool might include questions like: "Does the tool account for potential gender or racial biases in the hiring process?" or "Has informed consent been obtained from candidates for how their data will be used?"

2. Impact Assessments

Impact assessments are evaluations that focus on identifying and understanding the potential **social**, **economic**, and **legal** consequences of deploying a particular data-driven system. These assessments help anticipate the broader ramifications of a project before it is fully implemented, ensuring that risks are managed effectively and that potential harms are minimized.

Application:

- **Social Impact Assessment:** Consider how a model might affect different communities, particularly vulnerable or marginalized groups. For example, a predictive policing system might disproportionately target certain neighborhoods, leading to over-policing of already marginalized communities.
- **Economic Impact Assessment:** This includes evaluating the financial implications of a project. For instance, an AI-driven healthcare system might increase the efficiency of diagnosing diseases, but it could also lead to job displacement in certain areas of the healthcare industry.
- **Legal Impact Assessment:** It's important to evaluate how a project aligns with legal frameworks, such as data protection laws (e.g., GDPR or CCPA). It may involve ensuring that the data collection, processing, and usage comply with relevant privacy regulations.

Example: Before implementing a facial recognition system in public spaces, an **impact assessment** might examine how such a system could influence privacy rights, the potential for misuse by law enforcement, and its impact on specific demographics, such as minorities or activists.

3. Stakeholder Mapping

Stakeholder mapping is a tool that helps identify **who is affected** by a project and **how** they are impacted. By mapping out stakeholders early in the process, data scientists can ensure that the interests, concerns, and needs of all relevant parties are considered when making decisions.

Application:

- **Identifying Stakeholders:** This involves identifying individuals, groups, or organizations who are directly or indirectly impacted by the project. Stakeholders might include:
    - End-users (those directly affected by the model's decisions, such as job applicants or patients).
    - Developers and data scientists (who build and maintain the systems).
    - Regulatory bodies (who ensure compliance with laws).

- Affected communities (who may experience positive or negative social impacts).

- **Assessing Impact:** Once stakeholders are identified, the next step is to assess how they are impacted. For example, does a predictive algorithm in healthcare disproportionately affect lower-income patients, or does it enhance healthcare delivery for rural areas?

Example: In a project involving the deployment of AI-driven algorithms for determining insurance premiums, stakeholder mapping would include not only the insurance company but also customers, regulatory bodies, and consumer protection groups. Each group's concerns would be evaluated, such as privacy risks for customers or legal risks for the company.

4. **Deliberative Workshops**

Deliberative workshops are structured, collaborative sessions that bring together a diverse group of stakeholders to **reflect on ethical issues** and explore the potential consequences of different design decisions. These workshops are used to facilitate **dialogue** and **reflection**, encouraging cross-functional teams to discuss ethical challenges, share perspectives, and come to a consensus on how to address key concerns.

Application:

- **Collaborative Reflection:** In these workshops, diverse stakeholders—such as engineers, business leaders, ethicists, and community representatives—are invited to provide input on critical ethical questions. The goal is not just to reach a decision but to foster deeper ethical thinking and understanding within the team.
- **Scenario Planning:** The workshop might involve presenting hypothetical scenarios and discussing the ethical implications. For instance, the team could role-play various situations involving data misuse or algorithmic bias and brainstorm ways to mitigate these risks.

Example: For an AI system used in criminal justice, a deliberative workshop might bring together legal experts, criminologists, civil rights organizations, and technology developers to discuss how best to ensure fairness and avoid racial bias in risk assessments. They might discuss potential solutions, such as ensuring diverse training datasets or implementing bias mitigation techniques in the algorithms.

These practical tools—**ethics checklists**, **impact assessments**, **stakeholder mapping**, and **deliberative workshops**—help ensure that data scientists and technologists are not only aware of the ethical challenges in their work but are actively engaging with these challenges in structured, meaningful ways. By incorporating these tools into the development cycle, data science professionals can navigate complex ethical issues with greater clarity, responsibility, and collaboration, ultimately fostering the creation of technologies that are beneficial and fair for all stakeholders.

2.2.3 Ethical Dilemmas in Practice: Case Studies

Ethical dilemmas in data science and technology often present challenging scenarios where different moral frameworks clash. In these cases, applying ethical theories provides a structured approach to evaluating potential actions and their consequences. Below are three case studies that illustrate how these moral frameworks—**rights-based ethics**, **utilitarianism**, **deontology**, **care ethics**, and **virtue ethics**—can be applied to real-world issues in the context of data science.

1. Social Media Moderation: Balancing Freedom of Speech (Rights-Based) Against the Prevention of Harm (Utilitarianism)

Scenario: Social media platforms face the ethical dilemma of moderating content to prevent harm, such as the spread of hate speech, misinformation, and violence, while also respecting users' rights to freedom of speech. Platforms must strike a balance between enforcing community standards and protecting individuals' rights to express their opinions.

Ethical Frameworks:

- **Rights-Based Ethics (Freedom of Speech):** This perspective emphasizes the fundamental right to freedom of expression. From this viewpoint, social media companies should minimize censorship, allowing users to express diverse ideas, even if those ideas may be controversial or offensive. However, the application of this right is not absolute; it may need to be restricted if the speech violates other important rights or causes harm.
- **Utilitarianism (Preventing Harm):** A utilitarian approach weighs the potential harms of harmful content against the benefits of allowing freedom of expression. The goal is to

maximize the well-being of society. If certain speech leads to harm (e.g., inciting violence or spreading false information), a utilitarian would argue for moderation to protect the public good. This might involve censoring harmful content to prevent social unrest or widespread misinformation, even at the cost of limiting some users' ability to speak freely.

Example: In 2020, platforms like Facebook and Twitter faced backlash over their handling of misinformation related to the COVID-19 pandemic and the U.S. presidential election. Balancing users' right to express opinions about these issues against the risk of harmful misinformation spreading was a key challenge. The platforms implemented fact-checking measures and content moderation to prevent the spread of false information, thus limiting certain types of speech in the interest of public safety.

Dilemma: Should platforms prioritize users' right to express themselves freely, or should they prioritize preventing harm through content moderation? The challenge is determining where to draw the line between free speech and the protection of society.

2. Predictive Policing: Duty to Protect Public Safety (Deontology) vs. Risk of Reinforcing Racial Bias (Care and Fairness)

Scenario: Predictive policing systems use historical crime data to predict where crimes are likely to occur and allocate police resources accordingly. However, these systems have faced criticism for reinforcing racial bias, as they often rely on historical data that disproportionately targets minority communities, perpetuating cycles of over-policing in those areas.

Ethical Frameworks:

- **Deontology (Duty to Protect Public Safety):** From a deontological perspective, the primary duty of law enforcement is to protect public safety and prevent crime. Predictive policing can be justified as a tool for law enforcement to deploy resources efficiently, acting in accordance with the duty to protect citizens. The emphasis here is on the moral responsibility of the police to ensure safety and justice, regardless of the consequences of potential biases in the system.

- **Care Ethics (Concerns About Vulnerable Communities):** Care ethics emphasizes the importance of relationships, empathy, and responsibility toward others. In this case, care ethics highlights the disproportionate impact that predictive policing has on vulnerable populations, particularly racial minorities. A care ethics perspective would argue that the use of biased data harms these communities by perpetuating racial inequality and eroding trust in law enforcement. The ethical responsibility, therefore, is to take care in how predictive policing tools are designed and used, ensuring that the harms to vulnerable groups are minimized.
- **Fairness and Equality:** The fairness approach focuses on ensuring that algorithms and systems do not discriminate against individuals based on race or ethnicity. From this viewpoint, predictive policing systems need to be critically evaluated to ensure that they do not perpetuate unfair treatment of certain groups.

Example: In cities like Chicago, predictive policing systems like "Strategic Subject List" (SSL) used historical arrest data to predict future offenders. Critics argued that these systems reinforced racial biases by targeting predominantly Black and Latino neighborhoods. The ethical dilemma arises in balancing the moral duty to protect public safety with the need to ensure fairness and avoid reinforcing systemic bias.

Dilemma: How should law enforcement balance the duty to protect public safety with the risk of reinforcing racial bias? Is it justifiable to use predictive policing if it disproportionately harms minority communities?

3. Data Monetization: Profit Motives vs. Individual Privacy Rights and Informed Consent

Scenario: Data monetization is the practice of selling or using consumer data to generate revenue. Many tech companies collect vast amounts of personal data to sell targeted advertising or develop new products. However, this raises concerns about privacy violations and the exploitation of personal information without informed consent.

Ethical Frameworks:

- **Utilitarianism (Maximizing Benefit):** A utilitarian might argue that data monetization can bring significant benefits to society, such as funding innovative technologies or offering free services to users (e.g., social media platforms or search engines). The economic benefits generated by monetizing data could improve services, create jobs, and contribute to the overall good. However, the potential harms, such as privacy violations, must be weighed against these benefits.
- **Rights-Based Ethics (Privacy and Autonomy):** From a rights-based perspective, individuals have a fundamental right to privacy and control over their personal information. Data monetization without informed consent violates individuals' rights by commodifying their personal data without permission. This framework prioritizes autonomy and personal freedom, arguing that companies must seek explicit consent from users before collecting or selling their data.
- **Virtue Ethics (Honesty and Integrity):** Virtue ethics emphasizes the importance of character and moral virtues, such as honesty and integrity. A data-driven company should act with transparency and honesty when it comes to how it collects, stores, and uses consumer data. Data monetization practices that obscure or manipulate consent undermine trust and violate the ethical principle of integrity.

Example: Companies like Facebook and Google have faced backlash over their data practices, particularly regarding the collection of user data without clear consent. For example, Facebook's Cambridge Analytica scandal, in which personal data was harvested without proper consent and used for political profiling, sparked widespread ethical debates about data monetization and user privacy.

Dilemma: Should companies prioritize the financial benefits of data monetization, or should they respect individuals' rights to privacy and ensure that users provide informed consent before their data is used for profit?

These case studies illustrate how ethical frameworks can guide decision-making in real-world data science dilemmas. Whether it's balancing freedom of speech with the prevention of harm, ensuring that predictive policing doesn't reinforce bias, or navigating the ethical implications of data monetization, these frameworks help practitioners weigh competing moral values and make more informed, responsible choices. By applying ethical reasoning to these complex challenges, data scientists can create systems that not only deliver technical benefits but also uphold fundamental ethical principles such as fairness, privacy, and respect for individual rights.

2.2.4 Organizational Ethics Infrastructure

To ensure that ethical considerations are consistently integrated into data science practices, organizations must develop a robust infrastructure that supports responsible decision-making and accountability. The infrastructure must promote ethical standards across all levels of an organization, ensuring that ethical challenges are addressed proactively rather than reactively. The following are key components that constitute a comprehensive organizational ethics infrastructure.

1. Codes of Ethics and Conduct

A **code of ethics and conduct** is a foundational document that outlines the ethical principles and standards that govern behavior within the organization. This document serves as a reference for employees to understand the organization's stance on critical ethical issues, guiding their decisions and actions in complex situations.

Importance in Data Science: In the context of data science, a code of ethics is crucial for addressing issues like data privacy, transparency, fairness, and accountability. It helps establish clear guidelines on how to ethically handle personal data, ensure fairness in algorithms, and mitigate bias.

Example: The **IEEE Global Initiative on Ethics of Autonomous and Intelligent Systems** has developed a comprehensive code of ethics that provides guidance on the ethical development and deployment of AI technologies. It emphasizes values such as transparency, fairness, and respect for human rights. Such a code helps guide developers and organizations to ensure that their technologies are ethically sound.

Key Elements:

- Commitment to privacy and data protection
- Transparency in algorithmic decision-making
- Ensuring fairness and equity in AI systems
- Accountability for the consequences of technological outcomes

2. Internal Review Boards and Data Ethics Committees

An **internal review board (IRB)** or **data ethics committee** is a group within the organization that is responsible for reviewing data-related projects, policies, and practices to ensure they align with ethical standards. This committee typically includes individuals with diverse expertise in ethics, law, technology, and data science.

Importance in Data Science: Ethical decision-making in data science requires continuous evaluation, especially when new technologies or methodologies are introduced. Having a dedicated group to review and assess the ethical implications of data-driven projects ensures that ethical concerns are considered throughout the development and deployment phases.

Example: For instance, **Google's AI ethics board** (which was later disbanded) was initially set up to assess the ethical implications of AI technologies developed within the company. Such bodies can evaluate potential risks, such as bias in machine learning models or the potential for privacy violations.

Key Functions:

- Evaluate the ethical implications of data collection and analysis methods
- Review projects to identify and mitigate bias and harm
- Advise on compliance with data protection laws, such as GDPR
- Ensure the consideration of long-term societal impacts

3. Training Programs in Ethical Reasoning

Organizations must develop and offer **training programs in ethical reasoning** to ensure that employees, especially those involved in data science and AI, are equipped to navigate the ethical challenges they may face. These training programs should focus on building critical thinking skills and providing employees with the tools to assess ethical dilemmas from multiple perspectives.

Importance in Data Science: Given the complex ethical landscape of data science, it's essential for data professionals to understand both the technical and ethical aspects of their work. Training programs that emphasize ethical reasoning help create a workforce that is capable of making responsible and informed decisions in their everyday work.

Example: IBM has developed an **AI Ethics Training Program** for its employees to promote ethical AI practices. The program includes learning modules that explore how to avoid bias in algorithms, ensure fairness, and understand the potential impact of AI on society.

Key Components:

- Ethical decision-making frameworks (e.g., deontology, consequentialism, virtue ethics)
- Case studies on ethical dilemmas in data science
- Practical tools for evaluating ethical challenges in real-world projects
- Role-playing and simulations to encourage ethical discussions

4. Policies that Align Incentives with Responsible Behaviour

Incentive structures and policies within an organization play a crucial role in encouraging ethical behavior. To ensure consistent ethical practices, policies should align employee incentives with responsible, ethical decision-making. This means that both the rewards and penalties associated with employees' work should reflect the ethical standards of the organization.

Importance in Data Science: Without proper alignment between incentives and ethical behavior, employees may feel pressured to prioritize performance metrics (such as profitability or model accuracy) over ethical considerations. By incorporating ethical standards into performance evaluations, organizations can create an environment where employees are motivated to prioritize responsible practices.

Example: A tech company might include ethical performance criteria, such as transparency and fairness in algorithmic design, in the performance reviews of data scientists and engineers. This encourages them to consider the societal impacts of their work and to ensure that their projects meet ethical standards.

Key Policies:

- Ethical conduct as part of performance reviews and promotions
- Rewarding employees for developing ethical AI systems or reducing bias in models
- Accountability for decisions that lead to negative societal impacts
- Regular audits to evaluate whether projects meet ethical standards and regulations

Developing a strong **organizational ethics infrastructure** is crucial for fostering a culture of ethical decision-making in the context of data science and AI. By implementing **codes of ethics**, establishing **internal review boards**, providing **training programs in ethical reasoning**, and ensuring that **incentives are aligned with responsible behavior**, organizations can ensure that their data science practices are grounded in ethical principles. This not only promotes responsible innovation but also builds trust with consumers, stakeholders, and society at large, ensuring that technology serves the greater good while minimizing harm.

Moral frameworks are far from being abstract or theoretical constructs—they are critical for guiding the ethical conduct of data science. These frameworks offer a structured approach to addressing the complex ethical challenges that arise in data-driven technologies. They help practitioners navigate how systems are designed, how stakeholders are engaged, how potential consequences are evaluated, and how responsibilities are assigned.

When applied to the fast-evolving field of data science, classical moral frameworks, such as deontology, consequentialism, virtue ethics, and care ethics, provide the necessary grounding to address ethical dilemmas. For instance, a deontological approach may emphasize the importance of privacy and informed consent, while a consequentialist viewpoint may focus on maximizing societal benefits, such as using predictive algorithms for public health improvements. Meanwhile, virtue ethics would guide data scientists to cultivate a moral character, ensuring that they act with honesty, fairness, and integrity throughout the data lifecycle.

By interpreting and applying these frameworks in the context of modern technological practices, we can ensure that progress in fields like artificial intelligence and machine learning aligns with fundamental human values such as dignity, justice, and the common good. Far from being a checkbox for compliance, ethical excellence in data science reflects the kind of world we want to shape, where technology serves to enhance human flourishing rather than harm it.

In the next chapter, we will shift our focus to **fairness in algorithmic systems**. This will involve exploring how bias can manifest in data and models and investigating strategies for promoting greater equity and inclusiveness in machine learning systems.

Summary

This chapter delves into the critical role of ethics in data science, highlighting how classical moral frameworks can guide decision-making in the development and deployment of data-driven technologies. With the increasing influence of AI and machine learning on society, ethical considerations are not optional—they are foundational. The chapter opens with an exploration of key ethical trade-offs, such as the tension between transparency and security, and the conflict between fairness and accuracy. These dilemmas illustrate that ethical decision-making often involves navigating competing priorities, where every choice can have significant consequences.
To help practitioners make responsible decisions, the chapter introduces practical tools that bridge theory and practice, including ethics checklists, impact assessments, stakeholder mapping, and deliberative workshops. These tools are essential for ensuring ethical issues are systematically addressed at every project stage.
Real-world case studies bring ethical theory to life, demonstrating how frameworks like rights-based ethics, utilitarianism, and care ethics can be applied to pressing challenges in content moderation, predictive policing, and data monetization. Through these examples, the chapter illustrates the complexity of balancing individual rights, societal good, and corporate responsibility.

The final section underscores the need for strong organizational ethics infrastructure. This includes adopting formal codes of ethics, forming internal ethics committees, providing ethical reasoning training, and aligning employee incentives with ethical behavior. These components work together to embed ethical awareness into the culture and operations of data-driven organizations.

Ultimately, ethical excellence in data science is about more than avoiding harm—it's about designing systems that uphold dignity, justice, and the common good. The chapter closes by setting the stage for a deeper investigation into algorithmic fairness in the next chapter.

Test your Understanding

1. **Which of the following is NOT a classical moral theory?**

   a) Utilitarianism

   b) Deontology

   c) Virtue Ethics

   d) Algorithmism

2. **Utilitarianism is primarily concerned with:**

   a) Following rules

   b) Maximizing happiness

   c) Acting with virtue

   d) Protecting privacy

3. **Deontological ethics focuses on:**

   a) Outcomes

   b) Moral duties and rules

   c) Emotions

   d) Public opinion

4. **Virtue ethics emphasizes:**

   a) Consequences

   b) Rules

   c) Character and moral virtues

   d) Technology adoption

5. **Which ethical theory would most likely oppose using biased data even if it improves outcomes?**

   a) Utilitarianism

   b) Deontology

   c) Libertarianism

   d) Pragmatism

6. **Which framework encourages identifying stakeholders and considering their values in design?**

   a) Black box modeling

b) Value-Sensitive Design

c) Predictive Analytics Framework

d) Agile Methodology

7. **The principle of "the greatest good for the greatest number" aligns with:**

a) Deontology

b) Virtue Ethics

c) Utilitarianism

d) Kantianism

8. **A data scientist refusing to use personal data without consent is acting on which principle?**

a) Beneficence

b) Justice

c) Autonomy

d) Utility

9. **Ethical intent in data projects must be balanced with:**

a) Business goals

b) Practical application

c) Competitive advantage

d) Political opinion

10. **What does the FAT framework stand for?**

a) Fast, Accurate, Transparent

b) Fairness, Accountability, Transparency

c) Freedom, Access, Truth

d) Functionality, Agility, Trust

11. **According to Rawls' theory of justice, decisions should be made from:**

a) A place of authority

b) The veil of ignorance

c) The perspective of utility

d) A data-driven model

12. **Ethical design is MOST likely to fail when:**

a) Developers are trained in AI

b) Stakeholders are consulted

c) Trade-offs are openly discussed

d) Ethics is considered only at the end

13. **Which framework integrates user values into system development?**

a) Waterfall model

b) Value-Sensitive Design

c) Rapid Prototyping

d) Systems Thinking

14. **What is a key challenge of applying moral frameworks to data science?**

a) Too much regulation

b) Lack of programming skills

c) Complex trade-offs and ambiguities

d) Availability of ethical tools

15. **Aristotle's virtue ethics suggests ethical behavior is rooted in:**

a) Adherence to laws

b) Avoidance of harm

c) Development of moral character

d) Algorithmic fairness

16. **Which moral theory is MOST outcome-oriented?**

a) Utilitarianism

b) Deontology

c) Virtue Ethics

d) Social Contract Theory

17. **Designing a system that minimizes harm and promotes social good reflects the principle of:**

a) Transparency

b) Justice

c) Beneficence

d) Utility

18. **Which ethical model would justify surveillance for greater national safety?**

a) Virtue Ethics

b) Deontology

c) Utilitarianism

d) Libertarianism

19. **A critique of utilitarianism in data science is that it may:**

a) Ignore long-term outcomes

b) Violate individual rights

c) Overvalue intuition

d) Overemphasize technical detail

20. **Embedding ethics into machine learning design primarily helps to:**

a) Speed up development

b) Reduce operational costs

c) Ensure responsible innovation

d) Eliminate the need for regulation

Short Answer Questions

1. What is the main focus of **deontological ethics** in data science?
2. Define **consequentialism** in the context of ethical decision-making.
3. What does **virtue ethics** emphasize in a data science setting?
4. Name one key value emphasized by **care ethics**.
5. Which ethical framework prioritizes individual rights such as privacy and autonomy?
6. What is a **trade-off** commonly faced between transparency and security?
7. How does **Value-Sensitive Design** contribute to ethical system development?
8. What is the purpose of a **stakeholder map** in ethical data practice?
9. Give an example of a practical tool that helps apply ethics in data science.
10. Why is it important to balance **ethical intent with practical application**?

Long Answer Questions

1. Analyze how a data scientist might apply **deontological ethics** when designing a machine learning model that uses personal health data.

2. Discuss how **utilitarianism** can both support and challenge the use of large-scale social media data for public benefit.
3. Explain how **virtue ethics** can be promoted within a data science team or organization.
4. Apply the concept of **care ethics** to the ethical management of data collected from marginalized communities.
5. Compare and contrast **rights-based approaches** and **utilitarianism** in the context of surveillance technologies.
6. Evaluate the ethical dilemma of **predictive policing** using at least two different moral frameworks discussed in the chapter.
7. Describe how **ethical checklists** and **impact assessments** can help prevent ethical oversights during AI development.
8. Analyze the conflict between **fairness** and **accuracy** in algorithmic decision-making, using a real-world or hypothetical example.
9. Propose an organizational strategy to embed **ethical reasoning** into every stage of a data science project lifecycle.
10. Given a case of data monetization by a social platform, apply at least two ethical theories to assess its implications for user consent and rights.

Answers

1. d
2. b
3. b
4. c
5. b
6. b
7. c
8. c
9. b
10. b
11. b
12. d

13. b
14. c
15. c
16. a
17. c
18. c
19. b
20. c

Short Answer Questions – Answer Key Points

1. **Deontological ethics** focuses on following moral duties and rules, such as obtaining informed consent and protecting privacy.
2. **Consequentialism** judges actions based on their outcomes—maximizing benefits and minimizing harm is the central concern.
3. **Virtue ethics** emphasizes the moral character of the decision-maker, valuing traits like honesty, fairness, and integrity.
4. **Care ethics** values empathy, compassion, and the responsibility to nurture relationships, especially with vulnerable populations.
5. **Rights-based approaches** prioritize protecting individual freedoms such as autonomy, privacy, and freedom of expression.
6. **Transparency vs. Security**: Sharing algorithmic details may increase trust but can also expose systems to risks or leak proprietary information.
7. **Value-Sensitive Design (VSD)** helps integrate stakeholder values into system development, ensuring ethical alignment from the ground up.
8. **Stakeholder mapping** identifies individuals or groups affected by a data project and clarifies their interests and potential impacts.
9. Examples include: **ethics checklists**, **impact assessments**, **stakeholder mapping**, and **deliberative workshops**.
10. Ethical goals often clash with real-world limitations like deadlines, costs, or technical feasibility, requiring thoughtful compromise.

Long Answer Questions – Answer Key Points

1. **Deontological ethics & health data**: A data scientist might refuse to use personal health data without explicit consent, even if it improves model performance, due to the duty to respect privacy and autonomy.
2. **Utilitarianism & social media data**:
    - **Support**: Can be used to track public sentiment or prevent harm (e.g., suicide prevention).
    - **Challenge**: May ignore individual rights or privacy if focused only on aggregate benefits.
3. **Promoting virtue ethics in teams**:
    - Hire and reward ethical individuals.
    - Encourage open dialogue about moral values.
    - Model virtues like fairness, honesty, and humility in leadership.
4. **Care ethics & marginalized data**:
    - Prioritize community involvement.
    - Ensure data use benefits the community.
    - Avoid exploitation by understanding cultural and contextual needs.
5. **Rights vs. Utilitarianism in surveillance**:
    - **Rights-based**: Focuses on protecting individual freedoms and privacy.
    - **Utilitarianism**: Justifies surveillance if it leads to greater public safety, even at the cost of some rights.
6. **Predictive policing ethics**:
    - **Deontology**: Duty to protect public safety but must follow fair procedures and avoid discrimination.
    - **Care ethics**: Concerns about harm to communities, especially those already marginalized.
7. **Ethics tools in action**:
    - **Checklists** ensure ethical concerns are considered at each step.
    - **Impact assessments** predict societal and legal outcomes, helping avoid negative externalities.

8. **Fairness vs. Accuracy**:
   - Equalizing model performance across demographics might reduce accuracy.
   - Example: A credit scoring model adjusted for fairness may misclassify low-risk applicants.
9. **Embedding ethics in the project lifecycle**:
   - Train teams in ethics.
   - Use ethics checkpoints in development.
   - Establish review boards.
   - Incentivize ethical behavior.
10. **Data monetization & ethical theories**:

- **Rights-based**: Users should control how their data is used.
- **Utilitarianism**: May be acceptable if it benefits many users (e.g., funding free services), but should consider consent and harm.

Chapter 3: Ethical Data Collection Practices

Learning Outcomes

1. Recall the key principles of ethical data collection, including consent, clarity, and privacy protection.
2. Explain the importance of informed consent in research and data collection processes.
3. Apply ethical guidelines in data collection practices, ensuring voluntary participation and privacy protection.
4. Summarise the ethical considerations and challenges associated with collecting data from public platforms and online sources.

Introduction

In the modern age, data collection has become a cornerstone of research, business operations, and technological development. However, as data is collected at an unprecedented scale, ensuring that the data is gathered ethically becomes increasingly important. Ethical data collection practices protect individuals' privacy, respect their autonomy, and ensure that information is used responsibly. This section outlines three primary areas of ethical data collection: consent, clarity, and voluntary participation; avoiding intrusion and protecting identities; and responsible sourcing from public platforms.

3.1 Consent, Clarity, and Voluntary Participation

The Importance of Informed Consent

Informed consent is a foundational principle in both ethical research and data collection practices. It ensures that individuals are fully aware of what is happening with their personal data and that their participation is grounded in a clear understanding of the process. Informed consent requires that individuals know what data is being collected, the purpose of its collection, how it will be used, and how it may impact them. Crucially, consent should not be assumed or implied—it must be explicitly granted, ensuring transparency and respect for autonomy.

Example: Research Studies in Healthcare

In healthcare research, ensuring informed consent is critical to protect patients' rights and welfare. For example, in clinical trials, researchers are required to provide participants with detailed consent forms. These forms outline the study's goals, the types of data being collected (such as medical history, genetic data, or test results), any potential risks (e.g., side effects of a new drug), and the benefits of participation. It is not enough for participants to simply sign a form; they must actively understand and agree to the terms, ensuring their consent is both informed and voluntary. Only once participants fully comprehend these elements should they be asked to give explicit consent.

Clarity in Communication

Clear communication is paramount in obtaining informed consent. The language used in consent forms and during data collection must be straightforward and easily understandable. Technical terms, complex jargon, or legal language can confuse participants, which undermines the essence of informed consent. Clear and simple explanations ensure that individuals can make well-informed decisions about whether to participate.

Example: Online Surveys

Consider an online survey that gathers consumer data for market research. The survey should clearly state its purpose, such as analyzing consumer behavior or preferences for a specific product, and explain how the data will be used, whether it is for advertising strategies or product development. Ambiguous language or an overly complex form may obscure the true purpose of the data collection. For example, a consent form might read: "By clicking 'Agree,' I consent to my data being used for internal research purposes," but it's better to state explicitly, "I consent to my responses being used to analyze trends in consumer behavior, which may help develop new products or marketing strategies." A single, clear sentence is often more effective than a long paragraph filled with unnecessary legal or technical language.

Voluntary Participation and the Right to Withdraw

Participation in any data collection process should always be voluntary, meaning individuals are not coerced or unduly influenced to participate. They must also be clearly informed of their right to withdraw from the study at any time, with no adverse consequences. This is especially crucial in research involving vulnerable populations, who may feel pressured to participate due to a lack of alternatives or awareness of their rights.

Example: Social Media Data Mining

In studies that analyze data from social media platforms like Twitter or Facebook, researchers must ensure participants' autonomy and respect their right to opt-out. Even if the data is publicly available, the ethical principle of voluntary participation still applies. For instance, if a researcher is conducting a study based on the content of public social media posts, they must notify users about how their data will be used and allow them to withdraw consent. Users should be informed that they can opt-out of the research at any time and that doing so will not impact their access to the platform or any other services. This also applies to situations where data scraping or mining is used to collect information from publicly available profiles or posts—consent is still required from the users whose data is being utilized.

The principles of informed consent, clarity in communication, and voluntary participation are essential in ensuring ethical data collection and research practices. These principles promote transparency, respect for autonomy, and trust between researchers and participants. By ensuring that consent is explicitly obtained, that language is clear and accessible, and that participants have the right to withdraw without consequences, data scientists and researchers can uphold the ethical standards necessary for responsible data collection. In an increasingly data-driven world, these practices are critical in protecting individuals' rights and ensuring that data is collected in a manner that respects human dignity.

3.2 Avoiding Intrusion and Protecting Identities

In the realm of data collection, particularly within the context of smart cities, the ethical imperative to avoid intrusion and protect individual identities is paramount. This principle ensures that data collection practices respect personal privacy and uphold the dignity of individuals. Below, we delve into the risks associated with intrusive data collection, the role of data anonymization in mitigating these risks, and the ethical considerations surrounding surveillance-based data collection.

The Risk of Intrusion in Data Collection

Intrusion occurs when data collection practices exceed what is necessary, thereby violating an individual's right to privacy. This can manifest in various forms, such as:

- **Excessive Data Collection**: Gathering more information than is required for the intended purpose.
- **Lack of Transparency**: Failing to inform individuals about what data is being collected and how it will be used.
- **Inadequate Consent**: Collecting data without obtaining explicit and informed consent from individuals.

Example: Mobile Data Collection

Many mobile applications collect a wide range of data from users, such as location history, contacts, and usage patterns. While this data can be useful for personalizing experiences, it is crucial that users are aware of what data is being collected and why. An example of intrusion would be an app that collects GPS data when users have not explicitly agreed to share this information or an app that collects location data continuously without informing users.

Example: Smart City Projects

Smart city initiatives often involve the deployment of sensors and cameras to collect data on public behavior, traffic patterns, and environmental conditions. While these projects aim to enhance urban living, they can lead to continuous monitoring of individuals without their explicit consent. For instance, Amsterdam decided to cancel its plans for smart traffic lights due to privacy concerns, as the system would have allowed authorities to track users via GPS data collected from mobile apps.

The Role of Data Anonymization

Data anonymization is a technique used to protect personal information by removing or encrypting identifiable details. This process ensures that individuals cannot be readily identified from the data, thereby reducing the risk of privacy violations.

Example: Data Analytics in Retail

Retail companies often collect data on consumer purchases to personalize marketing campaigns. To prevent intrusion and ensure anonymity, data should be aggregated and anonymized, such that no single consumer's purchasing habits can be identified. By doing so, companies can still gain valuable insights into shopping trends while respecting customer privacy.

Ethical Considerations

While anonymization is a valuable tool, it is not foolproof. Advances in data analysis techniques can sometimes re-identify anonymized data, leading to potential privacy breaches. Therefore, organizations must implement robust anonymization methods and continuously assess the effectiveness of these measures to ensure ongoing protection of individual identities.

The Ethics of Surveillance-Based Data Collection

Surveillance-based data collection, especially in public spaces, raises significant ethical concerns. While such methods may be effective for certain purposes, like crime prevention or traffic monitoring, they can also infringe on individuals' rights to privacy.

Example: AI Surveillance at the Olympics

During the 2024 Olympics in Paris, AI algorithms were utilized to monitor CCTV footage at transport stations to identify potential security threats. This approach was criticized by human rights groups for its potential to infringe on privacy and for the biases inherent in AI surveillance systems .

Ethical Challenges

- **Lack of Consent**: Individuals are often unaware that they are being monitored, and thus cannot provide informed consent.
- **Potential for Misuse**: Data collected for one purpose may be used for another, potentially infringing on privacy rights.
- **Bias and Discrimination**: AI systems may perpetuate existing biases, leading to unfair treatment of certain groups.

Balancing Privacy and Innovation

To address these ethical challenges, it is essential to balance the benefits of surveillance technologies with the rights of individuals. This can be achieved by:

- Implementing clear policies that define the scope and purpose of data collection.
- Ensuring transparency in data collection practices.
- Obtaining explicit consent from individuals when possible.
- Regularly auditing surveillance systems to assess their impact on privacy.

Ethical data collection practices are fundamental to maintaining trust and protecting individual rights in an increasingly data-driven world. By avoiding unnecessary intrusion, anonymizing data, and carefully considering the ethics of surveillance, organizations can uphold the principles of privacy and respect for individuals. As technology continues to evolve, it is imperative that ethical considerations remain at the forefront of data collection practices to ensure that innovation does not come at the expense of personal dignity and freedom.

3.3 Responsible Sourcing from Public Platforms

In the digital age, data from public platforms—such as social media, online forums, and governmental databases—serve as invaluable resources for research, analysis, and marketing. However, the accessibility of this data does not diminish the ethical obligations associated with its use. Researchers and organizations must navigate the complexities of privacy, consent, and responsible data handling to ensure ethical practices.

The Ethical Implications of Public Data

While data from public platforms is often readily accessible, its use raises significant ethical considerations:

- **Privacy Expectations**: Users may share content publicly without anticipating its use for research or commercial purposes. The mere public availability of data does not equate to informed consent for its use in studies or marketing campaigns.
- **Contextual Integrity**: Data extracted from its original context can lead to misinterpretations or misuse. For instance, a tweet expressing personal sentiment may be repurposed for commercial advertising, which could be perceived as an ethical violation.
- **Informed Consent**: Even when data is publicly available, the ethical principle of informed consent should guide its use. Users may not be aware of how their data is being utilized, especially when aggregated or anonymized.

Example: Social Media Data Research

Researchers often analyze social media data to gauge public sentiment or consumer behavior. However, the context of the posts is crucial. For instance, a tweet about a political issue might be publicly accessible, but using that tweet for commercial purposes without the user's explicit consent can breach ethical standards. Additionally, the user's intent to participate in data collection, such as through likes or comments, should be considered.

Protecting Privacy on Public Platforms

Even though data on public platforms may be accessible to anyone, users may not expect their information to be used for research or commercial purposes. Therefore, platforms and researchers must take proactive steps to protect user privacy:

- **Anonymization**: Removing personally identifiable information (PII) from datasets to prevent the identification of individuals.

- **Data Minimization**: Collecting only the data necessary for the research purpose to limit exposure.
- **Transparency**: Clearly communicating to users how their data will be used and obtaining consent where feasible.
- **Ethical Review**: Subjecting research proposals to ethical review boards to assess potential risks and benefits.

Example: Research on User Behavior in Online Communities

Online communities generate a wealth of user-generated content valuable for understanding behavior and preferences. However, even when data is publicly available, it is essential to consider whether participants consented to its use for research purposes. Researchers should ensure that the anonymity of participants is maintained and that sensitive content is handled with care.

The Role of Data Brokers

Data brokers collect and sell public data from various sources, including public records and online activity. While some of this data is publicly available, the practices of data brokers often lack transparency, and individuals may not be aware of how their information is being used or sold. This raises significant ethical concerns:

- **Lack of Transparency**: Data brokers often operate without clear disclosure of their data collection and selling practices.
- **Informed Consent**: Individuals may not have provided explicit consent for their data to be sold or used by third parties.
- **Data Accuracy**: The data sold by brokers may be outdated or inaccurate, leading to potential harm.

Example: Selling Consumer Data

A company that purchases consumer data from data brokers might target individuals with personalized advertisements without their consent. Ethical data collection would require that companies obtain permission from individuals before purchasing their data or using it in any form of targeted marketing.

Ethical data collection practices are paramount in ensuring that individuals' rights and privacy are protected while still allowing for valuable research and data-driven insights. These practices include:

- **Obtaining Informed Consent**: Ensuring that individuals are aware of and agree to how their data will be used.
- **Maintaining Clarity in Communication**: Using straightforward language to explain data collection practices.
- **Ensuring Voluntary Participation**: Allowing individuals to opt out without facing negative consequences.
- **Protecting Identities**: Anonymizing data to prevent the identification of individuals.
- **Being Responsible When Sourcing Data**: Ensuring that data collection from public platforms adheres to ethical standards.

By adhering to these ethical guidelines, organizations and researchers can foster trust with the public and avoid potential harms associated with irresponsible data collection. As technology continues to evolve, the importance of ethical data collection will only grow, and the framework for responsible practices will need to adapt to new challenges. Ethical standards should not be static but should evolve in response to new developments in technology, data science, and societal norms.

Recent Developments in Data Brokerage Regulations

The ethical concerns surrounding data brokers have prompted regulatory actions:

- **CFPB's Proposed Rule**: The Consumer Financial Protection Bureau (CFPB) has proposed a rule to limit data brokers from selling sensitive personal information without explicit consent. This rule aims to provide individuals with greater control over their data and enhance transparency in data brokerage practices.

- **FTC's Enforcement Actions**: The Federal Trade Commission (FTC) has initiated actions against data brokers for illegally collecting and selling sensitive location data. These actions underscore the importance of adhering to ethical standards and legal requirements in data collection and usage.

These developments highlight the growing recognition of the need for ethical oversight in data brokerage and the importance of protecting individuals' privacy rights.

Summary

This chapter discusses the ethical principles surrounding data collection, focusing on three key areas: consent, clarity, and voluntary participation; avoiding intrusion and protecting identities; and responsible sourcing from public platforms. Consent, Clarity, and Voluntary Participation Informed consent is vital in ensuring individuals understand what data is being collected, its purpose, and its impact. Clear communication in consent forms is crucial, avoiding technical jargon that could confuse participants. Consent should be voluntary, and individuals must have the right to withdraw at any time without consequences. This is important in research, such as healthcare studies and social media data mining, where transparency and respect for participants' autonomy are essential. Avoiding Intrusion and Protecting Identities Ethical data collection should avoid unnecessary intrusion, such as collecting excessive data or using surveillance technologies without consent. Privacy risks are mitigated through techniques like data anonymization, which removes identifiable information. However, anonymization is not foolproof, and there are ongoing challenges in preventing the re-identification of anonymized data. Ethical concerns also arise from surveillance systems, as seen in the 2024 Olympics, where AI was used to monitor public spaces. Balancing privacy with innovation is key to maintaining ethical standards. Responsible Sourcing from Public Platforms Even though data from public platforms is easily accessible, ethical issues arise when it is used for research or commercial purposes without informed consent. Researchers must ensure privacy protection through anonymization and minimize data collection to what is necessary. Data brokers, who sell public data, raise concerns about transparency, consent, and accuracy. Recent regulatory developments, like the CFPB's proposed rule, aim to address these issues by ensuring better control and transparency for individuals over their data.

Ethical Considerations in Data Collection and Use

In the age of data-driven innovation, ethical data practices are crucial to protecting individual rights, maintaining trust, and ensuring responsible innovation. Several key principles guide ethical data collection, especially when working with public platforms and personal data.

1. Informed Consent and Transparency

Ethical data collection begins with **clear and informed consent**. Individuals must be told what data is being collected, why, how it will be used, and who it will be shared with. Consent must be explicit, not assumed, and participation should be voluntary, with the right to withdraw at any point. This is particularly critical in sensitive areas like **healthcare research** and **online surveys**, where clarity in communication avoids confusion and exploitation.

2. Avoiding Intrusion and Protecting Identities

Respecting privacy involves collecting **only necessary data** and avoiding overreach. Practices such as **data anonymization** help prevent identification and reduce privacy risks. Ethical concerns also arise in surveillance systems, such as **smart cities**, where constant monitoring can infringe on individual rights. Transparency and limited data access are essential in such contexts.

3. Responsible Use of Public Platform Data

Even publicly available data from **social media** or **online communities** must be used thoughtfully. Users may not expect their content to be analyzed for research or commercial use. Ethical practices include respecting context, anonymizing data, and, where feasible, obtaining consent. The use of **data brokers**, who often sell public and personal data without user knowledge, adds complexity and concern to this space.

4. Regulatory and Practical Responses

Regulatory bodies like the **FTC** and **CFPB** are responding to unethical data practices, especially regarding data brokers and the unauthorized use of sensitive personal information. Meanwhile, ethical research practices recommend tools like **ethics checklists, impact assessments,**

stakeholder mapping, and **deliberative workshops** to ensure theory translates into responsible action.

Ethical data practices are not just legal requirements—they reflect the values we bring into our digital systems. Responsible data collection requires **consent, clarity, minimal intrusion, and contextual sensitivity**, especially when using public data. As technology evolves, so must our ethical standards, ensuring that data science continues to serve the public good while respecting individual dignity.

Check Your Understanding

Fill in the blanks

1. Informed ________ is the process by which participants are made aware of how their data will be used and give explicit permission.
2. ________ participation means that individuals have the freedom to decide whether or not they want to take part in a data collection process.
3. Data ________ involves removing personally identifiable information to protect privacy.
4. ________ consent means that individuals must have the option to withdraw from a study or data collection at any time.
5. ________ platforms are online services where data is often gathered for research or marketing purposes.
6. When data is collected for research, it is important that participants are told about the ________ of the study.
7. ________ data refers to information that cannot be traced back to any specific individual.
8. The practice of ________ involves ensuring that the data collected does not intrude on an individual's personal privacy beyond what is necessary.
9. ________ forms are essential documents where participants agree to take part in data collection activities.
10. The principle of ________ ensures that data is collected for the sole purpose that participants have agreed to.
11. ________ is a key principle of data collection that emphasizes the importance of clarity and transparency when communicating with participants.
12. The ________ principle requires that data collectors inform participants about how their personal information will be used and stored.
13. Researchers must ensure that their data collection methods are not ________ by collecting excessive amounts of irrelevant information.
14. Ethical data collection involves protecting an individual's ________ when their information is being analyzed or shared.
15. The practice of ________ involves protecting individuals' identities in research data by removing identifiable information.

16. ________ is the term used to describe data collected from publicly available sources, such as social media.
17. The ________ principle states that data collection should only gather information necessary for the purpose of the study or project.
18. In an ethical data collection environment, ________ should be used to ensure participants understand the language and terms in consent forms.
19. A study or survey should clearly inform participants of their ________ to withdraw at any point during the research process.
20. When using data from social media platforms, researchers must ensure that users' ________ is not violated by using their information without consent.

Short Answer Questions

1. What does informed consent mean in the context of data collection?
2. Explain the importance of voluntary participation in research.
3. What is data anonymization, and why is it important in ethical data collection?
4. Define the term "public data" and provide one example.
5. Why is transparency crucial when collecting data from participants?
6. What does the principle of "no harm" entail in ethical data collection practices?
7. What is the role of clarity in consent forms?
8. What are the potential risks of collecting data without participant consent?
9. How can organizations protect identities when collecting data?
10. Why is it necessary to ensure data collected from public platforms is used responsibly?

Long Answer Questions

1. Discuss the ethical implications of collecting personal data from online platforms, and describe how researchers can ensure transparency and consent in this process.
2. Explain the steps involved in ensuring informed consent for participants in a research study. How does this process protect participants and enhance the quality of the research?
3. Evaluate the effectiveness of data anonymization techniques in safeguarding individuals' privacy. Provide examples of methods commonly used to anonymize data.

4. Analyze the ethical challenges involved in collecting data from vulnerable populations, such as children or people with disabilities. How should researchers navigate these challenges?
5. Discuss the potential conflicts between data collection for research purposes and the protection of personal privacy. How can researchers address these conflicts while maintaining ethical standards?
6. Explain how the principle of "avoiding intrusion" is applied in ethical data collection. Provide examples of when data collection can cross the line into intrusive practices.
7. Evaluate the ethical considerations of using data collected from social media platforms. What measures should researchers take to ensure ethical data use and respect user privacy?
8. Critically examine the practice of data mining in business and marketing. How can companies collect and use consumer data responsibly without violating ethical standards?
9. Assess the role of data brokers in the modern data economy. Discuss the ethical concerns surrounding the buying and selling of consumer data.
10. Discuss how ethical data collection can contribute to building trust between organizations and their participants. What strategies can be employed to ensure that data collection practices are transparent and respectful of privacy?

Answers

Fill in the blanks:

1. Consent
2. Voluntary
3. Anonymization
4. Informed
5. Public
6. Purpose
7. Anonymized
8. Avoiding intrusion
9. Consent
10. Purpose limitation

11. Transparency

12. Confidentiality

13. Intrusive

14. Privacy

15. De-identification

16. Publicly available

17. Data minimization

18. Simple language

19. Right

20. Privacy

Short Answer Questions (Answer Key)

1. Informed consent means that participants are fully aware of what data is being collected, how it will be used, and the potential risks involved, and they voluntarily agree to participate in the study or research process.
2. Voluntary participation ensures that individuals have the freedom to choose whether or not they want to participate in a research study without being coerced or pressured. This upholds participants' autonomy and respects their rights.
3. Data anonymization is the process of removing personal identifiers from data so that individuals cannot be easily identified. It is important because it protects participants' privacy and reduces the risk of misuse of sensitive information.
4. Public data refers to information that is freely available and accessible to the public. An example of public data would be government statistics, such as census data.
5. Transparency ensures that participants fully understand how their data will be used, stored, and shared. It builds trust and allows participants to make informed decisions about their involvement.
6. The principle of "no harm" means that data collection should not cause any physical, emotional, or psychological harm to participants. It requires careful consideration of risks and safeguards to minimize potential negative impacts.

7. Clarity in consent forms ensures that participants clearly understand what they are agreeing to. This includes understanding the purpose of the data collection, the types of data being collected, how the data will be used, and any potential risks involved.
8. Collecting data without consent can lead to privacy violations, loss of trust, legal consequences, and potential harm to participants. It can also damage an organization's reputation and result in the unauthorized use of personal information.
9. Organizations can protect identities by anonymizing or pseudonymizing the data, limiting access to sensitive information, and ensuring that personal identifiers are removed or encrypted before analysis.
10. Even if data is publicly available, individuals may not expect it to be used for research or commercial purposes. Responsible use includes ensuring that users' privacy is protected, their consent is obtained where possible, and their data is not exploited or misused.

Long Answer Questions (Answer Key)

1. Collecting personal data from online platforms, such as social media, raises significant ethical concerns related to privacy and consent. Many users may not be aware that their data is being used for research purposes. Researchers must ensure that they obtain explicit consent before using such data, even if it is publicly available. Transparency involves informing users about how their data will be used, who will access it, and how it will be protected. Ethical research should anonymize personal identifiers and limit data usage to the original research purpose, with clear options for participants to withdraw at any time.
2. The steps involved in ensuring informed consent include providing participants with clear and comprehensive information about the study's purpose, methods, risks, and how their data will be used. Researchers must offer the information in understandable language and provide an opportunity for participants to ask questions. Consent must be voluntarily given, without coercion. This process protects participants by ensuring they are fully aware of the study's risks and benefits, fostering trust. Informed consent also enhances the quality of the research by ensuring that participants are willing, knowledgeable participants, which strengthens the validity and reliability of the findings.
3. Data anonymization techniques are highly effective in safeguarding privacy, as they ensure that personal identifiers such as names, addresses, and contact details are removed or

disguised. Common anonymization methods include data aggregation (combining data into larger groups), pseudonymization (replacing personal identifiers with pseudonyms), and masking (altering identifiable parts of data). While anonymization reduces the risk of privacy violations, it is not foolproof, and there are always risks when combining datasets. As a result, researchers must carefully assess the level of anonymization needed for each dataset.

4. Collecting data from vulnerable populations raises ethical challenges, including ensuring proper informed consent, protecting participants' autonomy, and minimizing risks of harm. Special considerations are needed when working with children, such as obtaining consent from a parent or guardian. In the case of individuals with disabilities, additional accommodations may be necessary to ensure understanding and participation. Researchers should ensure that the benefits of the research outweigh the risks and should consult with ethics boards and use a rigorous informed consent process to safeguard participants' rights and well-being.
5. A potential conflict arises when data collection for research purposes may intrude on personal privacy. Researchers need to balance the value of the research with the ethical responsibility to protect participants' rights. This can be addressed by anonymizing data, securing participant consent, limiting data access, and ensuring data is used only for the specified purpose. Ethical standards can be maintained by following best practices, such as conducting ethical reviews, implementing robust data protection measures, and being transparent with participants about the potential uses of their data.
6. The principle of avoiding intrusion ensures that data is collected in a way that respects individuals' privacy and does not go beyond what is necessary for the research. For example, collecting sensitive data, such as personal health information, without the participant's explicit consent would be an intrusion. Ethical data collection requires that researchers ask only for the minimum amount of data needed, avoid intrusive methods such as surveillance without permission, and ensure that personal information is protected.
7. Social media data presents ethical challenges, including concerns about privacy, consent, and data ownership. Researchers must ensure that they obtain explicit consent from users if they intend to use their data, even if it is publicly available. To respect user privacy, data should be anonymized, and personally identifiable information should not be used without

consent. Additionally, researchers should be transparent about their use of social media data and explain the purpose of their research to users.

8. Data mining in business and marketing often involves the collection and analysis of vast amounts of consumer data to inform advertising strategies. Companies must ensure that they collect data with consumer consent, use it for specific, agreed-upon purposes, and avoid using it for unethical practices such as manipulation. Transparency, clear consent mechanisms, and data protection measures are critical for ethical data mining.
9. Data brokers play a significant role in the data economy by collecting and selling consumer data to businesses. Ethical concerns include the lack of transparency in how data is collected, the potential for misuse of personal information, and the fact that individuals are often unaware of their data being sold. Ethical practices require data brokers to ensure transparency, obtain consent, and respect privacy by offering individuals control over their data.
10. Ethical data collection builds trust by ensuring that participants' privacy is respected and that their data is used responsibly. Organizations can foster trust by being transparent about how data is collected, used, and protected. Strategies to ensure ethical data collection include clear consent forms, data anonymization, regular audits of data collection practices, and offering participants the option to withdraw at any time.

Chapter 4: Handling and Securing Sensitive Data

Learning Outcomes

1. Recall the definition and types of sensitive data commonly handled in digital environments.
2. Identify the basic tools and strategies used to safeguard personal and confidential information.
3. Understand the importance of secure infrastructure in maintaining user trust and privacy.
4. Explain ethical principles and responsibilities associated with data storage and retention.

Introduction

In today's digital landscape, the creation, collection, and transmission of sensitive data have reached unparalleled levels. From healthcare records and financial information to personal identifiers and behavioral data, organizations now manage vast quantities of data that carry significant ethical, legal, and societal implications. As digital systems grow in complexity and reach, so does the responsibility to protect the individuals whose information is being handled.

The handling of sensitive data is not merely a technical concern—it is fundamentally an ethical one. Organizations must ensure that data is gathered with informed consent, stored securely, used responsibly, and eventually discarded with care. When these responsibilities are neglected, the consequences can be severe: individuals may suffer privacy violations, identity theft, or discrimination, while institutions risk losing stakeholder trust, facing regulatory penalties, and damaging their reputations irreparably.

Building secure, trustworthy systems is therefore essential not only for compliance but for upholding public confidence in digital technologies. Establishing clear data protection policies, applying robust encryption techniques, and ensuring transparency in data practices are just a few of the measures that organizations must implement. Beyond technical safeguards, ethical considerations also come into play—such as determining how long data should be retained and ensuring that it is only used for its intended purpose.

This chapter ponders into the core principles and practical strategies for handling sensitive data ethically and securely. It outlines the importance of safeguarding information throughout its lifecycle, explores how to foster trust through transparent and secure systems, and examines the ethical challenges around data retention and disposal. As we move deeper into the data-driven age, cultivating responsible data practices will be crucial to protecting both individual rights and the integrity of digital ecosystems.

4.1 Safeguarding Personal and Confidential Information

In the era of digital expansion, the volume of sensitive data being generated and shared is growing at an extraordinary rate. This surge of data requires organizations to adopt rigorous strategies to ensure that such information is not only collected ethically but is also adequately protected throughout its lifecycle. Sensitive data includes personally identifiable information (PII), such as names, social security numbers, financial records, health information, and other details that can compromise an individual's privacy if mishandled. Therefore, it is crucial for organizations to implement stringent safeguards to avoid privacy breaches, identity theft, legal penalties, and erosion of trust.

Core Principles of Data Protection

To effectively secure sensitive information, three key principles guide data protection efforts, collectively referred to as the CIA Triad:

1. **Confidentiality**: This principle focuses on ensuring that sensitive information is accessible only to individuals with the proper authorization. Only authorized personnel should have access to personal data, ensuring that it is not exposed to unauthorized individuals, whether they are external attackers or even internal personnel with unnecessary access.
2. **Integrity**: Integrity ensures that the data is accurate, unaltered, and reliable throughout its lifecycle. This includes protections against unauthorized alterations, ensuring that the information remains trustworthy and accurate for decision-making, reporting, and operations.

3. **Availability**: Data must be accessible to authorized individuals when necessary. Availability ensures that systems are designed with redundancy and disaster recovery plans to ensure continuous access to data even in cases of system failures or attacks.

Best Practices for Securing Sensitive Data

To safeguard personal and confidential information effectively, organizations should adopt a combination of preventive measures:

- **Encryption**: Encrypting data both in transit and at rest is one of the most effective ways to protect sensitive information. Encryption transforms data into an unreadable format, ensuring that even if it is intercepted or accessed by unauthorized parties, it cannot be understood or misused without the appropriate decryption key.

Example: A **financial services company** that processes transactions online uses **SSL encryption** (Secure Socket Layer) to protect customer data during the checkout process. If someone intercepts the data, they will only see encrypted information, which is useless without the decryption key. Additionally, the company uses **encryption for data at rest**, meaning that customer financial records are encrypted even when stored in the database, making it hard for hackers to access sensitive information.

Why it matters: Encryption helps protect data both in **transit** (as it's being transmitted over the network) and **at rest** (when stored in databases or file systems).

- **Access Control Mechanisms**: Role-based access control (RBAC) ensures that only those who need specific data to perform their job functions can access it. By implementing strong access restrictions, organizations can minimize the risk of sensitive information being accessed by individuals without a legitimate need.

Example: In a **healthcare system**, only doctors and specific healthcare professionals have access to patient health records. The system uses **role-based access control (RBAC)** to ensure that administrative staff only has access to billing information and not to sensitive patient data such as medical history. In addition, the system restricts access to certain records based on security clearance levels, ensuring data confidentiality is maintained.

Why it matters: Implementing proper access control prevents unauthorized access and ensures that individuals can only view the data necessary for their roles, minimizing the risk of data exposure.

- **Regular Audits**: Conducting periodic audits of who is accessing what data and why can help detect potential vulnerabilities and prevent unauthorized access. Audits also play a significant role in regulatory compliance, ensuring that organizations are meeting the necessary standards for handling sensitive data.

Example: A **global e-commerce company** implements **audit logs** to track customer data access. For example, every time an employee accesses a customer's personal details, the system logs the action, capturing the employee's identity, time of access, and the data accessed. This log is regularly reviewed by an **internal audit team** to ensure no unauthorized access is occurring, especially to sensitive customer data such as payment details.

Why it matters: Regular audits not only help detect and prevent misuse of data but also allow organizations to demonstrate compliance with regulations such as **GDPR** or **HIPAA**, which mandate such tracking.

- **Secure Authentication**: Using multi-factor authentication (MFA) enhances security by requiring users to verify their identity through multiple forms of authentication, such as passwords, biometrics, or tokens. MFA adds an extra layer of protection, especially for sensitive data access points.

  Example: A **banking institution** uses **multi-factor authentication (MFA)** for its online banking system. To log in, users must enter their username and password, followed by an additional verification code sent to their phone. Even if an attacker manages to steal a customer's password, they would still need the phone to complete the login process, providing an extra layer of security.

Why it matters: MFA adds a significant barrier to unauthorized access, making it more difficult for hackers to gain access even if they have compromised login credentials.

- **Data Minimization**: Collecting only the essential data that is necessary for a specific purpose reduces the potential for exposure. By minimizing the amount of data collected, organizations can reduce their risk and the complexity of managing and securing excess information.

Example: An **online clothing retailer** collects only the essential data for processing customer orders: name, shipping address, and payment details. Instead of storing unnecessary data like customer preferences or browsing history, which would increase the complexity of securing this information, the retailer focuses on keeping only the essential information required for fulfilling orders. If additional data, such as order preferences, is needed, they ask for it explicitly, and the customer has the option to decline.

Why it matters: By minimizing data collection, organizations reduce the potential exposure of unnecessary data, thereby reducing the risk of a security breach and simplifying compliance with privacy regulations like **GDPR**.

Real-World Examples of These Practices in Action:

1. **Encryption Example (Financial Industry): PayPal**, a global online payment system, encrypts sensitive transaction data such as credit card information. This ensures that even if data is intercepted during transmission between PayPal's server and the bank, it cannot be read or misused by attackers.
2. **Access Control Example (Healthcare Industry): The Mayo Clinic**, a renowned healthcare provider, uses **RBAC** to ensure that only authorized medical staff have access to patients' medical records. Non-medical staff, such as billing or administrative staff, can only access the necessary parts of the system, such as appointment details, without being able to view sensitive health records.
3. **Audit Example (E-commerce Industry): Amazon**, the global e-commerce giant, conducts detailed **audit logs** for every action performed within its systems. These logs

track which employee accessed which customer account data and the reason for the access, ensuring transparency and accountability within their platform.

4. **Authentication Example (Banking Industry): Chase Bank** provides secure online banking services with **multi-factor authentication (MFA)**. To log into their accounts, customers use a combination of their login credentials (username and password) and an authentication code sent via text or email, which helps to secure accounts against unauthorized access.
5. **Data Minimization Example (Retail Industry): Zara**, a fashion retailer, only collects basic customer information such as name, address, and payment details when processing orders, avoiding excessive personal information. This minimizes the data stored and lowers the risk associated with customer data breaches.

Safeguarding personal and confidential information is a continuous process that involves employing best practices, including encryption, access control, secure authentication, data minimization, and regular audits. By adopting these practices, organizations not only protect sensitive data but also foster trust with their customers. The examples provided showcase how these strategies are implemented across different industries, illustrating the importance of data protection in maintaining security and complying with relevant regulations.

Example 2: Protecting Healthcare Data

Consider a healthcare provider using a secure cloud-based platform to store sensitive patient data. To ensure confidentiality, the data is encrypted both at rest and during transmission. Role-based access controls ensure that only authorized doctors and administrative staff can view specific patient information. Multi-factor authentication is required for login to the system, adding an additional layer of security. Regular access audits track which staff members accessed patient records, ensuring compliance with healthcare privacy regulations such as HIPAA. By following these practices, the healthcare provider ensures that patient data is protected from unauthorized access while maintaining regulatory compliance.

The protection of personal and confidential information is a critical responsibility for any organization in the digital era. By adhering to the principles of confidentiality, integrity, and availability, organizations can establish a robust framework for securing sensitive data. Implementing industry best practices such as encryption, access control, secure authentication, and data minimization allows organizations to safeguard data from unauthorized access, corruption, and loss. Ultimately, these practices help build trust with customers, clients, and stakeholders by ensuring their data is handled securely and ethically.

4.2 Building Trust Through Secure Infrastructure

In the modern digital era, data security is paramount in fostering and maintaining trust between organizations and their stakeholders. Whether it's a business-client relationship or a government-citizen dynamic, the assurance that personal information is handled with care is essential. When individuals feel secure about how their data is protected, they are more likely to engage and share information. Building trust requires a multi-layered approach, combining secure infrastructure with transparent practices and user empowerment. This section explores the key elements of a secure infrastructure, alongside the human aspects of building trust in digital spaces.

Elements of a Secure Infrastructure

1. Data Encryption Encryption is the most fundamental and effective way to protect sensitive data. Encryption transforms data into a coded format that can only be deciphered with the appropriate key, ensuring that unauthorized parties cannot access it. Robust encryption standards such as **AES-256** (Advanced Encryption Standard with a 256-bit key) offer a high level of security for sensitive information.

Example: A **global e-commerce platform** like **Amazon** uses encryption for all financial transactions. When a customer enters their payment details, the information is encrypted before it leaves the customer's device and is only decrypted by Amazon's secure servers. This ensures that sensitive details like credit card numbers and billing addresses are kept private, even if hackers intercept the data during transmission.

Why it matters: Encryption guarantees that even if data is intercepted or accessed by unauthorized parties, it remains unreadable and secure.

2. Firewalls and Intrusion Detection Systems (IDS) Firewalls act as a protective barrier between internal networks and the outside world, preventing unauthorized access and monitoring incoming and outgoing traffic. An **Intrusion Detection System (IDS)** is designed to detect suspicious or malicious activity in a network, alerting administrators of potential breaches.

Example: A **banking institution** implements a **firewall** to prevent unauthorized access to its customer database, while also using an IDS to monitor and analyze network traffic for any signs of unusual behavior. The IDS would alert the security team if a hacker attempts to access sensitive customer data, enabling swift action to mitigate the threat.

Why it matters: Firewalls and IDS are essential for identifying and blocking malicious activities before they can cause harm. They ensure the internal network remains secure against external threats.

3. Secure Software Development Practices Security should be integrated into the development process from the outset. This approach, known as **security by design**, ensures that applications are built with robust defenses against vulnerabilities that could be exploited by attackers.

Example: A **healthcare technology company** that develops electronic health record (EHR) systems adopts **secure software development practices**. Before releasing the software, the company conducts rigorous **code reviews**, **penetration testing**, and security audits to ensure there are no exploitable vulnerabilities that could compromise patient data. They also integrate continuous monitoring tools to detect any weaknesses as the software evolves.

Why it matters: By integrating security at every stage of development, businesses can significantly reduce the risk of vulnerabilities being present in the final product, thus ensuring the safety of sensitive data.

4. Regular Software Updates and Patch Management Cyber attackers often exploit **known vulnerabilities** in outdated software. Regular software updates and patch management programs are critical to ensuring that security vulnerabilities are addressed promptly. This is particularly important for operating systems, web servers, and other software critical to business functions.

Example: Microsoft routinely releases **security patches** for its operating systems, such as **Windows 10**, to address newly discovered vulnerabilities. A **large financial institution** implements a policy of regularly updating their systems and applying patches as soon as they are released to protect their internal network and customer data.

Why it matters: Failure to apply patches and updates in a timely manner leaves systems exposed to attacks that can exploit these known vulnerabilities. Keeping systems updated ensures that an organization stays ahead of potential threats.

5. Backup Systems In the event of a data breach, system failure, or ransomware attack, having secure and regular **backup systems** in place ensures that data can be restored without significant loss. Backup systems should be encrypted and stored in a secure location to prevent unauthorized access.

Example: A **cloud storage provider** like **Dropbox** offers automated backups of user data, encrypted in transit and at rest. Even if a user's account is compromised, the company can restore the data from its secure backup systems, minimizing the impact of the breach.

Why it matters: Backups ensure that data loss does not result in permanent harm to the organization or its clients, enabling recovery in case of unforeseen disasters or malicious attacks

6. Third-party Risk Management Organizations frequently rely on third-party vendors to provide services or support. However, the security of these vendors is just as important as the organization's own. Proper third-party risk management involves assessing vendors' security practices to ensure they meet the same standards and policies as the organization itself.

Example: A **retail chain** partners with an external payment processor to handle customer transactions. The retailer conducts thorough **due diligence** on the payment processor's security measures, including **PCI DSS compliance** (Payment Card Industry Data Security Standard), to ensure that it can securely handle sensitive credit card data. They also require regular security audits and access to the processor's security reports to ensure ongoing compliance.

Why it matters: Third-party vendors are often a weak point in security, and poor practices by these vendors can expose an organization to unnecessary risks. Effective third-party risk management mitigates these risks.

The Human Element of Trust

While a secure infrastructure is essential, trust is also built through transparent communication, user autonomy, and visible commitment to privacy. People must feel confident that their data is not only secure but also used ethically.

1. Clear Communication About Data Usage Transparency is critical in fostering trust. Organizations must clearly communicate how customer data is collected, used, and protected. Clear communication builds confidence and eliminates uncertainty.

Example: A **fintech startup** provides customers with **privacy notices** that detail exactly what data is being collected, how it will be used (e.g., for providing financial recommendations), and what measures are taken to secure the data. The company also informs customers of their rights under **GDPR** and other relevant privacy laws, giving them a sense of control over their data.

Why it matters: Transparent communication reassures customers that the organization is committed to protecting their data and not using it in ways they have not consented to.

2. User Controls Over Data Sharing Preferences Allowing users to control their data-sharing preferences is an essential component of building trust. This includes giving users the ability to opt in or out of specific data collection practices.

Example: A **social media platform** like **Facebook** offers users granular control over who can see their posts and what data is shared with third-party advertisers. Users can access their privacy settings and adjust what information they are willing to share, such as location data or browsing history.

Why it matters: Giving users control over their own data fosters a sense of ownership and trust, empowering them to make informed decisions about how their personal information is used.

3. Visible Commitment to Privacy Organizations should not only have clear privacy policies but also make visible commitments to protect user data. These can include public statements, certifications, or independent audits of security practices.

Example: Apple has built a reputation for its commitment to privacy. The company regularly makes public statements about how it secures customer data, employs end-to-end encryption in its messaging apps, and has a clear privacy policy that is easily accessible on its website. This visible commitment has helped Apple maintain customer loyalty and trust.

Why it matters: Visible commitments demonstrate an organization's dedication to user privacy and serve as a trust-building mechanism.

Example in Practice:

Fintech Startup Example: Consider a **fintech startup** that provides digital banking services. The company earns customer trust by taking the following steps:

1. **Public Sharing of Security Protocols**: The startup clearly communicates its security practices, such as using **end-to-end encryption** for transactions, and publicly shares its **security audits** to show it adheres to best practices.
2. **User Controls**: It allows customers to control how their data is shared with third-party service providers and offers them the option to opt in or out of certain data uses.
3. **Visible Commitment to Privacy**: The company publishes annual **transparency reports** and participates in **third-party security audits**, demonstrating its ongoing commitment to safeguarding user information.

These efforts, combined with a robust secure infrastructure, result in a strong foundation of trust between the startup and its users.

Building trust through secure infrastructure is an ongoing process that requires a multifaceted approach. By ensuring a secure environment through encryption, firewalls, regular updates, and third-party risk management, organizations can protect sensitive data. Additionally, transparent communication, user autonomy, and visible commitment to privacy strengthen the relationship between organizations and their users. Trust is not a one-time achievement but a continuous effort to maintain security, privacy, and transparency. Organizations that invest in both technical infrastructure and human trust-building strategies will foster long-lasting, loyal relationships with their customers.

4.3 Navigating Ethical Dilemmas in Data Retention

Data retention refers to the practices and policies surrounding how long organizations keep data, how they store it, and when they choose to delete it. Striking a balance between maintaining data for necessary business operations and respecting privacy concerns is a critical challenge. Storing data for too long can pose legal, ethical, and privacy risks, while deleting it too soon may hinder business operations or violate compliance regulations. In this section, we explore the common ethical dilemmas organizations face in data retention, the best practices to navigate these dilemmas, and provide examples of how organizations can implement ethical data retention policies.

Common Ethical Dilemmas in Data Retention

1. **How Long is Too Long?**

   One of the most prominent ethical issues in data retention is determining the appropriate amount of time to store data. While retaining data for extended periods can offer valuable insights and improve business analytics, it also presents significant risks. Storing sensitive data indefinitely increases the chances of it being exposed in a breach, and it can infringe on privacy rights. Prolonged retention of personal data may also conflict with evolving privacy norms and regulations, leading to legal risks for organizations.

   Example: A social media platform may retain user data, including posts, messages, and interactions, for an extended period to improve user experience and personalize advertisements. However, if the platform holds onto this data far beyond what is necessary or legally required, it could face privacy concerns or legal consequences. Users may feel their data is being exploited, even if they are unaware of how long it is retained.

2. **Balancing Business Needs vs. User Rights**

   Organizations often face a dilemma when they need to retain data for business purposes, but this may conflict with users' rights to privacy and control over their data. For example, retaining user transaction history for customer service purposes or providing better recommendations may enhance business operations, but it could infringe on a user's desire for privacy and control over their personal information.

   Example: An online retailer may retain purchase history to improve personalized recommendations or assist with customer service inquiries. However, users may prefer that their data be deleted after a certain period, especially if they no longer use the platform. Finding a balance between operational needs and respecting user preferences becomes crucial in such situations.

3. **Right to be Forgotten**

   The right to be forgotten, especially under regulations like the **General Data Protection Regulation (GDPR)**, allows individuals to request that their personal data be deleted. This provision can create ethical dilemmas for organizations that must balance users' rights to delete their data with the need to retain certain information for legal, regulatory, or business purposes. For example, an organization may be legally obligated to retain certain data for a specific period, but an individual might request its deletion sooner.

   Example: Under **GDPR** regulations, a user of a social media platform may request that their data be deleted entirely. However, if the platform retains certain data for compliance with tax laws or to preserve business records, the organization faces an ethical dilemma in fulfilling both legal obligations and the user's request. In some cases, organizations may be forced to strike a compromise, such as anonymizing data rather than fully deleting it.

Best Practices for Ethical Data Retention

To navigate the ethical dilemmas surrounding data retention, organizations should adopt the following best practices:

1. **Data Retention Policies**

   Establishing clear, documented data retention policies is vital for ensuring data is kept only for as long as necessary. These policies should be based on legal, regulatory, and business requirements, and they should specify the retention period for different types of data.

   Example: A **financial institution** may retain transaction records for a minimum of seven years to comply with regulatory requirements. However, non-essential data such as promotional emails or browsing history could be deleted after a shorter period, in line with company policy and user preferences.

2. **Periodic Review of Data**

   Conducting regular reviews of the data stored by an organization is crucial to ensuring that only the necessary data is retained. This process helps organizations identify outdated or unnecessary data, which can then be deleted or anonymized. Periodic audits also provide an opportunity to check for compliance with internal policies and legal requirements.

   Example: An **e-commerce company** reviews its customer data every year to ensure that it only retains purchase history, contact information, and billing details for active customers. Inactive accounts, or accounts with outdated information, are flagged for review, and customers are notified about the possibility of data deletion.

3. **Automated Deletion Mechanisms**

   Implementing automated deletion systems can help organizations comply with retention policies while also minimizing the risk of holding onto data longer than necessary. By setting expiration dates for certain data types, organizations can automate the deletion process once the retention period has passed.

   Example: An **online subscription service** uses automated deletion software to ensure that users' payment information is deleted after a certain period of inactivity (e.g., two years). This ensures compliance with **GDPR** and similar regulations while maintaining transparency with users regarding how long their data is retained.

4. **User Consent and Notification**

   Transparency about data retention practices is essential to building trust with users. Organizations should notify users about their data retention policies, giving them the ability to control how long their data is kept. Providing users with the ability to request deletion or modify their preferences ensures that their rights are respected.

   Example: A **cloud storage provider** sends users notifications when their data is nearing the end of its retention period, offering them the option to delete it sooner. The company also provides users with the ability to adjust their retention preferences via their account settings.

5. **Compliance with Laws**

   Aligning data retention policies with local, regional, or international regulations is essential for ensuring that the organization adheres to legal requirements. Laws like **GDPR**, **HIPAA**, and the **California Consumer Privacy Act (CCPA)** mandate that certain data types be retained for specific periods. Non-compliance can lead to severe financial and reputational damage.

   Example: A **healthcare provider** retains medical records for a minimum of ten years in compliance with **HIPAA** regulations. At the same time, it ensures that any non-medical data, such as marketing preferences, is deleted as per the user's request and in line with **GDPR** guidelines.

Case Example: E-Commerce Platform

An **e-commerce platform** illustrates how data retention policies can be implemented ethically and transparently. The company retains user purchase history for five years in compliance with warranty and legal requirements. However, after two years of inactivity, the platform automatically anonymizes the account details, ensuring that personal information is not linked to any user. Users are notified via email about this anonymization process, and they are given the option to delete their data at any time before the automatic anonymization occurs.

This approach balances the company's business needs (retaining purchase records for warranty purposes) with user privacy rights (anonymizing data after two years of inactivity). It also complies with privacy regulations like **GDPR**, which requires companies to be transparent about data usage and offer users the right to manage their data.

Navigating the ethical dilemmas in data retention requires a delicate balance between business needs, legal obligations, and user privacy rights. By adopting clear data retention policies, conducting regular audits, implementing automated deletion systems, and ensuring compliance with legal requirements, organizations can safeguard user privacy while maintaining operational efficiency. Clear communication, transparency, and respect for users' rights are essential in fostering trust and avoiding ethical pitfalls. As privacy regulations continue to evolve, organizations must remain adaptable and proactive in ensuring that their data retention practices align with both legal standards and ethical principles.

The ethical handling and protection of sensitive data go beyond technological solutions. It requires a strategic blend of policy, infrastructure, and organizational culture centered around privacy, transparency, and responsibility. By safeguarding data, building trust through secure systems, and making thoughtful choices about data retention, organizations not only comply with legal requirements but also earn long-term loyalty and credibility.

Summary

In the digital age, managing sensitive data is essential for protecting privacy and ensuring the security of individuals and organizations. Sensitive data includes personally identifiable information (PII), health records, financial data, and more. Organizations must implement key principles of data protection such as confidentiality, integrity, and availability to secure data from unauthorized access.

Best practices for safeguarding sensitive data include encryption, access controls, regular audits, secure authentication, and data minimization. For example, healthcare providers use encryption and multi-factor authentication to safeguard patient records and ensure compliance with regulations like HIPAA.

Building trust with stakeholders requires secure infrastructure that includes robust encryption, firewalls, secure software development, timely software updates, and backup systems. Additionally, organizations should focus on transparency and clear communication about data usage and protection. A fintech company might earn customer trust by sharing security protocols and offering privacy controls for users.

Data retention is another key ethical issue, involving decisions about how long to keep data and when to delete it. Ethical dilemmas arise around issues like data retention periods, user rights, and compliance with regulations such as GDPR, which grants individuals the right to request data deletion. Organizations should establish clear data retention policies, conduct periodic reviews, implement automated deletion mechanisms, and ensure compliance with laws. For instance, an e-commerce platform might retain purchase history for five years for legal reasons but anonymizes account details after two years of inactivity to protect privacy.

Ultimately, organizations must find a balance between retaining necessary data for business operations and respecting user privacy. Ethical data retention practices should be transparent, comply with legal standards, and be regularly reviewed to ensure ongoing compliance. By following these best practices, organizations can build trust, protect sensitive data, and navigate the complex ethical challenges of the digital era.

Check your understanding

1. Data that must be protected from unauthorized access is called __________ data.
2. The process of turning data into unreadable code to protect it is known as __________.
3. __________ ensures that only authorized individuals can access certain data.
4. Multi-factor authentication enhances __________ security.
5. __________ access ensures that users can only access data relevant to their role.
6. __________ systems are used to detect unauthorized access attempts or threats.
7. The principle of __________ refers to storing data only for as long as it is needed.
8. Backup systems are crucial for ensuring data __________ in case of failures.
9. A __________ breach occurs when sensitive information is exposed or stolen.
10. The __________ element is crucial in building user trust around data security.
11. Organizations should collect only the minimum data needed, known as __________.
12. Firewalls act as a __________ between trusted and untrusted networks.
13. __________ by design means embedding security into software development from the beginning.
14. Confidentiality, integrity, and availability form the foundation of data __________.
15. A __________ policy outlines how long data is stored and when it should be deleted.
16. Regular __________ of systems and permissions helps maintain security standards.
17. Secure data handling builds __________ between organizations and their users.
18. The right to request the deletion of personal data is known as the "right to be __________."
19. __________ controls restrict system access based on user roles and needs.
20. __________ information includes data like health records and financial details.

Short Answer Questions

1. What is meant by "sensitive data"?
2. Define data encryption.
3. What is the purpose of a firewall in data security?
4. List two examples of personally identifiable information (PII).
5. What does "data minimization" mean?
6. Why is role-based access control important in data security?

7. What is meant by "secure infrastructure"?
8. Name two ways to build trust with users when handling their data.
9. What is the "right to be forgotten"?
10. How does multi-factor authentication improve data security?

Long Answer Questions

1. Discuss the key principles of safeguarding personal and confidential data. Provide examples from real-world applications.
2. Explain how a secure infrastructure contributes to user trust. Include both technical and human elements in your answer.
3. Analyze the role of encryption and access control in preventing data breaches. How do they work together?
4. Evaluate the ethical considerations of storing user data beyond its intended purpose.
5. Describe a scenario where poor data retention policies could lead to ethical or legal issues.
6. Compare and contrast proactive vs. reactive security strategies in data protection.
7. Discuss how organizations can balance business needs with ethical responsibilities in data retention.
8. Explain how organizations can navigate data retention laws like GDPR while maintaining operational efficiency.
9. Examine the role of regular security audits in maintaining secure systems. Why are they necessary?
10. Propose a data retention strategy for a healthcare organization that respects both legal requirements and patient rights.

Answers

Fill in the Blanks – Answers Only

1. Sensitive
2. Encryption
3. Confidentiality
4. Login/account **(or** authentication**)**

5. Role-based
6. Intrusion Detection
7. Data retention
8. Recovery
9. Data
10. Human
11. Data minimization
12. Barrier
13. Security
14. Security
15. Retention
16. Audits
17. Trust
18. Forgotten
19. Access
20. Confidential

Short Answer Questions – Answer Key

1. **Sensitive data** refers to personal or confidential information that must be protected from unauthorized access, like financial or health records.
2. **Data encryption** is the process of converting information into a code to prevent unauthorized access.
3. A **firewall** is a security system that monitors and controls incoming and outgoing network traffic based on predetermined rules.
4. Examples include: **Name, address, phone number, Social Security number.**
5. **Data minimization** means collecting only the information that is necessary for a specific purpose.
6. **Role-based access control** ensures users only have access to the data necessary for their job roles, reducing risk of exposure.
7. A **secure infrastructure** includes tools, systems, and practices that ensure data is protected from breaches or unauthorized access.

8. By **being transparent** about data usage and **offering users control** over their data, trust can be built.
9. The **"right to be forgotten"** allows individuals to request deletion of their personal data from databases or systems.
10. **Multi-factor authentication** adds extra verification steps (e.g., a code sent to your phone) beyond just a password, increasing security.

Long Answer Questions – Answer Key

1. Key principles include **confidentiality, integrity, and availability**. For example, encrypting medical records or using access controls in banking platforms ensures data is kept safe from misuse.
2. A secure infrastructure uses **encryption, firewalls, regular audits**, and **human transparency** (such as clear privacy policies) to build trust with users.
3. **Encryption** scrambles data to make it unreadable to unauthorized users, while **access control** ensures only approved personnel can access the data. Together, they protect against internal and external threats.
4. Storing user data beyond its purpose can lead to privacy violations, legal non-compliance, and loss of user trust, especially when data is used without consent.
5. If a company keeps old customer data indefinitely, and that data is stolen in a breach, they may face legal consequences for not deleting it in accordance with regulations like GDPR.
6. **Proactive security** includes planning and prevention (like regular system updates), while **reactive security** involves responding to breaches after they occur. A combination is best.
7. Businesses must collect enough data to function but also respect privacy by setting clear limits and regularly deleting outdated or unnecessary information.
8. GDPR requires data to be retained only as long as necessary. Companies can use **automated retention schedules** to comply while still retaining critical data for operations.
9. **Security audits** review access logs, system configurations, and vulnerabilities, ensuring that best practices are being followed and weaknesses are addressed.
10. A good strategy includes: storing essential records for the minimum legal period, **encrypting data**, allowing patients to access and delete their own data, and performing periodic reviews.

Chapter 5: Dealing with Bias and Promoting Equity

Learning Outcomes

1. Define the key concepts of data protection, including confidentiality, integrity, and availability.
2. Identify the ethical principles involved in data collection and retention practices.
3. Explain the role of encryption, access controls, and regular audits in safeguarding personal information.
4. Describe the process of mitigating bias in predictive models and the importance of inclusive data collection.

Introduction

In the age of data-driven decision-making, predictive models and machine learning systems are increasingly shaping critical aspects of our lives—from determining loan approvals and hiring candidates to guiding healthcare interventions and influencing criminal justice outcomes. While these technologies offer powerful tools for efficiency and innovation, they also pose significant ethical challenges, particularly when it comes to fairness and equity.

At the heart of these challenges lies bias—often hidden within the data used to train models, in the way features are selected, or in how outcomes are interpreted. If left unchecked, these biases can lead to discriminatory practices, reinforcing societal inequalities and producing outcomes that are unjust or harmful to marginalized groups. Addressing bias isn't just a technical task; it's a moral imperative for data scientists, developers, and organizations committed to building inclusive and ethical systems.

This chapter delves into the complexities of bias in data science, beginning with an exploration of the types of biases commonly found in datasets and the methods used to detect them. It then examines how predictive models can unintentionally perpetuate these biases, and presents a comprehensive set of strategies for ensuring fairness in their design and deployment. By combining technical tools, ethical frameworks, and ongoing evaluation, organizations can work toward building systems that promote equity and reflect the diversity of the real world.

5.1 Uncovering Hidden Bias in Datasets

In data science, one of the most critical challenges is uncovering hidden biases within datasets. Bias in datasets is an insidious issue that can lead to unfair, inaccurate, and unethical outcomes. When datasets contain hidden biases, the models trained on them may perpetuate or amplify these biases, leading to discriminatory results. This section explores the various types of biases that can exist in datasets, how to detect them, and the steps organizations can take to mitigate them.

Types of Bias in Datasets

1. **Sampling Bias** Sampling bias occurs when the dataset is not representative of the population it is intended to reflect. This can happen if certain groups or characteristics are overrepresented or underrepresented in the data. Sampling bias can lead to models that perform well for certain demographic groups but poorly for others.

   Example: A facial recognition system trained primarily on images of light-skinned individuals may struggle to recognize people with darker skin tones. If the dataset predominantly consists of photos of one ethnicity, the model may perform poorly for people of other ethnicities.

2. **Label Bias** Label bias refers to the biases introduced when human annotators assign labels to data. This can happen when the annotators have their own prejudices, stereotypes, or cultural assumptions that influence how they label the data. This is particularly common in datasets used for supervised learning.

   Example: In a dataset of job applicants, if the annotators label resumes as "qualified" or "unqualified" based on their unconscious bias toward certain gender or ethnic groups, this will create a biased model that might favor one group over another, even if the qualifications are identical.

3. **Measurement Bias** Measurement bias occurs when the tools or methods used to collect data are flawed, leading to inaccurate or skewed data. This could involve using outdated technology, poorly calibrated instruments, or inconsistent data collection practices.

Example: In healthcare, if a dataset of blood pressure readings is collected using faulty equipment that consistently underestimates high blood pressure, the resulting model may fail to detect hypertension in patients who are truly at risk, leading to inadequate treatment.

4. **Exclusion Bias** Exclusion bias happens when certain relevant data points are omitted or excluded from a dataset, leading to a model that does not account for all variables that could influence outcomes.

   Example: In predictive policing, if the dataset excludes certain neighborhoods or demographics, the model might disproportionately target certain communities, reinforcing stereotypes about crime rates based on incomplete data.

5. **Historical Bias** Historical bias arises when datasets reflect past prejudices, inequalities, or injustices. These biases are often baked into historical data because societal systems may have been unjust or discriminatory at the time the data was collected.

   Example: A dataset used for hiring predictions might reflect historical hiring practices that favored men over women. If the data from previous years shows an underrepresentation of women in leadership roles, a model trained on this data may perpetuate this gender gap.

Techniques for Uncovering Hidden Bias in Datasets

1. **Exploratory Data Analysis (EDA)** EDA is a crucial step in identifying potential biases within datasets. By visualizing data distributions, performing statistical analyses, and inspecting correlations, data scientists can uncover patterns that may indicate the presence of bias.

   Example: Using box plots or histograms to compare the distribution of data across different demographic groups can reveal imbalances in the data that need to be addressed.

2. **Bias Audits** A bias audit is a systematic evaluation of a dataset to identify and measure potential sources of bias. Bias audits involve evaluating both the input data and the output predictions of machine learning models to determine if there are discrepancies in how different groups are treated.

Example: A company using an AI-powered hiring tool could conduct a bias audit to see whether the tool disproportionately rejects candidates from specific racial or ethnic backgrounds, even if they have the same qualifications as other candidates.

3. **Fairness Metrics** Fairness metrics are quantitative methods used to assess whether a model treats different demographic groups equitably. There are several fairness metrics that can be applied depending on the context, including:
    - **Demographic Parity**: Ensures that outcomes (e.g., positive predictions) are distributed equally across groups.
    - **Equalized Odds**: Requires that the false positive rate and false negative rate are equal across groups.
    - **Predictive Parity**: Ensures that the predictive accuracy is consistent across groups.

   Example: When testing a credit scoring model, the company might evaluate whether the approval rate for loans is the same for men and women, as well as for people from different racial or socioeconomic backgrounds.

4. **Algorithmic Bias Detection Tools** Several tools and frameworks have been developed to help identify bias in machine learning algorithms. These tools often involve statistical tests or audits that flag disparities in how different groups are treated by the model.

   Example: The IBM AI Fairness 360 toolkit offers a suite of algorithms to detect and mitigate bias in datasets and models. These tools help organizations evaluate whether their algorithms treat different groups fairly and, if not, how to adjust the models to promote fairness.

5. **Bias in Feature Engineering** Sometimes, bias can be introduced during the feature engineering process, where certain variables or features are selected in ways that disproportionately favor certain groups. It's essential to assess which features are included in the model and whether they might inadvertently contribute to bias.

Example: A predictive model for criminal recidivism that includes features like "neighborhood of residence" or "family history of incarceration" might inadvertently incorporate historical biases against certain communities, leading to biased predictions.

Strategies for Mitigating Bias in Datasets

1. **Diversifying Data Sources** One of the most effective ways to reduce bias is to ensure that datasets are diverse and representative of all relevant groups. This involves sourcing data from multiple channels and ensuring that underrepresented groups are adequately represented in the data.

   Example: A facial recognition system should be trained on a dataset that includes a balanced representation of people from various ethnicities, genders, and age groups. By ensuring diversity in the training data, the model is less likely to favor one group over others.

2. **Bias Detection During Data Collection** Proactively identifying potential sources of bias during data collection is critical. This can involve checking for any imbalances or exclusions and actively addressing these issues before the data is used for modeling.

   Example: A healthcare research study that collects data on patients with chronic diseases might monitor the distribution of participants by age, gender, and ethnicity to ensure that the dataset is representative of the general population and not skewed toward a particular demographic group.

3. **Regularly Updating Datasets** Bias can creep into models over time as societal norms change. It is essential to regularly update datasets to reflect these changes and ensure that historical biases do not continue to influence predictions.

   Example: A dataset used for predicting home loan approvals might need to be updated periodically to account for evolving social and economic conditions, ensuring that the model remains fair and equitable.

4. **Transparency and Accountability** Organizations should foster a culture of transparency and accountability when it comes to data collection and model deployment. Providing transparency about how data is collected, used, and analyzed can help mitigate bias by allowing stakeholders to understand and challenge potential issues.

   Example: A social media company might release transparency reports outlining how its content moderation algorithm works, including any potential biases it might have in

Uncovering and addressing bias in datasets is a vital step in ensuring fairness and equity in data science and machine learning. By using a combination of exploratory data analysis, fairness metrics, and bias audits, data scientists can identify hidden biases that could otherwise lead to harmful or unfair outcomes. Organizations must take proactive steps to diversify data sources, mitigate bias during data collection, and continually assess their models for fairness. Through these efforts, it is possible to build more equitable and inclusive systems that reflect the diversity of the real world.

5.2 Ensuring Fairness in Predictive Models

Predictive models have become an essential tool for decision-making across industries, from healthcare to finance to criminal justice. However, these models, if not carefully managed, can perpetuate existing biases and inequalities, leading to unfair outcomes. Ensuring fairness in predictive models is crucial for creating systems that are just, unbiased, and equitable for all users. This section explores the various challenges in ensuring fairness in predictive models, key strategies for promoting fairness, and real-world examples to illustrate how these strategies can be applied effectively.

Challenges in Ensuring Fairness

1. **Bias in Data** The first challenge in ensuring fairness is the inherent bias in the data that predictive models are built on. Data bias is often introduced during the data collection phase, where certain groups or characteristics may be overrepresented or underrepresented. When the model learns from biased data, it can replicate or even amplify these biases, leading to discriminatory outcomes.

Example: In a hiring algorithm, if historical data shows that men have been more frequently hired for leadership positions, the model may unintentionally favor male candidates, even if women are equally qualified.

2. **Complexity of Fairness** Fairness is not a one-size-fits-all concept. What constitutes fairness may differ based on the context and the stakeholders involved. For instance, a model that works fairly for one demographic group may be unfair to another. Defining fairness requires careful consideration of trade-offs, and achieving fairness in one area may lead to imbalances in another.

   Example: A healthcare model may be designed to optimize patient outcomes, but focusing solely on improving the health outcomes of one group (e.g., elderly patients) could result in neglecting the needs of other groups (e.g., children or low-income patients), leading to unequal treatment.

3. **Historical Inequities** Historical inequalities and systemic biases that exist in society can be reflected in the data. If not addressed, predictive models can inadvertently perpetuate these disparities. For example, models trained on historical criminal justice data may reflect and perpetuate racial biases that have existed in policing and sentencing practices.

   Example: Predictive policing models that are trained on past crime data may disproportionately target minority communities due to biased data, further exacerbating the over-policing of those communities.

4. **Legal and Ethical Constraints** Legal frameworks such as the General Data Protection Regulation (GDPR) and the Equal Credit Opportunity Act impose constraints on how data can be used, especially when it comes to sensitive attributes such as race, gender, or age. Ensuring fairness while complying with legal requirements can be a complex balancing act.

   Example: In credit scoring models, if race or gender is removed from the input features to avoid discrimination, the model might still indirectly use correlated features like zip codes, which could still reflect demographic disparities.

Strategies for Ensuring Fairness in Predictive Models

1. **Defining Fairness Metrics** One of the first steps in ensuring fairness in predictive models is to define what fairness means in the context of the model. There are various fairness metrics that can be used to evaluate and ensure equity. Some commonly used fairness metrics include:
    - **Demographic Parity**: Ensures that the positive prediction rate is the same across different demographic groups.
    - **Equalized Odds**: Ensures that the false positive and false negative rates are the same across different groups.
    - **Predictive Parity**: Ensures that the predictive accuracy is consistent across groups.
    - **Individual Fairness**: Ensures that similar individuals receive similar outcomes.

    Example: In a loan approval model, demographic parity would ensure that individuals from different racial backgrounds have an equal likelihood of receiving a loan approval. However, this might need to be balanced with other fairness metrics, such as equalized odds, to ensure that applicants with similar credit profiles are treated similarly, regardless of their demographic group.

2. **Pre-processing Techniques** Pre-processing techniques can be applied to datasets to mitigate bias before they are used to train models. These techniques typically focus on modifying the data to ensure that it does not unfairly represent one group over another. Some common pre-processing methods include:
    - **Re-sampling**: Adjusting the dataset by either oversampling underrepresented groups or undersampling overrepresented groups.
    - **Re-weighting**: Giving more weight to underrepresented groups in the training process.
    - **Disentangling Sensitive Attributes**: Removing correlations between sensitive attributes (e.g., race or gender) and other features in the dataset that could lead to biased outcomes.

Example: In a predictive policing system, re-sampling might involve adjusting the training dataset to ensure that neighborhoods with historically lower crime rates are not underrepresented, reducing bias in the model's predictions.

3. **In-processing Fairness Adjustments** In-processing fairness techniques involve modifying the learning algorithm itself to promote fairness. These techniques can help ensure that the model does not unfairly favor certain groups during the training process. Common in-processing fairness methods include:
    - **Adversarial Debiasing**: A technique that uses adversarial networks to reduce bias during training by penalizing the model if it learns biased patterns.
    - **Fairness Constraints**: Adding fairness constraints to the optimization process of the model to ensure that fairness objectives are prioritized during training.

    Example: In the case of a healthcare prediction model, adversarial debiasing might involve introducing an adversarial network that penalizes the model for learning features that are correlated with sensitive attributes like race or gender, promoting fairness in the predictions.

4. **Post-processing Fairness Adjustments** Post-processing fairness methods involve making adjustments to the model's predictions after they have been generated. These techniques are used to correct any bias that has been identified in the model's outputs. Common post-processing techniques include:
    - **Equalized Odds Post-processing**: Adjusting the model's output to ensure that the false positive and false negative rates are equal across different demographic groups.
    - **Calibration by Group**: Adjusting the predicted probabilities for different demographic groups to ensure that the model is fair across those groups.

    Example: In a credit scoring model, post-processing could be used to adjust the model's predicted approval rates to ensure that applicants from different demographic backgrounds are treated equally, even if the model's raw predictions are biased.

5. **Transparent and Explainable AI** To promote fairness, it is essential that predictive models are transparent and explainable. This allows stakeholders to understand how decisions are made and identify potential sources of bias. Explainable AI (XAI) methods can help provide insights into why certain decisions are made by the model, which is critical for identifying and mitigating unfair outcomes.

   Example: A bank that uses an AI model to predict loan approval may use explainability techniques to provide clear reasons for why an applicant was either approved or denied. This transparency can help ensure that the model's decisions are not influenced by hidden biases and can be easily audited for fairness.

6. **Bias Audits and Continuous Monitoring** Regular audits and continuous monitoring of predictive models are essential to ensure that they remain fair over time. Bias can creep into models as societal conditions change, so it is important to evaluate models periodically and adjust them to reflect evolving norms and standards.

   Example: A health insurance company using an AI model to predict patient risks should regularly audit the model to ensure it continues to provide fair outcomes across different demographic groups, especially as healthcare policies and societal attitudes change.

Real-World Example: Fairness in Hiring Algorithms

A tech company develops an AI system to streamline its hiring process by evaluating resumes and recommending candidates for interviews. However, after deploying the system, the company notices that the model disproportionately favors male candidates for technical roles, even when female candidates have similar qualifications.

To address this issue, the company:

- Conducts a bias audit and finds that the training data was skewed toward male candidates, reflecting historical gender imbalances in tech.
- Implements pre-processing methods, such as re-sampling and re-weighting the training data to ensure more equal representation of male and female candidates.

- Introduces fairness constraints during model training to minimize gender bias while maintaining performance.
- Continuously monitors the model's predictions and adjusts it based on feedback from diverse groups of employees.

As a result, the company is able to improve the fairness of its hiring model and increase the representation of women in technical roles.

Ensuring fairness in predictive models is a multifaceted challenge that requires a combination of strategies, including defining fairness metrics, applying pre-processing, in-processing, and post-processing techniques, promoting transparency, and regularly auditing models for bias. It is essential for organizations to be proactive in addressing fairness concerns to prevent unintended discrimination and promote equitable outcomes for all users. By leveraging these strategies, organizations can create more inclusive and just systems that benefit everyone, regardless of their demographic background.

5.3 Strategies for Inclusive and Balanced Outcomes

Creating inclusive and balanced outcomes in predictive models is a critical goal for organizations that aim to build fair, equitable, and socially responsible systems. Inclusivity ensures that all individuals, regardless of their demographic characteristics, are treated fairly and benefit equally from the decisions made by data-driven systems. A balanced outcome means considering the diverse needs of all groups involved and minimizing the disparities between them. This section outlines key strategies for promoting inclusivity and balance, along with real-world examples to illustrate how these strategies can be applied effectively.

Key Strategies for Promoting Inclusive and Balanced Outcomes

1. **Diverse Data Collection and Representation** Ensuring that data used to train predictive models is diverse and representative of all affected groups is the foundation of an inclusive system. Models trained on unrepresentative datasets risk perpetuating biases that disproportionately affect underrepresented or marginalized groups. Thus, it is essential to

ensure that data collection methods actively seek diverse data sources and that every group of people is adequately represented.

Best Practices for Data Collection:

- Actively seek diverse sources of data, ensuring that all groups, particularly historically marginalized groups, are included.
- Work with community representatives or focus groups to identify potential gaps in data collection.
- Use techniques like stratified sampling to ensure balanced representation of various subgroups within the data.

Example: In facial recognition technology, if training data primarily consists of images of white men, the model may perform poorly on women or people of color. To create an inclusive model, the dataset should be carefully curated to include a balanced representation of different genders, races, and ethnicities.

2. **Inclusive Model Design** Inclusive model design focuses on developing algorithms that take into account the needs and characteristics of all user groups. This involves making design choices that explicitly consider the potential impact of the model on different demographic groups, ensuring that the system is flexible and adaptable to diverse user needs.

Best Practices for Inclusive Design:

- Involve diverse teams in the design and development process to ensure that different perspectives are considered.
- Use an iterative process that allows for continuous feedback and improvement from diverse user groups.
- Consider the context in which the model will be used, including factors like culture, socio-economic status, and regional differences.

Example: A health application designed to track and manage chronic conditions may include features tailored to different cultural beliefs, language preferences, and health literacy levels. By ensuring that the app's design accommodates various needs, it becomes more inclusive and equitable for all users.

3. **Avoiding Discriminatory Algorithms** Discriminatory algorithms are those that, due to biased training data or flawed model design, disproportionately disadvantage certain groups. To ensure that predictive models promote balanced outcomes, it is essential to actively work to eliminate discrimination by identifying and addressing potential sources of bias.

   Best Practices for Avoiding Discriminatory Algorithms:

   - Use fairness constraints during model development to limit the ability of the model to discriminate based on sensitive attributes like race, gender, or age.
   - Regularly audit models for signs of discrimination and take corrective actions if bias is detected.
   - Prioritize fairness in algorithmic decisions and evaluate trade-offs between fairness and model accuracy.

   Example: In a credit scoring model, if the model inadvertently uses variables that are correlated with race (such as zip codes), it may lead to discriminatory outcomes. To avoid discrimination, the model could be adjusted to exclude such variables and focus on factors directly related to creditworthiness, ensuring a more balanced and inclusive result.

4. **Stakeholder Involvement and Feedback Loops** Inclusivity in predictive models requires the active involvement of all stakeholders, particularly those who are directly impacted by the model's decisions. By involving diverse stakeholders in the design, development, and testing of predictive models, organizations can ensure that the systems they create serve the needs of all groups. Feedback loops allow organizations to make adjustments based on real-world impact and user experiences.

   Best Practices for Stakeholder Involvement:

- Engage stakeholders from different demographic backgrounds in the design and testing process to ensure that all voices are heard.
- Create clear channels for users to provide feedback on their experiences with the model.
- Use this feedback to make iterative improvements to the model and ensure it remains inclusive.

Example: In a job recruitment algorithm, the company might involve diverse employees and external experts to test how the algorithm impacts candidates from different racial, gender, and age groups. Feedback collected from these stakeholders would be used to refine the model and eliminate any unintended bias.

5. **Continuous Monitoring and Evaluation** Predictive models are dynamic, and the context in which they operate may change over time. Regular monitoring and evaluation are essential to ensure that the model continues to deliver inclusive and balanced outcomes. This means not only auditing the model periodically for fairness but also assessing the long-term impact of the model on different groups.

Best Practices for Monitoring and Evaluation:

- Implement mechanisms for continuous monitoring of model performance across different demographic groups.
- Regularly evaluate whether the model's predictions are leading to equitable outcomes and adjust as necessary.
- Conduct periodic impact assessments to understand how the model affects different groups over time.

Example: A bank using an AI-driven loan approval model might regularly assess whether applicants from different income groups are being treated fairly and whether the model's decisions are still aligned with the bank's goals of equitable access to credit. Any disparities that emerge would be addressed through model adjustments.

6. **Promoting Accessibility** Inclusivity also involves ensuring that predictive models and the platforms that use them are accessible to all users, including those with disabilities. This requires designing systems that can be easily accessed and used by people with a variety of abilities.

   Best Practices for Promoting Accessibility:

   - Design user interfaces that are accessible to people with disabilities, such as screen readers for visually impaired users or voice interfaces for those with limited mobility.
   - Ensure that the models themselves do not inadvertently exclude users with disabilities from benefiting from their predictions or services.

   Example: In a public service application, providing alternative communication methods such as text-to-speech or voice-activated commands can ensure that people with disabilities are able to access services and benefit from the predictive model just like other users.

7. **Promoting Transparency and Accountability** Transparency and accountability are crucial for fostering trust in predictive models. When users understand how a model works, how decisions are made, and who is responsible for those decisions, they are more likely to trust and accept the model's outcomes. This also ensures that organizations can be held accountable if the model leads to biased or unfair outcomes.

   Best Practices for Promoting Transparency and Accountability:

   - Provide clear explanations of how the model works, what data it uses, and how it makes decisions.
   - Implement accountability mechanisms to ensure that decision-makers can be held responsible for model outcomes.
   - Make documentation and audit trails available for external review to increase transparency.

Example: A company developing an automated recruitment system may publish detailed information on how the system works, the data it uses, and the fairness measures it has implemented. By being transparent about their approach, the company builds trust and shows its commitment to inclusive practices.

Real-World Example: Fairness in Healthcare Models

A healthcare organization develops an AI model to predict patient outcomes and determine the allocation of resources. However, the model initially shows biases, such as underestimating the risk of heart disease in women compared to men. To address these issues, the organization takes several steps to ensure the model is inclusive and balanced:

1. **Diverse Data Collection**: The organization revises its data collection process to ensure it includes a representative sample of women and men from various age groups and ethnic backgrounds.
2. **Inclusive Model Design**: The healthcare team consults with diverse experts to design the model, ensuring that it accounts for gender, ethnicity, and socio-economic status.
3. **Continuous Monitoring**: The model is regularly audited for bias, and feedback from diverse patient groups is actively sought and used to make improvements.

As a result, the healthcare organization achieves a more accurate and equitable model that better predicts heart disease risk for both men and women, regardless of their background.

Promoting inclusivity and balanced outcomes in predictive models is not just a technical challenge; it requires a holistic approach that involves diverse data collection, inclusive design, stakeholder engagement, continuous monitoring, and a commitment to transparency. By implementing these strategies, organizations can ensure that their predictive models serve the needs of all users and deliver fair, equitable, and transparent outcomes. This not only helps to mitigate bias but also fosters trust and acceptance among users, leading to better and more sustainable decision-making in the long term.

Summary

This comprehensive discussion delves into the ethical, privacy, and security challenges surrounding data collection, retention, and usage. In today's digital era, organizations are tasked with safeguarding sensitive data and ensuring its ethical handling at every stage. Key concepts such as informed consent, data minimization, and privacy protection are explored in detail, emphasizing the need for transparency, clear communication, and respect for individual rights.

1. Data Collection and Privacy

- **Informed consent** is essential in data collection, ensuring individuals are fully aware of how their data will be used, the potential risks, and their ability to withdraw consent at any time.
- **Data minimization** stresses the importance of only collecting necessary information, reducing risks related to over-collection and exposure.
- **Access controls** ensure that only authorized personnel can access sensitive data, protecting it from unauthorized exposure or misuse.
- **Anonymization** of personal data is vital to maintaining privacy when using data for research or analysis.

2. Safeguarding Sensitive Data

- **Encryption** protects sensitive data, making it unreadable to unauthorized individuals, whether at rest or in transit.
- **Regular audits** of who accesses data help in detecting unauthorized use and ensuring compliance with security protocols.
- **Backup systems** ensure data is protected against loss, be it from system failure or cyberattacks like ransomware.
- **Firewalls and intrusion detection systems** provide an additional layer of defense by blocking malicious activities.

3. Building Trust and Security Infrastructure

- A secure infrastructure consists of robust encryption, firewalls, secure software development practices, and regular software updates to minimize vulnerabilities.
- Building **trust** goes beyond security infrastructure—clear communication with users about how their data will be used, offering control over data sharing preferences, and demonstrating transparency regarding privacy policies are key elements.

4. Ethical Dilemmas in Data Retention

- **Data retention** policies must balance business needs with ethical considerations such as user privacy. Retaining data too long can lead to privacy violations, while deleting data too early can affect business operations.
- The **right to be forgotten** allows individuals to request the deletion of their personal data, creating ethical challenges when these requests conflict with business or legal requirements.

5. Dealing with Bias and Promoting Equity

- **Bias in datasets** can lead to unfair and discriminatory outcomes. Ensuring fairness in predictive models is essential by using diverse datasets, employing fairness algorithms, and regularly auditing models for bias.
- Promoting **inclusive and balanced outcomes** involves considering all stakeholders' needs, minimizing bias, and ensuring that all groups benefit equally from technological advancements.

6. Practical Solutions and Real-World Examples

- Real-world examples demonstrate the application of these principles in various sectors like healthcare, retail, and finance. In healthcare, encrypted patient data and multi-factor authentication (MFA) ensure privacy. In e-commerce, data retention policies comply with legal requirements while offering users control over their data.

Ethical data practices, from collection to retention, play a crucial role in ensuring that data usage aligns with privacy laws and ethical standards. Ethical guidelines like informed consent, data minimization, and transparency help build trust with users and ensure compliance with regulations. By integrating security measures, such as encryption and regular audits, organizations can protect sensitive information. Moreover, addressing bias and promoting fairness in algorithms ensures that technology benefits everyone equitably.

This content emphasizes the importance of ethical considerations in the digital world, providing guidelines to ensure that organizations collect, store, and use data responsibly and securely, fostering trust and equity across different platforms and industries.

This chapter has explored various strategies and methodologies for addressing bias, ensuring fairness, and promoting inclusivity in predictive models. By focusing on these critical areas, organizations can ensure that their AI systems not only function efficiently but also serve society in a fair and equitable manner. In the following chapter, we will delve deeper into practical tools for monitoring AI performance and ensuring continued fairness in real-world applications.

This chapter provides a comprehensive overview of the ethical, fairness, and inclusivity challenges surrounding predictive models and offers practical strategies for addressing them. It emphasizes that building fair and responsible AI systems requires a multi-layered approach that spans the entire AI lifecycle—from data collection to model deployment and monitoring.

A core focus is on fairness in predictive modeling, highlighting various methods such as pre-processing (e.g., reweighting biased data), in-processing (e.g., adversarial debiasing), and post-processing (e.g., equalized odds) techniques. These are essential to mitigate bias and promote equitable outcomes across different demographic groups. The chapter also underscores the importance of transparency and explainability, ensuring stakeholders understand and trust model decisions.

The discussion extends to fostering inclusive and balanced outcomes, advocating for diverse data collection, inclusive model design, and stakeholder involvement. Practical examples, like improving fairness in hiring and healthcare models, illustrate how these strategies can reduce bias and enhance equity. Ongoing monitoring and feedback loops are highlighted as critical for adapting models to evolving societal norms and maintaining fairness over time. The chapter covers ethical data practices, including informed consent, data minimization, encryption, and responsible retention policies. It stresses the importance of building robust security infrastructures and upholding privacy rights, such as the right to be forgotten.

Ultimately, the chapter argues that addressing algorithmic bias and promoting ethical AI is not just a technical challenge but a societal responsibility. Through strategic implementation of fairness techniques and ethical data practices, organizations can develop AI systems that are not only accurate but also inclusive, transparent, and trustworthy. The next chapter will build on these foundations, exploring tools and techniques for ongoing performance monitoring and fairness in real-world AI applications.

Check your Understanding

Fill in the Blanks

1. In data science, the process of removing personally identifiable information (PII) to protect privacy is called ________.
2. A technique used to ensure that data can be only accessed by authorized users is known as ________.
3. The practice of encrypting data while it is being transferred is called ________.
4. ________ is a principle of data protection that ensures the accuracy of the data and prevents unauthorized alterations.
5. In the context of data protection, ________ refers to ensuring that data is available to authorized users when needed.
6. ________ is a practice that ensures software and systems are continuously updated to close vulnerabilities.
7. A data model that includes a diverse range of demographic groups in its training data can help reduce ________ in algorithmic outcomes.
8. ________ occurs when a model disproportionately benefits one group while disadvantaging another group due to biased training data.
9. The ethical principle of ________ ensures that individuals can control how their personal information is used and shared.
10. Data retention policies specify how long data should be kept before being ________.
11. The ________ framework in data ethics focuses on the fairness and treatment of individuals, particularly in predictive modeling.
12. ________ systems monitor the flow of data and detect any unauthorized access or potential breaches.
13. Data retention without proper justification can lead to violations of the ________ privacy regulation.
14. ________ is a practice that involves periodically assessing data stored to ensure it is still needed.
15. The principle of ________ in data protection means that organizations must only collect data necessary for the task at hand.

16. Organizations must secure data in both ________ and while it is in transit to ensure confidentiality.
17. The ________ law grants individuals the right to request the deletion of their personal data from a company's records.
18. A system that uses ________ authentication requires more than one method to verify a user's identity.
19. The act of removing excess or irrelevant data to mitigate risks is referred to as ________.
20. The practice of ensuring that data is processed in a way that complies with relevant legal and ethical guidelines is called ________.

Short Answer Questions

1. What is meant by "informed consent" in data collection?
2. Define "data minimization" and explain its importance in data protection.
3. What are access controls, and why are they essential for data security?
4. Explain the term "data anonymization" and its role in protecting privacy.
5. What is a data breach, and how can encryption help mitigate it?
6. Why is stakeholder involvement important in creating inclusive data systems?
7. What is the difference between "data integrity" and "data availability"?
8. What is a "right to be forgotten," and how does it apply in data retention?
9. Why is it important to have periodic reviews of the data collected?
10. What are firewalls, and how do they contribute to cybersecurity?

Long Answer Questions

1. Discuss the ethical challenges associated with collecting data from public platforms, and propose strategies for mitigating these challenges.
2. How can predictive models in healthcare unintentionally perpetuate bias, and what steps can organizations take to ensure fairness in these models?
3. In the context of data retention, explain the ethical dilemmas surrounding data deletion requests, especially when business or legal obligations are in conflict with an individual's right to privacy.

4. Explain the role of data encryption in maintaining the confidentiality and security of sensitive data, providing real-world examples of its application.
5. Describe the key principles of ethical data collection and discuss their importance in fostering trust between organizations and users.
6. Analyze the impact of algorithmic bias on decision-making processes, and discuss potential solutions for reducing bias in machine learning models.
7. Discuss the significance of user consent in data collection and how organizations can ensure that consent is truly informed.
8. How do third-party service providers affect the security and privacy of sensitive data, and what steps should organizations take to ensure third-party vendors comply with the same security standards?
9. Evaluate the implications of data retention policies on business operations, legal compliance, and ethical responsibility.
10. How can an organization create a secure infrastructure to protect sensitive customer data? Discuss the importance of having both technical and human elements involved in securing data.

Answers

Fill in the Blanks - Answers

1. Anonymization
2. Access Controls
3. Encryption
4. Integrity
5. Availability
6. Security
7. Bias
8. Discrimination
9. Privacy
10. Deleted
11. Fairness
12. Intrusion Detection Systems (IDS)

13. GDPR

14. Periodic Review

15. Data Minimization

16. Transit

17. GDPR

18. Multi-factor

19. Data Minimization

20. Compliance

Short Answer Questions – Answer Key

1. **Informed consent** refers to individuals being fully informed about how their data will be used, the purpose of data collection, the risks involved, and their right to withdraw consent.
2. **Data minimization** is the principle of collecting only the necessary data for a specific purpose. This reduces the risk of exposure and helps ensure compliance with data protection laws like GDPR.
3. **Access controls** are security measures that limit data access based on users' roles or responsibilities. They help protect sensitive data by ensuring only authorized users can access or modify it.
4. **Data anonymization** is the process of removing personally identifiable information from datasets, ensuring that individuals cannot be identified from the data. It helps protect privacy, especially when data is used for research.
5. A **data breach** occurs when unauthorized individuals gain access to sensitive data. **Encryption** helps mitigate this risk by making data unreadable to unauthorized parties even if intercepted.
6. **Stakeholder involvement** ensures that diverse perspectives are considered in the development of data systems, reducing bias and ensuring fairness in outcomes.
7. **Data integrity** ensures data accuracy and consistency, while **data availability** ensures that authorized users can access data when needed.
8. The **right to be forgotten** allows individuals to request the deletion of their personal data. This applies to data retention by giving individuals control over how long their data is stored.

9. **Periodic reviews** help ensure that only relevant, accurate data is retained, reducing the risk of holding unnecessary or outdated data and ensuring compliance with privacy laws.
10. **Firewalls** are security systems that monitor and control network traffic. They contribute to cybersecurity by preventing unauthorized access to systems and protecting sensitive data from external threats.

Long Answer Questions – Answer key

1. **Ethical challenges** in collecting data from public platforms include privacy concerns, misuse of data, and lack of consent. Mitigation strategies include anonymizing data, obtaining explicit consent when feasible, and ensuring transparency about data usage in the research process.
2. **Predictive models in healthcare** can perpetuate bias if trained on unrepresentative data, leading to unfair health outcomes for some groups. Solutions include using diverse datasets, fairness algorithms, testing for bias, and consulting diverse stakeholders in the development process.
3. **Ethical dilemmas in data deletion** occur when users request the deletion of data that the business needs for legal or operational reasons. Solutions involve transparency, allowing users to control data retention, and anonymizing data rather than deleting it entirely when needed.
4. **Data encryption** ensures data is transformed into unreadable text to protect it from unauthorized access. Real-world applications include healthcare systems encrypting patient data and financial institutions encrypting credit card information during transactions.
5. **Ethical data collection** requires informed consent, data minimization, transparency, privacy, and fairness. These principles ensure that individuals understand and agree to how their data will be used and that their privacy is respected.
6. **Algorithmic bias** arises when machine learning models produce biased outcomes due to skewed training data or flawed algorithms. Solutions include using diverse datasets, fairness constraints, auditing models, and involving diverse teams to ensure equitable outcomes.

7. **User consent** in data collection is vital for transparency and privacy. Organizations can ensure informed consent by providing clear, concise information about data collection purposes, risks, and how the data will be used. Consent should be voluntary and revocable at any time.
8. **Third-party service providers** can pose risks if they do not meet the same security standards. Organizations should audit third-party vendors, ensure contracts include data protection clauses, and only work with vendors compliant with privacy laws.
9. **Data retention policies** balance business needs and privacy. Ethical data retention involves ensuring data is stored only as long as needed for legal or business purposes, minimizing the risk of unnecessary exposure and ensuring compliance with privacy regulations.
10. A **secure infrastructure** involves using encryption, firewalls, intrusion detection systems, and regular updates. Human factors such as employee training, clear access control policies, and a culture of security awareness are critical in protecting sensitive data from breaches.

Chapter 6: Clarity in Algorithms and Decision-Making

Learning Outcomes

1. **Define** transparent and black-box models in machine learning.
2. **Explain** the importance of model explainability in AI systems from legal, ethical, and trust-building perspectives.
3. **Identify** and describe key methods used to make complex AI models interpretable, such as LIME and SHAP.
4. **Understand** the trade-off between accuracy and interpretability in AI models and its impact on system development.

Introduction

As machine learning and artificial intelligence (AI) become more deeply integrated into our daily lives, the importance of ensuring transparency, explainability, and fairness in these systems has never been more critical. AI systems, if left opaque, can turn into "black boxes," where the decision-making process is unclear to both users and developers. This lack of transparency can lead to significant challenges, especially when AI systems make decisions that directly impact individuals, such as determining loan eligibility, hiring decisions, or medical diagnoses. Without a clear understanding of how AI reaches its conclusions, people can lose trust in the system, and organizations may face ethical, legal, or reputational risks. Transparency in AI involves providing a clear view of how decisions are made, including information on the data used, the algorithms implemented, and the reasoning behind particular outcomes. This can help demystify the decision-making process, fostering trust and allowing users to feel confident in how their data is being used. However, achieving explainability goes beyond transparency—it is about making sure that these decisions can be explained in understandable terms, especially to the people most affected by them. For instance, if an AI system denies a loan application, the individual should be able to understand why, in clear and human-readable terms, allowing for accountability and the opportunity to rectify potential errors or biases. Furthermore, fairness plays a pivotal role in ensuring that AI systems do not perpetuate existing biases or discrimination. Since AI models are often trained on historical data, there is a risk that these systems might inherit and even amplify societal inequalities, leading to biased outcomes. A fair AI system must not favor certain demographic groups over others, and efforts should be made to mitigate bias through diverse data collection, fairness audits, and algorithmic adjustments. Despite these efforts, achieving fairness and explainability is challenging, especially as AI models grow in complexity. Some advanced AI models, like deep learning networks, are incredibly powerful but notoriously difficult to interpret. Striking a balance between performance and interpretability remains a significant hurdle. Moreover, the current lack of standardized guidelines for transparency and fairness in AI makes it difficult for organizations to adopt universal practices, potentially leading to inconsistent or inadequate approaches to ethical AI. Nonetheless, ongoing research and the development of explainable. AI (XAI) models are promising steps in making these systems more understandable and accountable. By focusing on clear communication, thoughtful design, and rigorous evaluation of AI systems, we can work toward AI technologies that operate ethically, treat individuals fairly, and promote long-term trust in their use.

6.1 Explaining Complex Models in Understandable Terms

Machine learning and artificial intelligence (AI) systems have revolutionized industries by enabling computers to make decisions based on vast amounts of data. However, as AI systems grow more complex, particularly with the use of deep learning, understanding how these models work becomes more challenging. This chapter explores how to explain complex machine learning models in simple, understandable terms, focusing on different methods for improving transparency and trust in AI systems.

Introduction to Complex Models

AI models can be broadly classified into two types based on their interpretability and complexity: **transparent models** and **black-box models**.

- **Linear Regression**: One of the simplest and most transparent machine learning algorithms, linear regression predicts a target variable based on linear relationships between input variables. The decision-making process is easy to understand because each input feature contributes to the final prediction in a straightforward manner.

- **Decision Trees**: A widely used model, decision trees break down decisions into a series of simple yes/no questions based on input features. Each decision node in the tree splits the data based on specific conditions, making the process of arriving at a decision relatively easy to interpret. Since the structure of decision trees can be visualized, they are inherently transparent.
- **Neural Networks**: Neural networks, particularly deep neural networks (DNNs), are often regarded as "black-box" models. They consist of multiple layers of interconnected nodes (or neurons) that transform the input data through complex mathematical functions. The decision-making process within these networks is not easily interpretable because of the large number of parameters and intricate transformations involved.
- **Deep Learning Algorithms**: Deep learning, a subset of machine learning that uses multiple layers of neural networks, is highly powerful in tasks such as image and speech recognition. However, as the number of layers increases, the decision-making process becomes even more opaque, making it difficult to understand the rationale behind a particular prediction.

Transparent Models such as linear regression or decision trees are easy to explain to stakeholders, as they provide a clear path from inputs to outputs. However, these models often sacrifice performance and accuracy for simplicity.

Black-box Models, particularly deep neural networks, offer exceptional accuracy but are difficult to interpret. This lack of interpretability can pose significant challenges, especially in high-stakes industries like healthcare, finance, and criminal justice, where understanding why a decision was made is critical.

Why Complexity Is a Challenge

The complexity of modern AI models—especially deep learning models—creates significant challenges for interpretability and explainability. Neural networks, for example, consist of thousands or even millions of parameters that influence the outcome. These parameters are adjusted during the training process through backpropagation, a method that fine-tunes the network's weights and biases. While the model becomes highly accurate over time, the intricate inner workings of deep neural networks make it nearly impossible for humans to trace how specific features contribute to a decision.

This **opacity** raises concerns in industries where decision-making processes must be transparent and accountable. For example, in the criminal justice system, AI systems used for sentencing or parole decisions must provide clear explanations to ensure fairness and prevent discrimination. Without transparency, there is a risk of perpetuating existing biases or making unfair decisions that affect individuals' lives.

The Need for Explainability

Legal and Ethical Considerations

The **General Data Protection Regulation (GDPR)** in the European Union has highlighted the need for explainability in automated decision-making processes. GDPR stipulates that individuals have the **right to an explanation** when subjected to automated decisions that significantly affect them, such as credit scoring or job application reviews. This regulation reflects a broader ethical obligation to ensure that automated systems do not perpetuate discrimination or biases.

In many jurisdictions, the lack of transparency in decision-making systems can lead to legal consequences. If a company or government agency uses an AI system that discriminates against a certain group (e.g., based on race, gender, or socioeconomic status), it can face lawsuits, regulatory fines, and a loss of public trust. Moreover, there is an ethical responsibility to ensure that AI systems do not propagate or amplify societal inequalities.

Impact on Trust

For AI to be trusted by the public, users must feel confident that they understand how decisions are made. Transparent AI systems increase the likelihood that individuals will trust these decisions, as they can verify that the model is acting based on logical, fair, and understandable criteria. For example, in healthcare, when doctors use AI systems to diagnose diseases or recommend treatments, they need to trust that the system's recommendations are based on sound reasoning and not biased data.

Trust is crucial in **high-stakes environments** like healthcare, finance, and criminal justice, where the consequences of a wrong decision can be dire. In these fields, transparency is not just desirable; it is necessary for ensuring that AI systems are used responsibly.

Methods to Explain Complex Models

As AI models become more sophisticated, researchers and practitioners have developed various methods to make black-box models more interpretable and understandable.

LIME (Local Interpretable Model-agnostic Explanations)

LIME is a popular technique that provides an explanation for individual predictions made by black-box models. Instead of trying to explain the entire model, LIME focuses on approximating the model with simpler, interpretable models (such as linear regression) for each individual prediction.

For example, if an AI system predicts whether a patient has a particular disease, LIME would show how small changes in individual patient features (such as age, symptoms, and medical history) influence the model's prediction. This helps healthcare professionals understand what factors contributed to the diagnosis, even though the underlying model (e.g., a deep learning algorithm) is a black-box.

SHAP (SHapley Additive exPlanations)

SHAP is another powerful method for interpreting black-box models. Based on **Shapley values** from cooperative game theory, SHAP assigns an importance value to each feature in a dataset, representing how much each feature contributes to the final prediction.

For example, in a credit scoring model, SHAP can show how features like income, credit history, and age influence the model's decision to approve or deny a loan. By assigning an importance value to each feature, SHAP helps users understand which aspects of the data are most influential in the decision-making process.

SHAP is particularly useful because it provides both **global interpretability** (explaining the model's behavior across all predictions) and **local interpretability** (explaining individual predictions).

Surrogate Models

Another approach to explain complex models is the use of **surrogate models**. A surrogate model is a simpler model (e.g., decision trees or linear regression) that approximates the behavior of a more complex model. The idea is that by creating a simpler model that mimics the behavior of the complex model, one can gain insights into the decision-making process.

For example, suppose a deep neural network is used for image classification. To explain the decision-making process, a decision tree might be trained on the same data to approximate the decisions made by the deep neural network. While the surrogate model may not capture all the intricacies of the complex model, it can provide a valuable explanation of how the complex model behaves in certain scenarios.

Feature Importance

Feature importance techniques, such as **Random Forest** or **XGBoost**, are also useful for interpreting black-box models. These techniques highlight which features have the most significant impact on predictions. For example, in a model predicting loan approvals, feature importance could reveal that income and credit history are the most influential features, while age and education level have less impact.

By using feature importance, data scientists and stakeholders can identify which factors the model is considering most heavily, helping to explain the decision-making process.

Challenges in Explainability

Accuracy vs. Interpretability

One of the primary challenges in explainability is the trade-off between **accuracy** and **interpretability**. While simpler models like decision trees or linear regression are easier to explain, they may not perform as well as more complex models, such as deep neural networks, which offer greater accuracy but are harder to interpret. This trade-off presents a dilemma: should we prioritize interpretability or the predictive power of the model?

For example, in medical diagnostics, a deep learning model may provide highly accurate predictions for disease diagnosis but be difficult for doctors to understand. On the other hand, a simpler model might be easier to explain but might not perform as well in predicting rare diseases.

Reducing Complexity for Clarity

Another challenge is the need to balance **simplification** with **accuracy**. As AI models become more complex, simplifying them for the sake of explanation can reduce their ability to capture intricate patterns in the data. In some cases, simplifying the model too much might result in a loss of valuable information, reducing its effectiveness.

For example, using a decision tree to explain a complex neural network model might miss important interactions between features that could lead to more accurate predictions. Therefore, it's essential to find a balance between making a model interpretable and maintaining its accuracy.

Real-World Example

Healthcare and AI

In healthcare, AI is increasingly used to predict patient outcomes, recommend treatments, and assist in diagnosis. However, when AI models are used to inform critical healthcare decisions, patients and healthcare professionals need to understand why certain decisions or recommendations were made.

Consider a scenario where an AI system predicts that a patient is at high risk of developing a particular condition after surgery. By using **LIME**, the hospital can explain to the patient how specific factors, such as age, pre-existing conditions, and surgical history, influenced the prediction. Additionally, the AI can provide a justification for the treatment recommendations, giving healthcare professionals the ability to trust the system's decision-making process and communicate it to the patient.

This transparent and understandable approach helps both healthcare professionals and patients make informed decisions, increasing trust in the system and improving patient engagement.

As AI systems become more integral to decision-making in various sectors, ensuring that these systems are interpretable and understandable is crucial. By utilizing techniques like **LIME**, **SHAP**, and **surrogate models**, we can bridge the gap between complex, black-box models and the need for transparency. This not only builds trust in AI systems but also ensures that these systems operate ethically, with accountability and fairness. As technology advances, ensuring clarity in decision-making processes will continue to be vital, particularly in high-stakes environments like healthcare, finance, and criminal justice.

6.2 Empowering Users Through Transparency

Transparency in Artificial Intelligence (AI) is vital for building trust, ensuring fairness, and empowering users to make informed decisions about how their data is used. As AI systems continue to play a significant role in various industries—from healthcare to finance—ensuring that these systems are transparent and accountable is key to their adoption and success. In this section, we will explore the concept of transparency in AI, its importance, the role of user-centric design, the benefits of empowering users, tools for enhancing transparency, and a real-world example.

Introduction to Transparency in AI

Defining Transparency

Transparency in AI refers to the clarity with which AI systems operate, allowing users to understand how decisions are made and on what basis they are grounded. In the context of AI models, transparency is not just about the visibility of the underlying algorithms but also about ensuring that users can grasp the decision-making processes and the factors that influenced a particular outcome. A transparent AI system should make its working mechanism understandable to stakeholders, enabling them to confidently interact with the system and its outputs.

For instance, consider a simple AI-based credit scoring system. A transparent system would explain how various factors, such as income, credit history, and outstanding debts, contribute to the score and what weight is assigned to each factor. Transparency in this context helps the user understand and trust the system, knowing that the decision is based on understandable and predictable rules.

Why Transparency is Vital

Transparency is critical because it provides stakeholders with the ability to question, challenge, and provide feedback on automated decisions. This level of scrutiny is essential for a few reasons:

1. **Promoting Accountability**: If users can see how decisions are made, they are more likely to hold organizations accountable for their actions. This can help organizations avoid mistakes, mitigate bias, and create fairer outcomes.
2. **Enhancing Trust**: Trust is an essential component of successful AI adoption. When users can see that an AI system works transparently, they are more likely to trust its predictions and decisions. Whether in healthcare, finance, or recruitment, trust in AI can significantly impact its widespread use and acceptance.
3. **Reducing Bias and Discrimination**: Transparent AI systems allow external parties, such as regulators or advocates, to monitor decisions and identify any potential biases in the data or algorithms. If users can understand the decision-making process, they can spot unfair treatment or discrimination and call for necessary changes.

User-Centric Design

Control Over Data

Empowering users begins with providing them with control over their own data. This is especially important in the digital age, where personal data is constantly collected, processed, and analyzed by AI systems. A transparent AI system should clearly explain how data is collected, why it is being collected, and how it will be used.

- **Consent Mechanisms**: Transparent AI systems should include easy-to-understand consent forms that explain the purpose of data collection and usage. Users should be able to opt-in or opt-out of data collection based on their preferences. Consent forms must be concise, clear, and free from jargon so that users fully understand what they are agreeing to.

- **Data Control**: Users should be able to manage their data, with the option to update or delete it when they choose. This gives them autonomy over their personal information and ensures that their data is not used beyond the agreed-upon scope.

Providing Feedback Mechanisms

To further empower users, AI systems should incorporate **feedback mechanisms** that allow users to voice concerns, provide insights, or correct any potential errors in predictions. This fosters a **collaborative environment** where users actively contribute to the improvement of AI systems, especially when the consequences of inaccurate or biased predictions can significantly impact their lives.

For example, in recruitment or hiring decisions, candidates should have the opportunity to contest decisions made by an AI system and provide additional context that could affect their chances. In this way, users have an active role in shaping the decisions that affect them.

Feedback mechanisms also allow users to point out any unintended biases in AI systems. For instance, if an AI algorithm is unintentionally favoring one demographic over others, users can report this discrepancy, prompting an investigation into potential issues with the training data or algorithm design.

Benefits of Empowering Users

Trust and Adoption

Empowering users through transparency builds **trust** and encourages the adoption of AI systems. Users are more likely to adopt technology if they feel in control and understand its decision-making processes. Transparency ensures that users are not left in the dark about how their data is being used or how decisions are being made.

For example, in **healthcare**, patients are more likely to trust and follow medical advice if they understand how the AI system arrived at a particular diagnosis or treatment recommendation. Transparent AI systems can show how different variables, such as symptoms, medical history, and test results, contribute to the diagnosis, thus increasing patient confidence in the technology.

Enhanced Accountability

Transparency also leads to enhanced accountability. When an organization's AI systems are transparent, users can hold the organization responsible for the decisions made by the system. This is especially important in sectors like **finance**, where AI algorithms often determine whether individuals can secure loans or mortgages. If the decisions made by an AI system are opaque, users may feel that they have no recourse for challenging unfair or biased decisions. However, with transparency, they can better understand the rationale behind the decisions and seek recourse when necessary.

Moreover, when organizations know that their algorithms are open to scrutiny, they are more likely to ensure fairness and accuracy in their decision-making processes.

Improved Model Performance

Empowering users through transparency can also help improve model performance. When users are given insights into how their data is used and the opportunity to provide feedback, they can offer valuable insights that help developers refine the system. This iterative process leads to better models over time.

For example, in an **AI-based recommendation system** (e.g., Netflix or Spotify), transparency about how recommendations are generated can lead to better user engagement. Users can provide feedback on inaccurate or irrelevant recommendations, which can then be used to fine-tune the system and improve the user experience.

Tools and Techniques for Transparency

Clear Consent Forms

One of the foundational aspects of empowering users through transparency is providing clear and concise **consent forms**. These forms should explain what data will be collected, why it will be collected, and how it will be used. The language used in consent forms must be straightforward and free from complex jargon, ensuring that users can make informed decisions about their participation.

An example of clear consent in practice might be a user being asked for permission to share their location data with a mobile app, with the consent form clearly stating the purpose of the data collection and how it will be used to improve user experience or provide location-based services.

Transparent Data Policies

Organizations can create **transparent data policies** to enhance user understanding. These policies should clearly outline how user data is stored, processed, and used for training AI models. It is crucial to avoid vague or overly technical language in these policies and instead use clear and simple explanations that are accessible to the average user.

For instance, a company's data policy could explain that user data will be anonymized before being used for model training, ensuring that individuals cannot be identified. Such transparency fosters trust between the organization and its users.

Data Anonymization and Security

Data anonymization is another essential technique for ensuring transparency while protecting user privacy. Anonymizing data means removing personally identifiable information (PII) so that individuals cannot be identified. This allows organizations to use user data for training AI models without compromising privacy.

Additionally, data security measures, such as **encryption**, must be in place to protect sensitive information. By ensuring that data is both anonymized and securely stored, organizations can build trust with their users while maintaining transparency about their data usage.

Real-World Example

Fintech Sector: Transparent Financial Advice

A prominent **fintech company** that provides personalized financial advice could be a great example of transparency in action. The company uses an AI-based system to analyze users' spending habits, income, debt, and savings patterns to provide tailored financial recommendations.

To empower users, the company makes the decision-making process behind the AI system fully transparent. For instance, when a user receives a suggestion to save more or invest in a particular way, the system explains which financial behaviors influenced the advice—whether it was based on spending patterns, income trends, or debt levels.

Moreover, the system offers users full control over the data they share. They can view the specific data points being used to generate the advice, update or remove certain pieces of information, and even see how changes in their financial behavior will affect future recommendations.

This transparency not only enhances the user experience but also builds trust in the company's financial advice system. Users are more likely to act on the recommendations if they understand the reasoning behind them and feel secure in the way their data is being handled.

Transparency is a cornerstone of responsible AI development and use. By empowering users through transparency, organizations can foster trust, ensure accountability, and enhance the performance of AI systems. Whether in the fintech sector, healthcare, or other industries, providing users with control over their data, clear consent mechanisms, and the ability to understand and challenge automated decisions will lead to more ethical and fair outcomes. Transparent AI systems also facilitate better user feedback, which can be used to improve model performance over time. As AI continues to shape various industries, prioritizing transparency will be key to ensuring that these systems are fair, accountable, and trusted by all stakeholders.

6.3 Navigating the Challenges of Black-Box AI

Black-box AI refers to machine learning models where the internal workings and decision-making processes are not transparent or easily understood by humans. These models are commonly used for complex tasks, such as predicting customer behavior, diagnosing medical conditions, or determining loan eligibility. Unlike more transparent models, such as decision trees, where the reasoning behind each decision is easily traceable, black-box models operate with a level of opacity that poses significant challenges. In this section, we will explore the concept of black-box AI, the challenges it presents, and strategies to mitigate these issues.

What is Black-Box AI?

Black-Box vs. Transparent AI

The term "black-box" in AI refers to models whose internal mechanisms are hidden from the user. In these models, data flows through various layers of computations, but the process by which the model arrives at a decision is not observable or easily interpretable. This lack of transparency contrasts with **transparent AI** models, where decision-making processes are easily understood. For example, in decision trees, each decision is based on clearly defined rules, and one can easily trace the exact path that the algorithm took to reach its conclusion.

In contrast, models like **deep neural networks** or **ensemble methods** (e.g., random forests) operate as black boxes. While these models can achieve high accuracy, the trade-off is that it becomes increasingly difficult to explain how the model arrived at a particular decision. For instance, a deep neural network can process millions of data points across multiple hidden layers, but its decision-making path is complex and opaque to both developers and end-users.

Black-Box Challenges

The complexity of black-box models gives rise to several challenges, particularly when it comes to **fairness**, **accountability**, and **trust**. Because the internal workings of these models are not transparent, it is difficult to understand why they make certain decisions or to ensure that the decisions are made fairly. This lack of interpretability can create serious issues, especially when the models are deployed in sensitive areas, such as healthcare, finance, and criminal justice.

One of the primary challenges of black-box models is the **lack of accountability**. When the model makes a decision that negatively impacts an individual, such as rejecting a loan application or misdiagnosing a medical condition, it is often unclear who or what is responsible. The decision-making process cannot be traced back to specific data points or features, making it difficult to challenge or correct the outcome.

Challenges with Black-Box Models

Bias and **Fairness**

One of the most significant concerns with black-box models is the risk of **bias**. Without the ability to interpret how the model works, it becomes challenging to detect and mitigate biases that may be present in the data. If the training data reflects biased historical decisions or systemic inequalities, the model will likely perpetuate these biases. This can lead to **discriminatory outcomes** that disproportionately affect marginalized or underrepresented groups.

For instance, in a **credit scoring** system, if the model is trained on biased historical data, it may unfairly deny loans to certain demographic groups, even if they are financially capable of repaying them. Without transparency, it is difficult to identify whether this bias is coming from the data itself or the way the model processes the data.

Accountability and Legal Concerns

The **lack of interpretability** in black-box models also raises significant legal and ethical concerns. In scenarios where AI systems make decisions that affect individuals' lives—such as denying insurance claims, determining criminal sentences, or approving loans—it is essential to be able to explain and justify those decisions. If a black-box model makes a harmful or unjust decision, it is nearly impossible to pinpoint exactly how the decision was made or whether the system operated fairly.

This lack of transparency is problematic from a **legal perspective**, particularly in regions with stringent regulations, such as the **GDPR** (General Data Protection Regulation) in Europe, which mandates that individuals have the right to receive an explanation for any automated decision made about them. Similarly, in the **US**, the **Equal Credit Opportunity Act** and other anti-discrimination laws require that decisions, such as those made in credit scoring, be non-discriminatory and based on transparent criteria.

Security Risks

Black-box models are also more vulnerable to **adversarial attacks**. Adversarial attacks involve making small, subtle changes to the input data in a way that causes the model to produce incorrect or biased outputs. Since the inner workings of black-box models are opaque, it is difficult to predict how they will respond to changes in input. This makes these models more susceptible to manipulation and exploitation, especially when deployed in critical systems like security or financial services.

For example, in the case of an **image recognition model** used for security purposes, an adversarial attack might subtly alter an image so that the system misidentifies a person or object. Because the model's decision-making process is not transparent, it is difficult to detect or prevent such attacks.

Strategies to Address the Black-Box Problem

Model Transparency Tools

To mitigate the challenges of black-box AI, various **model transparency tools** have been developed. These tools help to approximate the behavior of black-box models and make their decision-making processes more interpretable.

1. **LIME (Local Interpretable Model-agnostic Explanations)**: LIME is a popular technique that helps explain the predictions of complex models by approximating them with simple, interpretable models. It works by perturbing the input data and observing how the model's predictions change, allowing it to generate a local explanation for each individual prediction. For example, if a black-box model predicts a loan rejection, LIME could provide an explanation showing which features—such as income or credit score—were most influential in that particular decision.
2. **SHAP (SHapley Additive exPlanations)**: SHAP is based on **Shapley values** from cooperative game theory and offers a more global understanding of a model's behavior. It assigns a contribution value to each feature, explaining how each one influences the model's output. SHAP can be used to determine the most important factors that led to a particular decision, such as which data points or features (e.g., income, age, credit score) were most responsible for a loan approval or rejection.

These tools do not make the black-box model fully transparent but offer insights into the factors that influence its decisions. This transparency is critical for building trust and ensuring fairness in AI systems.

Explainable AI (XAI)

Explainable AI (XAI) is an emerging field that focuses on developing machine learning models that are interpretable while still maintaining high performance. The goal of XAI is to create AI systems that make decisions in a way that is understandable to humans without sacrificing accuracy.

XAI methodologies include designing models with built-in explainability, such as using attention mechanisms in neural networks that allow users to see which parts of the input data the model is focusing on. By integrating explainability into the model design itself, developers can make AI systems more transparent without compromising their predictive power.

For example, in a **medical diagnosis system**, an explainable model might allow healthcare professionals to see which symptoms or test results contributed most to the diagnosis, making the system easier to trust and use effectively.

Hybrid Models

One strategy for addressing the black-box challenge is to use **hybrid models**, which combine complex models with simpler, more interpretable ones. By doing so, developers can maintain the high accuracy of the complex model while making the decision-making process more understandable.

For instance, a hybrid model might use a deep learning model for predicting outcomes, such as loan approvals, but pair it with a decision tree to explain how the prediction was made. The decision tree can provide a clear and interpretable summary of the decision-making process, while the deep learning model ensures high predictive accuracy.

Real-World Example

Criminal Justice: Recidivism Risk Prediction

In the **criminal justice system**, AI models are often used to assess the **recidivism risk** of offenders, which influences parole decisions. These models typically take into account a wide range of factors, including prior convictions, age, rehabilitation efforts, and social factors.

However, many of these models are **black-box systems** that are difficult to interpret. The lack of transparency in these models has raised concerns about fairness, accountability, and bias. For example, if a model disproportionately predicts higher recidivism risk for certain demographic groups, it may be perpetuating existing biases in the criminal justice system.

To address this issue, researchers have begun using **SHAP** to explain the factors influencing recidivism risk predictions. SHAP allows for a detailed understanding of how individual features, such as prior convictions or age, influence the model's predictions. This transparency helps ensure that parole decisions are based on clear, understandable reasoning and that potential biases are identified and addressed.

Black-box AI systems offer high performance and accuracy, but their lack of transparency poses significant challenges in ensuring fairness, accountability, and trust. By using model transparency tools like LIME and SHAP, embracing the principles of explainable AI, and considering hybrid models, developers can mitigate the black-box problem. Transparency is critical, especially in high-stakes domains like criminal justice, healthcare, and finance, where decisions made by AI systems have significant consequences for individuals. As AI continues to evolve, addressing the challenges of black-box models will be essential for creating more ethical, fair, and accountable AI systems.

Summary

1. Explaining Complex Models in Understandable Terms

Complex AI models, such as deep learning and neural networks, process vast amounts of data but are often considered "black boxes" due to their lack of transparency in decision-making. While simpler models like decision trees are more interpretable, more complex models excel at achieving higher accuracy, which sometimes comes at the cost of explainability. The need for explainability in AI has grown, particularly due to legal and ethical concerns around automated decision-making, such as the General Data Protection Regulation (GDPR). Transparency builds trust in AI, especially in sensitive fields like healthcare and finance. Tools such as **LIME** (Local Interpretable Model-agnostic Explanations) and **SHAP** (SHapley Additive exPlanations) help explain black-box models by attributing decision-making to specific features, helping users understand how inputs influence outputs. However, balancing accuracy with explainability remains a challenge in AI model development.

2. Empowering Users Through Transparency

Transparency in AI refers to making the decision-making process of AI systems clear and accessible to users, enabling them to understand how their data is used and why decisions are made. Transparent AI systems foster trust and accountability, especially in sectors like healthcare, where decisions can significantly impact individuals' lives. Empowering users means providing them with control over their data and offering feedback mechanisms, where users can correct errors or challenge decisions. Transparent data policies, clear consent forms, and user control are essential for building trust and ensuring fairness in AI. In industries like fintech, organizations can employ transparent algorithms that show how data like income or spending habits influence financial decisions, further encouraging user participation and trust.

3. Navigating the Challenges of Black-Box AI

Black-box AI refers to machine learning models where the internal workings are not visible or understandable to the user. These models can achieve high accuracy but are challenging to interpret, raising concerns about fairness, bias, accountability, and trust. Biases in training data may result in discriminatory outcomes, and since the decision-making process is opaque, it's difficult to hold models accountable for harmful decisions. To address these challenges, transparency tools like **LIME** and **SHAP** help approximate black-box model behavior by showing how inputs influence predictions. The field of **Explainable AI (XAI)** also seeks to develop models that balance accuracy and interpretability. Hybrid models, combining complex and simpler interpretable models, offer another strategy to maintain model performance while making decisions more understandable. In sectors like criminal justice, where AI predicts recidivism risk, transparency tools help explain how certain features influence decisions, improving accountability and fairness.

Ensuring clarity in algorithms and decision-making is a fundamental responsibility for developers and organizations working with AI systems. As AI continues to influence nearly every aspect of society, transparency, explainability, and fairness are essential for building trust and ensuring that AI models are used ethically. By developing methods for explaining complex models, empowering users through transparency, and addressing the challenges of black-box AI, we can create systems that are not only accurate but also fair, accountable, and understandable.

Key Takeaways

- **Transparency** and **explainability** are crucial for building trust in AI systems, particularly in high-stakes fields like healthcare, finance, and criminal justice.
- Tools like **LIME** and **SHAP** are helping to make black-box models more interpretable by providing insights into how data influences AI predictions.
- There is a trade-off between **accuracy** and **interpretability**, where more accurate models like deep learning may be harder to explain.
- **Empowering users** through transparency involves giving them control over their data, providing feedback mechanisms, and ensuring that AI decisions can be questioned or corrected.
- Addressing the challenges of black-box AI is necessary for ensuring that AI systems are fair, accountable, and trustworthy in real-world applications.

Check your Understanding

Fill in the Blanks

1. Machine learning models such as ____________ are often referred to as "black-box" models.
2. ____________ algorithms are used in supervised learning to predict continuous outcomes.
3. The General Data Protection Regulation (GDPR) mandates transparency in automated decision-making processes for ____________ systems.
4. A common example of a transparent model is a ____________, which makes decisions by following a set of simple rules.
5. The trade-off between ____________ and interpretability is a significant challenge in AI systems.
6. ____________ is a method that approximates black-box models by creating simple interpretable models for each individual prediction.
7. ____________ values, derived from game theory, are used in SHAP to measure the contribution of each feature to the model's prediction.
8. ____________ models are simpler models, such as decision trees, that help explain the behavior of more complex algorithms.
9. One of the main ethical concerns in AI systems is preventing the model from ____________ bias in decision-making.
10. A common use of AI in the healthcare industry is predicting ____________ outcomes.
11. AI models are considered transparent when their decision-making process can be easily ____________ and understood by humans.
12. ____________ is a method used to determine which features of a dataset most influence the prediction made by the model.
13. Deep learning models can be highly accurate but often lack the ____________ needed to understand their decisions.
14. The ____________ method helps explain model predictions by assigning contributions to each feature based on Shapley values.
15. The ____________ algorithm is a type of tree-based model used to identify the most important features in data.

16. ____________ is often used as a surrogate model to approximate the behavior of complex AI systems.
17. In machine learning, ____________ involves a system being able to provide clear reasons for its predictions or actions.
18. A ____________ model is typically easy to interpret and can be used to approximate complex models in some cases.
19. ____________ is a field within machine learning that involves using neural networks to process vast amounts of data for tasks such as image recognition.
20. ____________ explains how small changes in input data affect a model's output, making the model's behavior more understandable.

Short Answer Questions

1. What is the difference between a transparent model and a black-box model in machine learning?
2. Define LIME and explain how it helps in explaining complex models.
3. What is SHAP, and how does it contribute to model explainability?
4. Why is explainability important in AI systems, particularly in legal and ethical contexts?
5. How does the trade-off between accuracy and interpretability affect AI model development?
6. What role does transparency play in building trust with users in AI systems?
7. What are surrogate models, and why are they used in machine learning?
8. Give one real-world example of how AI is used in healthcare.
9. How do feature importance techniques like Random Forest help in explaining model behavior?
10. What are the key challenges in making complex AI models interpretable?

Long Answer Questions

1. Discuss the ethical implications of using black-box models in critical applications such as healthcare and criminal justice. How can transparency mitigate these concerns?

2. Explain how LIME (Local Interpretable Model-agnostic Explanations) works in making black-box models more interpretable. Provide an example where LIME could be effectively applied.
3. Evaluate the role of SHAP (SHapley Additive exPlanations) in improving the transparency of AI systems. How does SHAP differ from other explainability methods?
4. Describe the trade-off between model accuracy and interpretability. How can developers ensure that they balance the two when building AI systems?
5. Discuss the challenges in explaining deep learning models. How does the complexity of neural networks impact their explainability, and what methods can be used to address this?
6. Analyze how regulatory frameworks like GDPR influence the need for explainability in AI systems. What are the legal requirements for explainability, and why are they important?
7. How can AI systems be designed to avoid perpetuating bias and ensure fairness in decision-making processes? Discuss the ethical responsibilities of AI developers in this context.
8. Explain the concept of surrogate models and how they help in approximating complex machine learning models. Why are they important for transparency?
9. What is the importance of feature importance techniques in making AI models more interpretable? Discuss how these techniques contribute to understanding how models make predictions.
10. Critically analyze the role of transparency in fostering trust in AI systems. Discuss examples of industries or applications where transparency is particularly crucial.

Answers

Fill in the Blanks

1. Deep learning
2. Linear regression
3. Automated **decision-making**
4. Decision trees
5. Accuracy
6. LIME **(Local Interpretable Model-agnostic Explanations)**
7. Shapley **values**
8. Surrogate

9. Perpetuate
10. Patient
11. Explained
12. Feature importance
13. Interpretability
14. SHAP **(SHapley Additive exPlanations)**
15. XGBoost
16. Decision tree
17. Explainability
18. Decision tree
19. Neural networks
20. LIME

Short Answer Questions – Answer key

1. **Transparent models** are those whose decision-making processes can be easily understood by humans (e.g., decision trees), whereas **black-box models** are more complex and their decisions cannot be easily interpreted (e.g., deep neural networks).
2. **LIME (Local Interpretable Model-agnostic Explanations)** is a technique that approximates black-box models by using simpler, interpretable models for each individual prediction, helping to explain why a particular decision was made.
3. **SHAP** stands for SHapley Additive exPlanations. It is based on Shapley values from cooperative game theory and is used to assign contributions to each feature in a model's prediction, allowing users to understand how each input feature influences the result.
4. Explainability is crucial because it ensures that AI systems are **transparent** and do not violate **legal rights** (e.g., GDPR requires transparency for automated decisions). It also helps address **ethical concerns** by preventing bias and ensuring that AI systems are fair.
5. The **trade-off between accuracy and interpretability** arises when highly accurate models (e.g., deep learning) are more difficult to explain. Simpler models (e.g., decision trees) are more interpretable but may sacrifice some accuracy.

6. **Transparency** in AI systems helps build **trust** with users because when they understand how decisions are made, they are more likely to believe that the system is fair and reliable. This is especially important in sensitive areas like finance, healthcare, and criminal justice.
7. **Surrogate models** are simpler models, such as decision trees, used to approximate the decision-making process of more complex models. They help explain how the complex model works in a more understandable way.
8. One real-world example is the use of AI in healthcare for **predicting patient outcomes** after surgery, where AI analyzes factors like age, health history, and lifestyle to assist doctors in making informed treatment decisions.
9. **Feature importance** techniques like **Random Forest** and **XGBoost** help to identify which features (variables) have the greatest influence on the predictions made by a model, making it easier to understand the key factors driving decisions.
10. The key challenges in explainability include the **complexity** of models like deep learning, which are highly accurate but difficult to explain, and the **trade-off** between accuracy and simplicity, where simplifying a model for interpretability may reduce its performance.

Long Answer Questions -Answer key

1. **Ethical implications of black-box models** in critical applications (e.g., healthcare, criminal justice) include the risk of **bias**, **discrimination**, and **lack of accountability**. Transparent models can mitigate these issues by allowing stakeholders to understand the reasoning behind decisions, ensuring fairness, and providing the opportunity to challenge outcomes. For example, in healthcare, a black-box AI system used for diagnosing diseases could perpetuate health disparities if it isn't transparent and doesn't account for bias in the data.
2. **LIME** works by creating simpler, interpretable models to explain complex, black-box models. It applies to individual predictions by showing how small changes in input data affect the model's output, helping users understand why certain predictions are made. For example, in a loan approval system, LIME can show how changes in an applicant's credit score, income, or other factors influence the approval decision.
3. **SHAP** improves transparency by providing a unified measure of feature importance, with each feature's contribution to the prediction calculated using Shapley values from game theory. Unlike other methods, SHAP accounts for all possible combinations of feature interactions,

giving a comprehensive view of how each feature impacts the model. This method is more detailed and accurate compared to other explainability techniques like LIME.

4. **The trade-off between accuracy and interpretability** happens because more complex models (e.g., deep neural networks) are highly accurate but hard to explain. In contrast, simpler models (e.g., decision trees) are easier to interpret but might sacrifice accuracy. To balance the two, developers can use techniques like LIME and SHAP to enhance explainability while maintaining the model's predictive power.
5. **Challenges in explaining deep learning models** include their multi-layered architecture, which processes vast amounts of data in ways that are not easily interpretable. Methods like **LIME**, **SHAP**, and **surrogate models** help to explain the decisions made by deep learning systems, but they often require simplifying the model or approximating its behavior, which may reduce some accuracy.
6. **GDPR** mandates that users have the right to understand automated decisions, which is why **explainability** is crucial. AI systems must be transparent to ensure that users can challenge decisions made about them, especially when those decisions have significant personal consequences. Legal requirements like **right to explanation** ensure that AI systems operate within ethical bounds, offering accountability and fairness.
7. To ensure **fairness** and **avoid bias** in AI, developers must address the **data biases** that could influence the model's predictions. Ethical responsibilities include making sure that training data is representative of diverse populations and ensuring that AI models do not favor one group over another. Techniques such as **bias detection**, **data auditing**, and **regular checks for fairness** are essential.
8. **Surrogate models** (e.g., decision trees) are simpler models used to approximate complex machine learning models. They provide an easier-to-understand explanation of the decision-making process without compromising the predictive power of the original, more complex model. Surrogate models help bridge the gap between accuracy and interpretability by offering a more transparent view of the model's behavior.
9. **Feature importance techniques**, such as **Random Forest** or **XGBoost**, rank features based on their impact on model predictions. These techniques help explain which factors the model is prioritizing, making it easier for users to understand how decisions are made. For example,

in a housing price prediction model, **square footage**, **location**, and **number of bedrooms** might be identified as the most important features driving the model's output.

10. **Transparency** in AI systems fosters **trust** by ensuring users understand how decisions are made. In industries like healthcare and finance, where decisions can have significant consequences, transparency helps to build credibility and ensures fairness. For example, in a loan approval AI, users will trust the system more if they understand the reasoning behind the approval or denial decision.

Chapter 7: Responsibility in Data-Driven Systems

Learning Outcomes

1. Understand the basic principles of accountability in AI systems.
2. Recognize the challenges of defining and assigning accountability in automated systems.
3. Identify the importance of transparency and fairness in AI design.
4. Describe the role of human oversight in mitigating bias and ensuring ethical decision-making in AI systems.

Introduction

In the age of artificial intelligence (AI) and machine learning, automated systems are becoming an integral part of various decision-making processes that impact individuals, organizations, and society as a whole. These systems process vast amounts of data, identifying patterns and delivering outcomes that can influence critical areas such as loan approvals, criminal sentencing, hiring decisions, and healthcare diagnoses. The ability of AI to process and analyze data at a speed and scale far beyond human capabilities offers the potential for increased efficiency, objectivity, and even accuracy in these areas.

However, the growing reliance on AI-driven decision-making also brings forth a complex set of ethical and practical challenges. As the decisions made by AI systems can directly affect people's lives, issues like accountability, fairness, and transparency become critical. For example, if an AI system is used to determine loan eligibility, how do we ensure that it does not perpetuate existing biases or discriminate against certain individuals or groups? Similarly, in healthcare, how do we ensure that AI algorithms provide accurate diagnoses without reinforcing any form of medical inequity?

This chapter delves into the evolving responsibility that comes with data-driven systems, focusing particularly on the need for accountability in automated outcomes. It examines how accountability can be assigned when AI systems make decisions, the importance of human oversight in ensuring ethical standards are met, and how organizations can incorporate ethical checks into the design of AI systems. Ultimately, the chapter aims to provide insights into the frameworks and best practices necessary to ensure that AI systems are developed, deployed, and operated responsibly, for the benefit of society.

7.1 Defining Accountability in Automated Outcomes

Introduction to Accountability in AI Systems

Accountability in the context of AI systems refers to the expectation that individuals, organizations, or algorithms are responsible for the decisions and actions they take. AI systems are increasingly capable of making independent decisions based on the data they process, often with minimal or no direct human intervention. While this autonomy offers benefits such as speed, efficiency, and consistency, it also creates challenges when things go wrong. When an AI-driven system produces a harmful, erroneous, or biased decision, the question arises: Who should be held accountable?

In traditional systems, accountability can usually be traced back to specific individuals or organizations that have clear roles and responsibilities. However, in AI systems, particularly those using advanced algorithms like deep learning or machine learning, decisions are made through complex processes that can be difficult to explain. This lack of transparency and clarity often obscures who should be held accountable, especially when something goes wrong. This section explores the challenge of defining accountability in automated outcomes, the principles that guide accountability in AI systems, and provides real-world examples where accountability becomes a critical issue.

The Challenge of Defining Accountability

In AI-driven systems, the question of who is accountable for decisions is not as straightforward as in traditional systems. The complexity and autonomy of AI make it difficult to assign clear responsibility, leading to several challenges:

1. **Lack of Transparency**: Many AI systems, especially deep learning models, are often referred to as "black boxes." These models are capable of learning patterns from vast datasets and making predictions or decisions based on these patterns. However, the internal

workings of these models are often opaque, even to the developers who built them. For example, a deep neural network might provide an accurate prediction or decision, but understanding the exact factors that influenced that decision is difficult. Without transparency into how the model arrives at its conclusions, it becomes challenging to hold anyone accountable when things go wrong.

2. **Ethical Responsibility**: AI systems are trained on data, and if the data is biased or flawed, the AI will likely produce biased or unfair outcomes. But who is responsible when an AI system makes a discriminatory or harmful decision? Is it the fault of the dataset creators who supplied the biased data, the developers who built the model without sufficient safeguards, or the organization deploying the AI system? Ethical responsibility for AI decisions is a complex issue because the decisions made by AI systems may not reflect the intentions of their creators. For example, if an AI algorithm used for recruitment ends up discriminating against women or minorities, it can be difficult to pinpoint where the ethical responsibility lies. Should the developers of the algorithm be held accountable for failing to account for potential bias, or is the organization deploying the algorithm at fault for not properly vetting it?
3. **Legal Accountability**: As AI continues to evolve and take on a more prominent role in decision-making, legal systems around the world are struggling to keep up. There is often no clear framework for assigning legal responsibility when an AI system causes harm. For example, if an AI system used in healthcare makes a misdiagnosis, who should be held legally responsible? Should it be the healthcare provider, who used the AI system in their practice? Or should it be the developers who created the algorithm, or perhaps the AI system itself? Legal frameworks such as the General Data Protection Regulation (GDPR) in Europe provide some guidance, but these regulations were developed in the early stages of AI technology and are still adapting to emerging issues related to automated decision-making.

Assigning Accountability in Automated Systems

Several key principles and best practices can guide the assignment of accountability in AI systems. These principles aim to ensure that AI technologies are used responsibly and that there is clarity when things go wrong:

1. **Clear Attribution of Responsibility**: One of the first steps in assigning accountability in AI systems is to clearly define who is responsible for each aspect of the system's lifecycle. This includes accountability for the data collection process, the development of the model, the deployment of the AI, and the ongoing monitoring of its performance. AI systems are complex and often involve multiple parties, so it is essential to establish clear lines of responsibility from the outset. For example, in the case of a biased AI system, accountability might be shared between the data creators, the algorithm developers, and the organizations that deploy the system. However, clear attribution is necessary to identify who should be held accountable in case of harm.
2. **Explainability and Transparency**: A key component of accountability is ensuring that AI systems are explainable and transparent. Transparent AI systems allow stakeholders to understand how decisions are made and why specific outcomes occur. This transparency is vital for identifying and correcting problems when they arise. If an AI system produces a discriminatory outcome, it is essential to be able to trace back the decision-making process to understand why the system behaved that way. Explainability tools such as Local Interpretable Model-agnostic Explanations (LIME) or SHAP (SHapley Additive Explanations) can be used to provide insights into complex models. These tools help to make the decision-making process of black-box systems more interpretable, thereby increasing transparency and making it easier to assign accountability.
3. **Monitoring and Auditing**: Regular monitoring and auditing of AI systems are essential to ensure that they operate as intended and remain in compliance with ethical and legal standards. Audits provide ongoing checks on the effectiveness, fairness, and accuracy of AI systems. These audits should be conducted both before the system is deployed and throughout its operational lifecycle. For example, an AI system used in criminal sentencing should be audited regularly to ensure that it is not perpetuating biases based on race or socioeconomic status. If the system is found to be making biased decisions, corrective

actions should be taken, and those responsible for the deployment of the system should be held accountable.

4. **Ethical and Legal Frameworks**: The development and deployment of AI systems should be governed by clear ethical and legal frameworks. International and national regulations, such as the GDPR, the Health Insurance Portability and Accountability Act (HIPAA), or the California Consumer Privacy Act (CCPA), provide guidelines for data collection, privacy, and automated decision-making. These frameworks help define who is responsible when AI systems cause harm, ensuring that individuals and organizations are held accountable for their actions. As AI technology continues to advance, it is essential that governments and regulators create new laws that address the unique challenges posed by automated systems.

Real-World Example: Self-Driving Cars

The case of self-driving cars is a particularly pertinent example when discussing accountability in AI systems. Autonomous vehicles, powered by AI, are designed to make decisions about navigation, speed, and safety without direct human input. However, if a self-driving car is involved in an accident, questions of accountability arise. Who should be held responsible for the harm caused?

Is it the manufacturer of the vehicle, who developed the AI software that powered the self-driving system? Is it the software developer who wrote the code that determines how the car behaves in various situations? Or should the car owner be held accountable, as they chose to use the vehicle in the first place? These questions are still unresolved and have sparked significant debate in legal and ethical circles.

Some argue that the manufacturer and software developer should bear the responsibility, as they are the ones who designed and programmed the AI system. Others suggest that car owners should be accountable, especially if they failed to properly maintain the vehicle or override the system when necessary. In either case, the lack of clear attribution of responsibility highlights the challenges of assigning accountability in AI systems.

As AI continues to play a larger role in decision-making, the question of accountability for automated outcomes becomes increasingly important. Clear attribution of responsibility, transparency, monitoring, and the establishment of ethical and legal frameworks are all essential in ensuring that AI systems are used in a way that benefits society and minimizes harm. While the issues of accountability in AI are complex, addressing these challenges will be crucial for the responsible development and deployment of AI technologies.

7.2 The Role of Human Oversight

Human Oversight in AI

Human oversight refers to the involvement of individuals in the decision-making processes of AI systems to ensure that these systems are used responsibly and ethically. Despite the increasing sophistication of AI technologies, the need for human oversight remains critical in ensuring that AI-driven decisions are aligned with societal norms, ethical principles, and legal frameworks. While AI systems are capable of autonomously making predictions and decisions based on data, they still lack the ability to fully comprehend human values, nuanced situations, and complex ethical dilemmas. Hence, human intervention provides the necessary safeguards to ensure that AI operates in ways that are transparent, accountable, and fair.

This section explores the importance of human oversight in AI systems, its role in mitigating potential risks, and the various types of oversight mechanisms that can be implemented to ensure AI systems function as intended. We will also look at real-world examples where human oversight has been critical to the success and ethical implementation of AI technologies.

The Need for Human Oversight

AI systems, no matter how advanced, are not infallible. They can still produce unintended, biased, or harmful outcomes due to limitations in the algorithms, training data, or unforeseen factors. Human oversight plays a vital role in addressing these challenges by ensuring that AI systems remain accountable, ethical, and effective in their decision-making.

1. Unforeseen Consequences

AI systems can evolve and learn from vast amounts of data, leading to decisions and behaviors that were not anticipated by the developers. This adaptability, while powerful, can also introduce unforeseen consequences. For example, an AI model trained to optimize for efficiency in a logistics company may prioritize speed over worker safety, leading to unsafe conditions in the workplace. In such scenarios, human oversight ensures that unintended consequences, such as unsafe practices or discriminatory outcomes, are caught and addressed before they become problematic.

Human involvement also helps identify cases where an AI model may produce outcomes that are not aligned with ethical or societal expectations. For instance, an AI system used in recruitment may inadvertently perpetuate bias by favoring candidates from certain demographic groups due to the data it was trained on. Human oversight helps recognize and correct such issues, ensuring that the system operates fairly and justly.

2. Ethical Judgments

AI systems, despite their computational prowess, lack the ability to make complex ethical judgments. These systems operate based on mathematical models and predefined rules, which means they may struggle with decisions that require human values, moral considerations, or ethical reasoning.

For instance, an AI system used in the criminal justice system may be tasked with predicting recidivism risk to inform parole decisions. However, such systems might not account for the socio-economic background, personal rehabilitation, or mental health conditions of the individual. These are factors that a human judge or parole officer might consider before making a decision. In this context, human oversight ensures that decisions made by AI align with ethical norms and legal frameworks, incorporating considerations that an algorithm may overlook.

3. Bias Mitigation

AI systems are only as unbiased as the data used to train them. If the training data is biased—whether due to historical inequities or unrepresentative samples—the AI model can perpetuate or even amplify these biases. This can lead to discriminatory outcomes, especially in sensitive areas like hiring, lending, and criminal justice.

Human oversight is essential in detecting and mitigating these biases. For instance, if an AI algorithm used for hiring purposes disproportionately favors male candidates for certain roles, human intervention is required to analyze and rectify the underlying biases in the data or algorithm. Oversight mechanisms can ensure that the system is tested for fairness, transparency, and equity before being deployed in real-world scenarios.

4. Ensuring Compliance

In industries such as healthcare, finance, and law, AI-driven decisions are often subject to strict regulatory frameworks and ethical standards. For example, healthcare professionals must ensure that AI-driven diagnostic systems comply with medical ethics, patient privacy laws, and industry standards. Human oversight plays a critical role in ensuring that these systems adhere to legal and regulatory requirements. It helps safeguard the rights of individuals and ensures that AI technologies are deployed in ways that do not harm or infringe upon privacy or human dignity.

For example, in the context of healthcare, AI systems that provide diagnostic support must be carefully monitored to ensure they comply with patient confidentiality standards such as HIPAA (Health Insurance Portability and Accountability Act) in the United States. If an AI model used in healthcare violates these regulations, human oversight can quickly intervene to rectify the situation, preventing further harm or legal violations.

Types of Human Oversight

Human oversight can take various forms depending on the context in which the AI system is being used. Different types of oversight ensure that AI systems operate correctly and that there is accountability for the outcomes they generate.

1. Real-Time Monitoring

In high-stakes environments, such as healthcare, autonomous vehicles, or critical infrastructure, real-time monitoring is essential. This type of oversight involves human supervisors actively observing the operation of AI systems and intervening when necessary to prevent harm or errors. For instance, an autonomous vehicle might be monitored in real-time to ensure that it navigates the roads safely. If the vehicle encounters a scenario that the AI is not trained to handle, a human operator may take control to avoid an accident.

Similarly, AI systems used in healthcare, such as those that assist with medical imaging or diagnostic recommendations, should be monitored in real-time by medical professionals. While the AI can analyze images and provide suggestions, it is the role of the human healthcare provider to ensure that the AI's analysis aligns with the patient's unique medical history and symptoms.

2. Decision Support Systems

Decision support systems involve the integration of AI as an assistive tool, rather than a fully autonomous decision-maker. In these systems, AI provides recommendations or suggestions based on data analysis, but the final decision is always made by a human. This type of oversight ensures that human judgment remains central to the decision-making process.

For example, in the field of finance, an AI system may assist in determining credit scores or recommending loans to applicants. However, the final decision to approve or deny the loan should be made by a human credit officer who takes into account the context, nuances, and additional information that the AI might not have considered.

In healthcare, AI-powered systems can provide diagnostic recommendations based on medical images, but the final diagnosis and treatment plan should always be made by a human doctor, who can consider the full spectrum of the patient's health and history.

3. Post-Decision Review

Post-decision review involves evaluating the decisions made by AI systems after they have been executed. In this model, humans review the outcomes of automated decisions to identify errors, biases, or areas for improvement. This type of oversight is especially useful when dealing with large-scale AI implementations where immediate real-time intervention may not be feasible.

For example, in the case of AI-driven loan approval systems, human auditors may review the loan decisions made by the system to ensure they comply with fairness and anti-discrimination regulations. If the system has made a biased decision, the review process provides an opportunity to correct the issue and take necessary action.

In criminal justice, post-decision review may involve human experts reviewing AI-driven risk assessments used in sentencing or parole decisions. This helps ensure that the AI system's recommendations align with legal standards and ethical guidelines, while also protecting individuals' rights.

Real-World Example: AI in Healthcare

In the healthcare industry, AI is increasingly being used to assist medical professionals in diagnosing and treating patients. For example, AI systems can analyze medical imaging data, such as X-rays or MRIs, to identify signs of diseases like cancer. However, despite AI's remarkable ability to analyze data quickly and accurately, the final diagnosis and treatment decisions are still made by human doctors. This is an example of human oversight in action.

The role of human oversight is crucial in ensuring that AI recommendations are validated and interpreted within the broader context of patient care. For instance, an AI algorithm might flag a potential abnormality in an image, but only a trained physician can assess the severity of the condition, review the patient's medical history, and consider other relevant factors. This collaborative approach between AI and human professionals helps to ensure that patient care is optimized, and errors or oversights in the AI system are minimized.

Human oversight is a critical component in ensuring that AI systems are used ethically, safely, and effectively. It helps address challenges such as unforeseen consequences, ethical dilemmas, bias mitigation, and regulatory compliance. By incorporating human judgment at various stages—whether in real-time monitoring, decision support, or post-decision review—AI systems can be deployed in ways that benefit society while minimizing harm. Human oversight ensures that AI remains a tool to enhance human decision-making rather than replace it, allowing for a more responsible and ethical use of technology across industries.

7.3 Building Ethical Checks into System Design

Introduction to Ethical System Design

Ethical considerations in AI design are paramount to ensuring that the technology is not only efficient and accurate but also fair, transparent, and aligned with societal values. As AI becomes increasingly embedded in decision-making processes that affect people's lives, from hiring and healthcare to criminal justice and finance, ensuring that AI systems are ethically designed is essential for maintaining public trust and preventing harm.

The development of AI systems should not focus solely on profit, efficiency, or technical performance but also prioritize ethical principles that reflect the values and needs of society. This involves creating frameworks and mechanisms that help ensure AI operates in a way that promotes justice, accountability, privacy, and sustainability. Ethical checks must be incorporated into AI system design from the beginning to ensure that potential risks, such as bias, discrimination, and privacy violations, are mitigated.

This section discusses the key principles for ethical system design in AI, explores how these principles can be built into AI systems, and provides a real-world example of how ethical considerations are applied in AI-driven hiring processes.

Key Principles for Ethical System Design

The following are the fundamental principles that should guide the design of AI systems to ensure they align with ethical standards:

1. Fairness Fairness is a core principle of ethical AI design. AI systems must be designed in ways that avoid biases that could lead to discriminatory or unjust outcomes. Biases in AI models can arise from biased data, flawed algorithms, or assumptions made during the design process. It is essential to ensure that AI systems do not discriminate based on race, gender, socioeconomic status, or other protected characteristics.

To achieve fairness, AI systems should be built with the following practices in mind:

- **Diverse Datasets:** Ensuring the training data used to develop AI models is representative of the diverse populations that the system will impact. This reduces the risk of reinforcing existing biases.
- **Fairness Metrics:** Implementing quantitative metrics to measure the fairness of an AI system's decisions and outputs. These metrics help identify potential discrimination or disparities in outcomes.
- **Continuous Evaluation:** Regularly assessing AI models to ensure they remain fair over time and identifying any emerging biases as new data is processed or as the system adapts to new contexts.

2. Transparency Transparency is vital to building trust in AI systems. A transparent AI system allows stakeholders—whether they are users, regulators, or developers—to understand how decisions are made, what data is used, and what assumptions are built into the model. Transparency is not just about openness; it is about making complex systems understandable to a wide audience.

Key approaches to ensuring transparency include:

- **Explainability:** AI systems should be designed to offer clear explanations of how they arrive at decisions. For example, in decision support systems used for healthcare or criminal justice, AI systems should be able to explain the factors that influenced a particular recommendation.

- **Clear Communication:** Developers should make the decision-making process of AI systems clear and accessible, avoiding jargon or overly complex models that hinder understanding.
- **Auditability:** Implementing mechanisms to allow external parties to audit and review the AI system's decision-making process. This ensures that stakeholders can verify that the system operates as intended and adheres to ethical principles.

3. Accountability As highlighted in earlier sections, accountability is a central aspect of ethical AI. AI systems should not operate in a vacuum; there must be clear mechanisms for holding the developers, organizations, and other stakeholders responsible for the outcomes of automated systems. The challenge is that accountability in AI systems can be complex, especially in cases where decision-making is automated, and the rationale behind decisions may not be transparent.

Effective accountability mechanisms involve:

- **Clear Attribution of Responsibility:** Identifying and assigning responsibility at each stage of the AI lifecycle, from design and development to deployment and monitoring.
- **Auditable Trails:** Ensuring that AI systems generate logs or trails that track how decisions are made, enabling organizations to trace errors, biases, or failures back to specific components or processes.
- **Legal and Ethical Frameworks:** Establishing legal and ethical frameworks that define responsibility and liability for AI-driven decisions, particularly in high-stakes areas such as healthcare or criminal justice.

4. Privacy and Security AI systems process vast amounts of sensitive data, and it is essential that designers incorporate measures to protect privacy and security. Privacy-enhancing technologies, such as encryption, data anonymization, and secure data storage, should be implemented to protect individuals' personal information. Ensuring data security helps prevent data breaches, identity theft, and other security threats.

In addition to data protection, AI systems must also be designed to respect individuals' rights to privacy:

- **Data Minimization:** Ensuring that only necessary data is collected and processed for the intended purposes, avoiding overreach in terms of data usage.
- **User Control:** Allowing users to control their data, including opting out of data collection and understanding how their data is being used by AI systems.
- **Compliance with Privacy Laws:** Adhering to privacy laws and regulations, such as the General Data Protection Regulation (GDPR) in the EU, which mandates that AI systems respect users' rights to privacy and data protection.

5. Sustainability As AI systems become more widespread, it is essential to consider their long-term impact on the environment and society. Sustainable AI design involves minimizing the environmental footprint of AI technologies and ensuring that their benefits are distributed equitably across society. This includes considering the energy consumption of AI models, especially those that require extensive computational resources, and ensuring that their deployment does not contribute to societal inequalities or exacerbate existing risks.

Key practices for building sustainability into AI design include:

- **Energy Efficiency:** Designing AI models that use computational resources efficiently, reducing the energy consumption associated with training and operating large models.
- **Long-Term Impact:** Considering the broader societal, environmental, and economic implications of AI deployment, including the impact on employment, resource distribution, and social structures.

Building Ethical Frameworks into System Design

To effectively incorporate ethical principles into AI design, organizations should establish comprehensive frameworks and strategies that ensure these principles are followed throughout the lifecycle of AI systems.

1. Ethical Audits Ethical audits are a critical tool for identifying and addressing potential ethical concerns in AI systems. These audits should be conducted regularly throughout the development, deployment, and maintenance of AI technologies. Ethical audits assess factors such as fairness, transparency, accountability, and bias, and they provide organizations with an opportunity to address issues before they cause harm.

Audits should include:

- **Pre-deployment Audits:** Assessing the AI system's design and data to ensure that it meets ethical standards before it is deployed in real-world scenarios.
- **Ongoing Audits:** Continuously evaluating the performance and impact of the AI system to ensure it remains fair and unbiased over time.
- **Post-deployment Audits:** Conducting audits after the system has been deployed to address any unintended consequences, biases, or ethical issues that may arise.

2. Inclusive Design Incorporating input from diverse stakeholders is crucial to creating AI systems that are fair and equitable. By involving people from underrepresented groups, organizations can better identify potential biases or blind spots in the design process. Inclusive design ensures that AI technologies benefit all members of society, not just a select few.

Inclusive design practices include:

- **Diverse Development Teams:** Involving individuals from different racial, gender, and socioeconomic backgrounds in the design and development of AI systems.
- **Stakeholder Input:** Engaging with affected communities and stakeholders to understand their needs, concerns, and experiences with AI technology.
- **Testing for Bias:** Actively testing AI systems for biases related to race, gender, age, and other factors to ensure that they do not perpetuate or exacerbate existing inequalities.

3. Human-Centered Design Human-centered design places the needs, values, and experiences of users at the core of the design process. By focusing on how AI systems impact real people, organizations can ensure that their technologies are both functional and beneficial to society. This approach emphasizes user empowerment, accessibility, and fairness.

Key elements of human-centered design include:

- **User Feedback:** Incorporating regular feedback from end users to refine and improve AI systems based on their experiences.
- **Ethical Decision-Making:** Ensuring that ethical considerations are integrated into every stage of the design and development process.
- **Focus on User Benefits:** Designing AI systems that prioritize the well-being of users and society, ensuring that technology is used to create positive outcomes rather than exacerbate problems.

Real-World Example: AI in Hiring

AI-driven hiring systems have the potential to revolutionize recruitment by streamlining the process, reducing human biases, and improving efficiency. However, these systems can also perpetuate existing biases if they are not designed ethically.

For example, an AI system trained on historical hiring data may unintentionally favor certain demographic groups (e.g., male applicants for tech roles or white applicants for executive positions) if the data reflects past hiring practices that were biased. Without ethical checks, such a system could reinforce these biases and result in unfair hiring practices.

To prevent this, companies can integrate ethical checks such as:

- **Fairness Metrics:** Using fairness metrics to assess whether the AI system is equally likely to recommend candidates from different demographic backgrounds.
- **Diverse Data Sources:** Ensuring that the training data includes a diverse range of candidates and experiences, reducing the risk of reinforcing biases.
- **Bias Audits:** Conducting regular bias audits to ensure that the AI system is not unintentionally favoring certain groups over others.

By incorporating these ethical checks into the design of AI-driven hiring systems, companies can help ensure that their recruitment processes are fair, inclusive, and equitable.

Building ethical checks into AI system design is essential for creating technologies that are fair, transparent, accountable, and aligned with societal values. By integrating key ethical principles such as fairness, transparency, accountability, privacy, and sustainability into AI development, organizations can ensure that their systems serve the public good rather than just profit. Ethical audits, inclusive design practices, and human-centered approaches further help organizations create AI technologies that are not only functional but also just and beneficial to all. Through these practices, AI can be a force for positive change, improving decision-making and outcomes while minimizing harm and promoting equity.

Summary

The integration of ethical considerations into AI system design is crucial as AI increasingly impacts key areas like healthcare, hiring, finance, and criminal justice. Ethical system design ensures that AI technologies are not only efficient but also fair, transparent, and aligned with societal values, promoting the overall well-being of society. By embedding ethics from the outset, organizations can create AI systems that prioritize societal good and prevent harmful outcomes.

Key Principles for Ethical System Design:

1. **Fairness**: AI systems must avoid bias and ensure equality in outcomes. This is achieved by using diverse datasets, fairness metrics, and ongoing evaluations to minimize discriminatory decisions.
2. **Transparency**: Systems should be understandable and provide clear explanations for decision-making. Transparency fosters trust and accountability, allowing stakeholders to verify AI decisions.
3. **Accountability**: Clear responsibility must be assigned for every aspect of the AI system, from development to deployment, ensuring that systems are auditable and responsible parties can be held accountable for negative outcomes.
4. **Privacy and Security**: Protecting data privacy and ensuring robust security are critical. Privacy-enhancing technologies like encryption and anonymization safeguard sensitive information.

5. **Sustainability**: AI systems should be designed with environmental and social sustainability in mind, minimizing their ecological impact and ensuring their long-term societal benefits.

Building Ethical Frameworks into System Design:

1. **Ethical Audits**: Regular ethical audits throughout an AI system's lifecycle ensure that it meets fairness, transparency, and accountability standards, identifying and addressing any issues before they escalate.
2. **Inclusive Design**: Engaging diverse stakeholders in the development process ensures that AI systems reflect a broad range of perspectives, reducing the risk of reinforcing existing societal biases.
3. **Human-Centered Design**: Focusing on users' needs and values ensures AI systems are designed to benefit society as a whole. This approach emphasizes user feedback and ethical decision-making at every stage of the process.

Real-World Example – AI in Hiring: AI can streamline hiring by improving efficiency and reducing human bias, but it also risks perpetuating past biases in the hiring process. For instance, AI systems trained on historical hiring data may favor specific demographic groups. Ethical checks like fairness metrics, diverse data sources, and regular bias audits ensure that AI hiring tools are equitable and do not discriminate against underrepresented groups.

Incorporating ethical checks into AI system design is essential for creating AI technologies that are not only functional but also just and beneficial to all. Through ethical audits, inclusive design, and human-centered approaches, AI systems can be developed to promote fairness, transparency, and accountability. These practices enable AI to be a positive force in society, improving decision-making and minimizing harm. Ethical AI design ensures that technology serves humanity, rather than contributing to inequalities or negative consequences.

Responsibility in data-driven systems is an evolving field that requires careful consideration of ethical, legal, and societal factors. Ensuring accountability in automated outcomes, integrating human oversight, and embedding ethical checks into system design are critical for the responsible use of AI and machine learning technologies. By fostering transparency, fairness, and accountability, organizations can build AI systems that not only perform well but also align with societal values and contribute to the common good.

Check your Understanding

Fill in the Blanks:

1. Accountability refers to the concept that entities, whether they are organizations, individuals, or __________, should be responsible for their actions and decisions.
2. AI systems that make decisions autonomously are known as __________ systems.
3. One challenge in defining accountability in AI systems is the lack of __________, which can make it difficult to trace how decisions are made.
4. When an AI system makes a biased decision, it can be challenging to determine if the fault lies with the __________, the model, or the organization that deployed it.
5. National and international legal standards, such as the __________ in Europe, provide frameworks for accountability in AI systems.
6. Self-driving cars are an example of an AI-driven system where accountability for accidents may be debated among the car manufacturer, the __________, or the car owner.
7. Human __________ ensures that AI-driven decisions comply with laws, regulations, and organizational policies.
8. Real-time monitoring in AI systems is a form of __________ oversight, where humans actively intervene during operation.
9. In decision support systems, the final decision is made by a __________, even though AI provides recommendations.
10. To ensure fairness, AI systems should be designed to avoid __________ that could lead to unfair outcomes.
11. One of the goals of ethical system design is to incorporate __________-enhancing technologies to safeguard individuals' privacy.
12. AI systems must be __________ to make sure they are transparent and their decisions can be explained and challenged.
13. ____ is a key principle in ethical AI system design, ensuring that all stakeholders understand how decisions are made.

14. The use of __________ datasets is essential to avoid bias and promote fairness in AI systems.
15. Ethical __________ should be conducted regularly to ensure AI systems comply with ethical standards.
16. AI-driven hiring systems can unintentionally reinforce __________ if they are trained on biased historical data.
17. __________ is the process of embedding ethical considerations into the design and deployment of AI systems.
18. Human-centered design ensures that AI systems prioritize the __________ and values of users.
19. The concept of __________ oversight involves reviewing decisions made by AI systems after they are executed.
20. AI systems in healthcare, such as diagnostic tools, require human __________ to ensure the correct application of AI recommendations.

Short Answer Questions

1. What is meant by accountability in AI systems?
2. Explain the concept of "black box" systems in the context of AI.
3. What is one challenge related to the legal accountability of AI systems?
4. What is the purpose of real-time monitoring in AI systems?
5. Define the term "decision support systems" in AI.
6. Why is fairness an important consideration in AI system design?
7. What is the significance of transparency in AI decision-making?
8. How does human oversight help in bias mitigation in AI systems?
9. Give an example of a real-world application of AI in healthcare.
10. What does the term "human-centered design" mean in AI?

Long Answer Questions

1. Discuss the challenges of assigning accountability in AI systems, especially in cases where automated decisions cause harm.

2. Explain the role of human oversight in preventing unforeseen consequences in AI-driven systems. How can human intervention improve the reliability of such systems?
3. How can organizations ensure AI systems are ethically designed? Discuss the integration of fairness, transparency, and accountability.
4. What are the potential ethical issues in self-driving cars, and who should be held accountable in case of an accident?
5. Describe the relationship between human oversight and compliance in regulated industries like healthcare and finance.
6. Analyze the importance of explainability and transparency in AI systems. How can these factors influence accountability?
7. What steps can be taken to ensure that AI hiring systems are free from bias? Provide practical examples.
8. How can an ethical audit help identify potential problems in AI systems before they lead to harmful consequences?
9. Discuss the importance of sustainability in the design of AI systems and its implications on long-term societal impact.
10. Compare and contrast the benefits and drawbacks of decision support systems and fully autonomous AI systems in high-stakes environments like healthcare and law enforcement.

Answers

Answers for Fill in the Blanks:

1. algorithms
2. autonomous
3. transparency
4. data
5. GDPR
6. software developer
7. oversight
8. human
9. human

10. biases
11. privacy
12. explainable
13. accountability
14. diverse
15. audits
16. biases
17. ethical system design
18. needs
19. post-decision review
20. oversight

Answer Keys for Short Answer Questions

1. **Accountability in AI systems** refers to the responsibility of organizations, individuals, or algorithms for their actions and decisions, especially when those decisions are made autonomously.
2. **Black box systems** in AI refer to systems whose decision-making processes are not transparent or easily understood, even by their creators.
3. One challenge related to **legal accountability in AI systems** is the lack of a clear legal framework to assign responsibility when automated systems cause harm.
4. **Real-time monitoring** in AI systems is the practice of human supervisors actively observing AI operations to ensure proper functioning and intervene if necessary.
5. **Decision support systems** in AI are systems where AI provides recommendations or suggestions, but the final decision is made by a human.
6. **Fairness** is important in AI design to avoid biases that could lead to discrimination against certain groups or individuals.
7. **Transparency** in AI decision-making is crucial for allowing stakeholders to understand how decisions are made, ensuring decisions can be challenged if necessary.
8. **Human oversight** helps in bias mitigation by identifying and correcting biases in data or algorithms, ensuring AI systems make more fair and accurate decisions.

9. A **real-world application of AI in healthcare** is diagnostic tools that assist doctors in analyzing medical images and making diagnoses.
10. **Human-centered design** in AI refers to designing systems that prioritize the needs, values, and well-being of users, ensuring that AI solutions benefit society as a whole.

Answer Keys for Long Answer Questions

1. **Challenges of assigning accountability in AI systems** include the complexity of tracing decision-making in autonomous systems, lack of transparency, and difficulty in determining the responsible party when harmful outcomes occur. For example, in healthcare, if an AI system makes a misdiagnosis, the question arises whether accountability lies with the healthcare provider, the AI developer, or the AI itself. Legal frameworks struggle to keep up with technology, which complicates assigning clear responsibility.
2. **Human oversight in preventing unforeseen consequences** ensures that AI systems are monitored for unintended behaviors, such as perpetuating biases or making inaccurate predictions. By involving humans in decision-making processes, they can address issues that AI might miss, such as considering the broader social context in decisions. Human intervention helps correct errors, adjust models, and ensure ethical guidelines are followed.
3. Organizations can ensure **AI systems are ethically designed** by embedding key principles such as fairness, transparency, and accountability. Fairness can be achieved by using diverse datasets and fairness metrics, transparency by making AI decisions explainable, and accountability by creating audit trails for every stage of the AI lifecycle. Ethical design involves evaluating the social impact of AI systems and ensuring they align with societal values.
4. The ethical issues in **self-driving cars** revolve around responsibility in case of an accident. If a self-driving car causes harm, it is unclear who should be accountable: the manufacturer, the software developer, or the car owner. These ethical issues raise questions about liability, consumer trust, and the development of laws to govern autonomous vehicles. Legal systems are still evolving to address these concerns.
5. **Human oversight and compliance** in regulated industries like healthcare and finance ensure that AI-driven decisions adhere to legal and regulatory requirements. In healthcare,

for example, AI diagnostic tools may assist in analyzing medical data, but human doctors are responsible for validating those diagnoses to ensure compliance with healthcare standards and patient safety regulations.

6. **Explainability and transparency** are vital in AI systems to ensure accountability and trust. Transparent AI systems allow stakeholders to understand how decisions are made, which is essential for identifying and addressing problems, ensuring that automated outcomes can be challenged and corrected. Explainable AI provides insights into the rationale behind decisions, fostering greater trust and accountability in its use.
7. To ensure that **AI hiring systems are free from bias**, companies must use diverse datasets, implement fairness metrics, and regularly audit the systems. Training AI systems on biased historical hiring data can reinforce discriminatory patterns. By using fairness checks and involving diverse stakeholders in the design process, AI hiring tools can be made more equitable and less likely to perpetuate past biases.
8. **Ethical audits** are important for identifying issues such as bias, fairness, and accountability in AI systems. These audits help organizations ensure that AI systems align with ethical standards before they are deployed, preventing harmful consequences. Regular audits provide an ongoing evaluation to address ethical concerns as AI systems evolve and are used in new contexts.
9. **Sustainability in AI systems** is critical to ensure that they do not harm the environment or create long-term societal risks. Sustainable AI design involves minimizing energy consumption, reducing waste, and ensuring that AI's impact on the environment and society is carefully considered. Organizations must prioritize sustainable practices in developing AI technologies to ensure they contribute positively to the future.
10. **Decision support systems** provide recommendations, while **fully autonomous AI systems** make decisions without human intervention. In high-stakes environments like healthcare, the benefit of decision support systems is that humans remain in control and can validate AI-generated suggestions. Fully autonomous systems, while efficient, may lack the nuanced judgment needed for complex decisions and could lead to unintended consequences. Both systems have their advantages and challenges, with decision support offering a balance of AI assistance and human oversight.

Chapter 8: Automated Systems and Ethical Limits

Learning outcomes

By the end of this unit, learners will be able to:

1. **Define** key concepts such as autonomous systems, self-learning technologies, and artificial intelligence.
2. **Identify** ethical concerns associated with the use of AI in replacing human roles.
3. **Describe** various frameworks and guidelines used for regulating autonomous technologies.
4. **Explain** the risks of self-learning systems and the strategies to manage them.

Introduction

As technology advances at an unprecedented pace, automated systems and artificial intelligence are reshaping how we live, work, and interact. These systems, capable of making decisions with minimal human input, bring remarkable benefits—enhancing efficiency, reducing human error, and unlocking new possibilities across sectors. However, alongside these advantages come significant ethical concerns.

This unit explores the crucial topic of *Automated Systems and Ethical Limits*, focusing on how society can responsibly navigate this transformation. It examines the need for clear boundaries in deploying autonomous technologies, highlights the potential risks of self-learning systems, and reflects on the moral challenges of replacing human roles with AI. By integrating concepts from Bloom's Taxonomy, the module also equips learners with foundational knowledge and understanding, encouraging them to think critically about the ethical, social, and legal implications of automation in today's world.

8.1 Setting Boundaries for Autonomous Technologies

In the ever-accelerating landscape of technological innovation, autonomous technologies have emerged as transformative tools reshaping the way we work, travel, communicate, and live. From self-driving cars to robotic surgeries, these systems promise increased efficiency, safety, and accessibility. However, with their growing capabilities comes an equally critical responsibility to ensure these systems act ethically, safely, and in alignment with societal values. This necessitates setting robust boundaries—ethical, legal, and operational—that define how, where, and to what extent these technologies should function. Establishing such boundaries is essential not only to prevent harm but also to maintain public trust and ensure these technologies serve humanity's best interests.

Definition and Scope of Autonomous Technologies

Autonomous technologies refer to systems capable of performing tasks or making decisions independently, without continuous human guidance. These systems rely on a combination of sensors, data processing algorithms, machine learning models, and artificial intelligence (AI) to interact with their environments, interpret inputs, and make real-time decisions.

Autonomous technologies are not monolithic. They span across physical and digital domains:

- **Physical Systems**: These include **autonomous vehicles**, **delivery drones**, **surgical robots**, and **industrial automation robots**. For instance, companies like Tesla and Waymo are leading the development of self-driving cars that can navigate urban streets with minimal human intervention.
- **Digital Agents**: Examples include **AI-driven chatbots**, **automated stock trading systems**, and **autonomous cybersecurity tools** that detect and respond to threats without human prompting.

Levels of Autonomy

To understand and regulate these systems effectively, we must recognize their varying levels of autonomy:

- **Level 0-2 (Assisted Automation)**: Systems operate with human control. For example, a car with lane assist or adaptive cruise control.
- **Level 3-4 (Conditional Automation)**: The system can handle tasks in specific conditions but may require human input during complex situations.

- **Level 5 (Full Automation)**: The system functions entirely independently, without any human oversight. An example would be a fully autonomous taxi that navigates any terrain or traffic scenario on its own.

Understanding where a system lies on this spectrum helps in identifying the level of human oversight needed, the risks involved, and the ethical and legal frameworks that must be applied.

The Need for Ethical Boundaries

While autonomous technologies offer immense benefits, they also introduce unprecedented ethical dilemmas. Machines that make decisions without human intervention must be guided by a strong ethical framework to prevent harm, ensure fairness, and maintain accountability.

1. Life-and-Death Decision Making: The Self-Driving Car Dilemma

One of the most discussed ethical challenges is the **"trolley problem"** applied to self-driving cars. Imagine a scenario where a car must choose between swerving to hit a wall—potentially killing the passengers—or continuing forward and hitting a group of pedestrians. Which choice should the car make? And who decides that logic?

Without clearly defined boundaries and ethical programming, autonomous systems could make choices that are legally or morally unacceptable. Some argue that vehicles should be programmed to minimize overall harm, while others believe they should prioritize the safety of their occupants. This dilemma shows the need for clear societal input on how such life-and-death decisions are programmed into machines.

2. Bias and Discrimination in AI

Autonomous systems often rely on **historical data** to make predictions or decisions. If that data reflects existing biases—such as racial or gender-based discrimination—these systems can perpetuate and even amplify those biases.

For example, AI recruitment tools have been found to favor male candidates over female ones due to biased historical hiring data. In the criminal justice system, tools like predictive policing algorithms have come under fire for disproportionately targeting minority communities. In both cases, the problem lies not just with the data but also with the lack of oversight and ethical boundary-setting during system development.

3. **Privacy** and **Surveillance Concerns**

The rise of **autonomous surveillance technologies** like drones, facial recognition systems, and smart city sensors raises serious concerns about privacy and civil liberties. In some countries, drones are already being used to monitor crowds, enforce curfews, and track individuals, often without adequate legal frameworks or public consent.

Autonomous technologies should not be allowed to operate in ways that violate basic human rights. Without strict boundaries, the misuse of such systems can lead to mass surveillance, unauthorized data collection, and erosion of personal freedoms.

4. Security Vulnerabilities and Weaponization

Autonomous systems, especially those connected to the internet, are susceptible to hacking and manipulation. Imagine a **hacked self-driving truck** rerouted into a crowd or an **autonomous drone** repurposed as a weapon. Furthermore, **autonomous weapons systems**, such as killer drones or robotic soldiers, pose a dangerous ethical question: should machines ever be given the authority to take human life?

Without global agreements and strict regulations, these systems can be misused by rogue actors or governments, leading to devastating consequences.

Frameworks and Guidelines for Regulation

Recognizing the risks posed by autonomous technologies, several international organizations, governments, and advocacy groups have introduced frameworks to guide their development and deployment responsibly.

1. The European Union's AI Act

The EU's Artificial Intelligence Act is one of the most comprehensive regulatory efforts to date. It classifies AI systems into different **risk categories**:

- **Unacceptable risk** (e.g., social scoring systems, manipulative technologies)
- **High risk** (e.g., biometric identification, credit scoring, hiring tools)
- **Limited risk** (e.g., chatbots)
- **Minimal risk** (e.g., video games, spam filters)

Each category comes with corresponding obligations regarding transparency, data governance, human oversight, and robustness. High-risk systems, for example, must undergo conformity assessments and ensure clear documentation and human accountability.

2. IEEE's Ethically Aligned Design

The **Institute of Electrical and Electronics Engineers (IEEE)** developed a framework titled *Ethically Aligned Design* to promote the creation of ethical autonomous systems. Key principles include:

- Respect for human rights
- Accountability
- Transparency
- Data privacy
- Societal well-being

This framework encourages developers to embed ethical considerations into the design phase rather than as an afterthought.

3. The Asilomar AI Principles

Drafted by AI researchers and philosophers, the **Asilomar AI Principles** serve as a foundation for long-term safety and responsibility in AI development. Among the principles are:

- **Value alignment**: Systems should align with human values.
- **Human control**: Humans should be able to oversee or override autonomous decisions.
- **Shared benefit**: The benefits of AI should be shared broadly across humanity.

These principles, while voluntary, have become a reference point in discussions about global AI ethics.

Stakeholder Roles and Responsibilities

Creating effective boundaries for autonomous systems is not a job for technologists alone. A wide array of stakeholders must collaborate to ensure these systems are safe, fair, and aligned with public interest.

1. Developers and Engineers

Developers are on the front lines of autonomous technology creation. They must prioritize **ethical design**, **inclusive data sets**, and **built-in accountability mechanisms**. For instance, companies building facial recognition systems must ensure their models perform equally well across all demographics to avoid racial or gender-based errors.

2. Policymakers and Regulators

Governments play a crucial role in **setting legal boundaries**, **enforcing standards**, and **creating incentives for responsible innovation**. For example, regulatory bodies could require that self-driving car manufacturers disclose their ethical algorithms and submit safety assessments before deployment.

3. Private Companies and Industry Leaders

Businesses adopting autonomous technologies must take responsibility for their ethical use. This includes training staff, ensuring transparency, and having clear protocols for human oversight. For example, a hospital using an AI diagnostic tool must ensure it is only used as a **support tool**, not a **replacement for human medical judgment**.

4. Civil Society and the Public

Citizens, consumer advocacy groups, and the media play an essential role in **holding organizations accountable** and **shaping public discourse**. For instance, public backlash against biased facial recognition systems has led several companies, including IBM and Microsoft, to scale back their involvement in such technologies.

The Future of Boundaries: A Collaborative Approach

Setting boundaries is not about stifling innovation but about guiding it in a direction that enhances human welfare. A future-focused approach should prioritize:

- **Global cooperation**: Ethical standards must transcend national borders.
- **Adaptive governance**: Rules should evolve as technologies and their applications do.
- **Ethics-by-design**: Ethical thinking must be embedded from the beginning of the development process.

Additionally, interdisciplinary collaboration—between technologists, ethicists, legal experts, and social scientists—is essential to anticipate future challenges and develop holistic solutions.

Autonomous technologies are reshaping the modern world with their potential to perform complex tasks, optimize systems, and improve quality of life. However, their increasing autonomy also introduces risks that cannot be ignored. From ethical dilemmas in self-driving vehicles to bias in AI decision-making and the threat of autonomous weapons, the importance of setting clear boundaries has never been greater.

By defining the levels of autonomy, embedding ethical considerations into design, and establishing strong regulatory frameworks, we can harness the benefits of these technologies while minimizing their harms. Achieving this balance requires the collective efforts of developers, governments, industry leaders, and the public. Only through shared responsibility and proactive boundary-setting can autonomous systems truly serve humanity in a fair, transparent, and safe manner.

8.2 Managing the Risks of Self-Learning Systems

As artificial intelligence (AI) technologies evolve, **self-learning systems** have emerged as a powerful class of tools capable of adapting to new information in real time. These systems, often underpinned by **machine learning (ML)** and **deep learning** architectures, excel at pattern recognition, prediction, and decision-making in complex and dynamic environments. They are integral to applications ranging from **personalized recommendations** on streaming platforms to **fraud detection**, **autonomous vehicles**, and **clinical diagnostics**.

Unlike traditional software that follows static, predefined rules, self-learning systems continuously adjust their behavior based on incoming data. This flexibility offers considerable benefits, but it also introduces **unique risks**—some of which challenge our current legal, ethical, and technical frameworks. As these systems become more embedded in critical infrastructure and public services, managing their risks becomes a matter of societal urgency.

Understanding Self-Learning Systems

Self-learning systems rely on algorithms that improve their performance over time without explicit reprogramming. These systems typically consist of:

- **Supervised learning models**, which learn from labeled datasets.
- **Unsupervised learning models**, which identify patterns in unlabeled data.
- **Reinforcement learning models**, which learn through trial and error by receiving feedback from their environment.

Such systems are already in use across diverse sectors:

- **Healthcare**: AI models assist in diagnosing diseases, analyzing radiological images, and predicting patient outcomes.
- **Finance**: Algorithms detect fraudulent transactions and optimize high-frequency trading strategies.
- **Transportation**: Self-driving vehicles learn from road conditions, user behavior, and traffic patterns to navigate safely.

However, the complexity of their learning processes and decision pathways often results in **opacity**, meaning users and even developers may not fully understand how specific outputs are generated. This lack of transparency is known as the **"black box" problem**, and it underpins many of the challenges associated with deploying self-learning systems responsibly.

Key Risks Associated with Self-Learning Systems

1. Bias and Discrimination

Perhaps the most publicly recognized risk of self-learning systems is their **propensity to absorb and amplify societal biases**. Since these systems learn from historical or real-time data, any skew in the dataset—intentional or unintentional—can lead to biased outcomes.

Case Example: Facial Recognition Technology

Facial recognition systems have been found to **misidentify people of color at much higher rates** than white individuals. A 2019 study by the National Institute of Standards and Technology (NIST) revealed that some algorithms were **up to 100 times more likely to misidentify Asian and African-American faces** compared to Caucasian ones. These errors stemmed from training data that underrepresented certain ethnic groups.

In high-stakes scenarios such as **law enforcement**, biased outcomes can lead to wrongful arrests or surveillance, raising serious **civil rights concerns**.

2. Loss of Control and Predictability

As self-learning systems evolve, they can develop behaviors that deviate from their original programming. This is particularly concerning in **safety-critical sectors** where precision and reliability are paramount.

Example: AI in Aviation

In aviation, AI-powered systems assist with auto-piloting, maintenance prediction, and weather analysis. If a machine learning model adapts to new flight data without adequate oversight, it could make decisions that are **unpredictable under extreme or rare circumstances**, potentially endangering lives.

Even well-trained systems may produce unexpected outcomes when encountering **data distributions they weren't exposed to during training**. This phenomenon, known as **"distributional shift"**, can render the model's decisions unreliable.

3. Security Vulnerabilities and Adversarial Attacks

Self-learning systems are not immune to malicious exploitation. One of the more concerning forms of attack is the **adversarial example**—a subtle manipulation of input data that causes the system to behave incorrectly.

Example: Adversarial Inputs in Autonomous Vehicles

Researchers have demonstrated how **slightly altered stop signs**—with stickers or paint—can fool self-driving car systems into interpreting them as speed limit signs. This is dangerous in real-world scenarios where misinterpretation can lead to collisions.

Moreover, attackers can target the training process itself, injecting **poisoned data** to skew outcomes, or engage in **model inversion attacks** to extract sensitive information.

4. Lack of Accountability

A fundamental problem with self-learning systems is that **the responsibility for their decisions is often unclear**. When an AI system evolves continuously, its creators may no longer fully understand its reasoning or have the ability to predict its actions.

Legal Dilemma: Who Is Liable?

If an autonomous system makes a mistake—like a self-driving car running a red light—**who is held accountable**? The manufacturer? The software developer? The car owner? The AI itself?

This diffusion of responsibility complicates legal proceedings and insurance frameworks, demanding new laws and ethical standards for **algorithmic accountability**.

Risk Mitigation Strategies

To mitigate the risks associated with self-learning systems, a combination of technical, procedural, and regulatory approaches must be employed.

1. Explainability and Transparency (XAI)

Efforts are underway to create **Explainable AI (XAI)**, which aims to make machine learning models more interpretable to humans. By offering insights into how a system reached a particular decision, XAI enhances trust and facilitates debugging.

Example: Healthcare Diagnostics

In medical AI systems, it's vital that clinicians understand why an algorithm recommends a diagnosis or treatment. Tools like **LIME (Local Interpretable Model-agnostic Explanations)** and **SHAP (SHapley Additive exPlanations)** help visualize which features (e.g., blood pressure, age) most influenced a model's decision.

2. Bias Auditing and Fairness Mechanisms

Fair AI begins with **clean, diverse, and representative data**. Ongoing audits can detect and address bias in both training data and model outcomes.

Best Practice: Fairness-Aware Algorithms

Techniques like **re-weighting datasets**, **pre-processing inputs to remove sensitive attributes**, and using **fairness constraints in model training** are increasingly used to ensure equitable performance across demographic groups.

Some companies now conduct **AI ethics reviews** and require teams to submit a **model card**—a document outlining the model's performance, limitations, and fairness assessments—before deployment.

3. Human-in-the-Loop (HITL) Systems

To counter the loss of control, organizations often adopt **HITL approaches**, where humans retain oversight over the AI system's decisions—especially in high-risk domains.

Example: Military and Medical Applications

In military applications, autonomous drones may identify targets, but final strike decisions are left to human operators. Similarly, in medicine, diagnostic AI tools assist doctors, but do not replace their clinical judgment. This balance maintains human responsibility while leveraging AI's capabilities.

4. Robust Testing and Validation

Before self-learning systems are deployed, they must undergo **extensive testing**—including exposure to **adversarial conditions** and **edge cases** (rare, unexpected scenarios).

Simulation Environments

In sectors like automotive and robotics, companies use simulation platforms like **CARLA** or **AirSim** to test how AI systems behave under different weather, traffic, and environmental conditions. This reduces the risk of unforeseen failures in real-world deployment.

Continuous monitoring post-deployment is also essential. Feedback loops should be established so the model can be retrained or adjusted when unexpected behavior is detected.

Ethical and Legal Considerations

Self-learning systems do not operate in a vacuum—they affect people, societies, and legal frameworks. Ethical and legal boundaries must evolve alongside these technologies.

1. Consent and Data Rights

AI systems learn from vast quantities of data, often collected from users—sometimes without explicit consent. Ethical design must prioritize **user autonomy**, **informed consent**, and **data protection**.

Legal Frameworks: GDPR and Beyond

Under the EU's **General Data Protection Regulation (GDPR)**, individuals have the right to understand how their data is used, to opt out of automated decision-making, and to request data deletion. Similar laws are emerging globally.

2. Impact on Employment

Self-learning systems have the potential to **displace human labor**, particularly in roles involving repetitive or analytical tasks. While they can increase productivity, they also **threaten job security** in sectors like transportation, finance, customer service, and manufacturing.

Ethical Obligation: Reskilling

Organizations and governments must take responsibility to support **reskilling programs**, invest in **digital literacy**, and ensure a just transition for workers affected by automation.

3. Algorithmic Accountability and Governance

There is an urgent need for **regulatory frameworks** that define standards for transparency, auditability, and liability.

Emerging Policies

- **The EU AI Act** requires certain AI systems to meet transparency and risk management criteria.
- **The Algorithmic Accountability Act (U.S.)** seeks to mandate impact assessments for high-risk automated systems.
- **AI ethics boards and independent audit mechanisms** are being implemented by tech firms to assess ethical compliance.

Self-learning systems are among the most transformative—and potentially disruptive—technologies of our time. Their ability to adapt and improve over time holds immense promise, from advancing medicine to improving logistics, security, and environmental monitoring. Yet, this same capability introduces a host of complex risks that must be carefully managed.

Bias, loss of control, security vulnerabilities, and unclear accountability are not merely technical issues—they are **societal challenges** that demand a collaborative and multi-disciplinary approach. Mitigating these risks requires investment in explainable AI, robust testing, fairness auditing, and continuous human oversight.

Moreover, ethics and law must evolve alongside technology. Societies must develop adaptive legal frameworks and strong data governance policies that protect rights and ensure equitable outcomes. Only through proactive, ethical design and responsible governance can we unlock the benefits of self-learning systems while minimizing their potential for harm.

8.3 Ethics of Replacing Human Roles with AI

Artificial Intelligence (AI) has transitioned from a futuristic concept to a powerful force reshaping the modern workforce. Its integration into industries, from manufacturing to healthcare, has transformed operations by enhancing productivity, reducing costs, and automating routine tasks. However, this technological revolution brings with it a profound ethical dilemma: **what happens to the human roles being replaced?**

The ethical concerns go beyond mere economic calculations. They touch on **human dignity**, **social equity**, the **meaning of work**, and the **psychological and emotional impact** of automation. As AI systems continue to outperform humans in areas once thought uniquely human—like creativity, decision-making, and empathy—the urgent question arises: **How can we integrate AI ethically into the workforce without undermining the human spirit or societal cohesion?**

The Scope of AI-Driven Replacement

AI's capabilities have rapidly expanded due to advancements in **machine learning**, **natural language processing**, and **robotics**. These systems are now able to replicate or surpass human performance in a wide range of tasks:

- **Routine and repetitive work**: Assembly line jobs, data entry, logistics coordination.
- **Cognitive tasks**: Financial analysis, fraud detection, legal document review.
- **Creative tasks**: AI-generated art, automated journalism, music composition.
- **Service-oriented roles**: Chatbots in customer service, virtual assistants, autonomous delivery vehicles.

Entire sectors are being reshaped:

- **Manufacturing**: Robotics now dominate car assembly and electronics production.
- **Retail**: Automated checkout systems and inventory robots are replacing clerks.
- **Transportation**: Self-driving technology threatens jobs in trucking and delivery.
- **Finance**: AI handles portfolio management and market forecasting.

- **Healthcare**: AI diagnoses medical conditions and interprets scans with increasing accuracy.

Even professions once thought safe from automation—such as writers, teachers, and counselors—are being partially encroached upon by sophisticated AI systems.

Economic Implications

1. Job Displacement and Unemployment

Perhaps the most immediate concern is **job displacement**, especially for low-skilled, repetitive roles. According to a McKinsey Global Institute report, by 2030, as many as **800 million jobs** could be automated worldwide. Those most vulnerable are workers in sectors like manufacturing, customer service, and transportation.

While automation may be beneficial to corporate efficiency, the **human cost**—especially for workers in vulnerable communities—can be severe. Without intervention, displaced workers may face prolonged unemployment, income insecurity, and mental health challenges.

2. Creation of New Roles

It is important to note that while AI displaces certain jobs, it also **creates new opportunities** in emerging fields:

- **AI development and engineering**
- **Data science and analytics**
- **Robotics maintenance and support**
- **Cybersecurity and AI ethics auditing**

However, a significant concern is the **skills gap**. The jobs being created often require advanced education and technical skills, leaving behind those without access to training or education.

3. Productivity Gains vs. Income Inequality

AI significantly boosts productivity and economic growth. Businesses that leverage AI enjoy **higher efficiency, lower operational costs**, and improved customer experiences. But these gains are not evenly shared. The majority of benefits tend to accumulate to:

- **Large corporations**
- **Highly educated workers**
- **Urban centers with technological infrastructure**

This leads to **widening income inequality** and the risk of creating a "two-tier" workforce—those who benefit from AI and those displaced by it.

Social and Ethical Challenges

1. Erosion of Human Dignity

Human work is not only a means of survival—it's a source of identity, purpose, and social connection. When AI replaces roles traditionally filled by humans, especially in **fields requiring empathy, judgment, or creativity**, there's a risk of **diminishing the value of human input**.

Example: AI in Creative Professions

AI-generated art, music, and writing challenge the notion of creativity as an inherently human trait. When a machine writes a poem or composes a symphony, it may be technically impressive—but does it carry the same emotional or cultural weight?

Some fear that over-reliance on AI may devalue **human expression**, reducing creative work to mere productivity.

2. Loss of Social Interaction

In sectors like healthcare, education, and customer service, human interaction is crucial. Replacing staff with AI-powered bots may improve efficiency but could degrade the **quality of service** and **emotional well-being** of those served.

Example: Elder Care Robots

In countries like Japan, AI robots are used to care for the elderly due to staff shortages. While helpful for basic tasks, these machines cannot replace **empathy, touch, and emotional companionship**—all of which are essential to human dignity and mental health.

3. De-skilling and Over-reliance on AI

As AI becomes more capable, there is a risk of **de-skilling**—where human workers lose proficiency in tasks because machines do them better or more conveniently.

Example: Aviation Autopilot Systems

Pilots heavily reliant on autopilot systems may find their manual flying skills deteriorating. In emergency scenarios requiring manual control, this can become a safety hazard.

Strategies for Ethical Integration

Rather than viewing AI as a replacement for humans, we should strive for **human-AI collaboration** that enhances rather than erodes human work.

1. Human-AI Collaboration

The most ethical path forward is designing systems that **augment human capabilities** rather than eliminate them. This approach maintains human agency and decision-making while leveraging the speed and accuracy of AI.

Example: Medicine

AI can assist doctors in analyzing MRI scans, flagging anomalies, and providing diagnostic suggestions. But final decisions should rest with the human physician, preserving the **ethical and relational aspects of care**.

2. Reskilling and Lifelong Learning

To mitigate the impact of job displacement, governments and private institutions must invest in **upskilling and reskilling programs**. These should focus on:

- **Digital literacy**
- **Technical skills**
- **Soft skills** such as critical thinking, communication, and emotional intelligence

Successful Model: Singapore's SkillsFuture Program

Singapore has implemented a national initiative that provides citizens with credits to pursue training in emerging industries. This ensures a **proactive response** to technological disruptions.

3. Inclusive and Accessible AI Design

Ethical AI must be designed to **include marginalized populations** and accommodate workers of all skill levels. This includes:

- Designing user-friendly interfaces
- Supporting diverse languages and learning styles
- Ensuring equitable access to new job opportunities

This helps ensure that **the benefits of AI are shared broadly**, not hoarded by elites or concentrated in tech hubs.

Policy Recommendations

1. Universal Basic Income (UBI)

As AI disrupts labor markets, some experts and economists suggest **Universal Basic Income** as a solution. UBI proposes a fixed, unconditional income for all citizens, regardless of employment status.

Pros:

- Provides a **safety net** during periods of job loss or transition.
- Encourages **entrepreneurship** and **creative pursuits**.
- Reduces poverty and income inequality.

Cons:

- **Costly to implement** on a large scale.
- Risk of **reducing work incentives** if not structured correctly.

Pilot programs in Finland and Canada have shown **modest benefits** in terms of well-being and mental health, but broader implementation remains a topic of debate.

2. Taxation of AI Labor

Economists like Bill Gates have proposed a **robot tax**—taxing companies for each job replaced by automation. The revenue could be used to fund:

- Reskilling programs
- Education
- Public services

This approach also **slows down rapid automation** by making it more financially comparable to employing human workers.

3. Ethical Standards for Employment Algorithms

AI systems are increasingly used in **hiring, performance evaluation, and termination decisions**. Without oversight, these systems may introduce bias or lack transparency.

Best Practices:

- AI hiring tools should be regularly **audited for fairness**.
- **Transparent criteria** should be shared with applicants.
- Final decisions should always involve a **human reviewer**.

Regulatory bodies must define **clear guidelines** for how AI can be used in employment contexts to ensure fairness, accountability, and privacy.

The rise of AI as a replacement for human labor is both **inevitable** and **transformational**. It holds the potential to solve pressing global problems—from labor shortages to inefficiencies in healthcare and logistics. However, without **ethical foresight**, we risk creating a world where productivity comes at the cost of human purpose and dignity.

Addressing these challenges requires a **multifaceted approach**—one that combines inclusive technology design, proactive public policy, and a reimagining of work itself. AI should not be seen as a competitor to human labor but as a **partner in building a more equitable and creative future**.

Through ethical integration, inclusive innovation, and compassionate leadership, we can ensure that the age of AI uplifts all members of society—not just a privileged few.

Summary

This module examines the growing impact of autonomous and self-learning technologies on society, ethics, and the workforce. As artificial intelligence (AI) becomes more integrated into our daily lives, it is essential to set boundaries that ensure safety, fairness, and accountability. The content is divided into three key sections:

1. Setting Boundaries for Autonomous Technologies

This section defines autonomous systems and explains why ethical boundaries are necessary. It highlights real-world dilemmas, such as how autonomous vehicles should make split-second decisions, and addresses concerns like privacy, safety, and biased decision-making. It also outlines global efforts—such as the EU AI Act and IEEE's ethical design principles—to regulate AI use responsibly.

2. Managing the Risks of Self-Learning Systems

Self-learning AI systems adapt based on data, but this flexibility brings unique risks. Challenges include biased outputs, security vulnerabilities, and the difficulty of interpreting decisions (known as the "black box" problem). Strategies like explainable AI (XAI), human oversight, and fairness audits are introduced to manage these risks. Legal and ethical issues, such as data privacy and accountability, are also discussed.

3. Ethics of Replacing Human Roles with AI

As AI increasingly takes over human tasks, ethical concerns grow. These include job displacement, loss of interpersonal interaction, de-skilling of workers, and threats to human dignity. Economic effects are considered, such as rising inequality and the need for reskilling programs. Solutions like human-AI collaboration, universal basic income, and inclusive design are suggested to help society transition ethically.

As automated and self-learning systems continue to evolve, it is imperative that ethical considerations guide their development and integration into society. Setting boundaries for autonomous technologies ensures they align with human values and legal norms. Managing risks in self-learning systems safeguards against unintended harm and fosters accountability. Finally, thoughtfully addressing the ethics of AI-driven job replacement can help balance technological advancement with social well-being. The future of automation depends not only on what machines can do but also on what they *should* do—and that responsibility lies with us.

Check your understanding

Fill-in-the-Blanks Questions

1. Autonomous technologies are systems capable of operating without ______ intervention.
2. The ______ problem refers to the difficulty in understanding how self-learning AI makes decisions.
3. The EU's proposed AI legislation is known as the ______ Act.
4. IEEE's ______ ______ Design offers ethical guidelines for AI systems.
5. Self-learning systems are often based on ______ ______ and neural networks.
6. Bias in AI systems is frequently caused by ______ training data.
7. Explainable AI is also referred to as ______.
8. One ethical concern in AI is the ______ of human dignity in the workplace.
9. AI can contribute to job ______ if not implemented responsibly.
10. Human-AI ______ ensures that humans remain involved in critical decision-making.
11. Systems that adapt without explicit programming are called ______ systems.
12. Universal ______ Income is a proposed solution to job loss from automation.
13. An AI that operates entirely on its own is referred to as ______ autonomous.
14. Ethical boundaries help ensure AI systems operate with ______ and accountability.
15. The Asilomar AI Principles advocate for responsible ______ of AI.
16. Robots and AI could potentially widen the economic ______ between social classes.
17. Surveillance drones raise ethical concerns regarding personal ______.
18. De-skilling refers to the loss of ______ due to reliance on AI.
19. Adversarial ______ can trick AI systems into making wrong decisions.
20. AI systems must be designed to reflect ______ values and norms.

Short Answer Questions

1. What is an autonomous system?
2. Define the term "self-learning system."
3. What are the main ethical concerns with AI in the workplace?
4. Name one international AI regulatory framework and its purpose.
5. How does biased data affect AI decision-making?

6. What is the "black box" problem in AI?
7. Describe the role of human oversight in self-learning systems.
8. Why is explainability important in AI systems?
9. What is meant by "human-AI collaboration"?
10. List one benefit and one drawback of using AI in healthcare.

Long Answer Questions

1. Discuss the ethical implications of replacing human roles with AI in healthcare and education.
2. Explain the various levels of autonomy in AI systems with examples.
3. What are the main challenges in managing risks associated with self-learning systems?
4. Analyze the social and economic impacts of job displacement due to AI automation.
5. How can governments and organizations ensure fairness in AI algorithms?
6. Describe in detail the key components of the IEEE's Ethically Aligned Design.
7. Compare and contrast different global regulatory approaches to autonomous technologies.
8. Explain the concept of adversarial attacks and how they affect AI systems.
9. What role does public discourse play in setting ethical boundaries for AI?
10. Suggest strategies for ethical integration of AI into existing human-centric industries.

Answers

Fill-in-the-Blanks

1. human
2. black box
3. AI
4. Ethically Aligned
5. machine learning
6. biased
7. XAI ***(Explainable AI)***
8. erosion
9. displacement

10. collaboration

11. self-learning

12. basic

13. fully

14. transparency

15. development

16. gap

17. privacy

18. skills

19. attacks

20. societal

Answer Key for Short Answer Questions

1. A system capable of performing tasks without human intervention by processing inputs and making decisions independently.
2. A system that modifies its behavior by learning from data without being explicitly programmed for each new situation.
3. Job displacement, erosion of human dignity, de-skilling of workers, and loss of interpersonal interactions.
4. The EU AI Act – it classifies AI based on risk and imposes regulations accordingly to ensure safety and accountability.
5. It can lead to discriminatory outcomes by replicating or amplifying existing social inequalities.
6. It refers to the lack of transparency in how AI systems make decisions, making their processes hard to interpret.
7. It ensures that critical decisions are reviewed and approved by humans, adding accountability and ethical judgment.
8. To help users understand how decisions are made, build trust, and ensure accountability.
9. The practice of AI systems working alongside humans to augment rather than replace their roles.

10. Benefit: Faster, data-driven diagnosis.
    Drawback: Potential loss of human empathy and misdiagnosis due to algorithmic error.

Answer Guide for Long Answer Questions

These responses are meant to be structured outlines. You can expand each into essays or reports as needed.

1. **Ethical implications in healthcare and education**

- Loss of human touch, empathy
- Data privacy issues
- AI misjudgments
- Benefits like scalability and efficiency

2. **Levels of autonomy**

- Manual, assisted, semi-autonomous, fully autonomous
- Examples: Cruise control (semi), self-driving cars (fully)

3. **Challenges in self-learning systems**

- Opacity in decision-making
- Data bias
- Security threats
- Legal liability

4. **Social and economic impacts**

- Widening income gaps
- Rise in tech-based jobs vs. low-skill job loss
- Pressure on welfare systems
- Need for retraining

5. **Ensuring fairness in AI algorithms**

- Diverse and representative data
- Regular audits
- Transparency in design
- Stakeholder input

6. **IEEE Ethically Aligned Design**

- Guidelines for ethical AI development
- Topics include transparency, well-being, and human rights
- Promotes value alignment and accountability

7. **Comparing global regulatory approaches**

- EU AI Act (risk-based)
- U.S. (sectoral regulation)
- China (focus on development with social control)

8. **Adversarial attacks**

- Malicious input manipulations
- Affect system reliability
- Example: fooling facial recognition with altered images

9. **Public discourse's role**

- Shapes cultural and ethical norms
- Informs policymaking
- Promotes transparency and accountability

10. **Strategies for ethical integration of AI**

- Augmentation, not replacement
- Reskilling programs
- Ethical design

Chapter 9: Sharing Data in a Responsible Manner

Learning Outcomes

By the end of this module, learners will be able to:

1. **Define** key terms such as open data, data ownership, and ethical reuse.
2. **Identify** ethical issues related to the misuse of open datasets.
3. **Explain** the importance of maintaining original data context during reuse.
4. **Recognize** best practices for collaboration and data sharing without exploitation.

Introduction

In today's data-driven world, access to information is a powerful catalyst for innovation, research, and social progress. With the rise of open data initiatives and publicly available datasets, individuals, organizations, and governments are sharing vast amounts of information at unprecedented rates. However, with great access comes great responsibility. The ethical handling of data is no longer just a technical challenge—it is a moral obligation.

Responsible data sharing involves a balance: promoting transparency and collaboration while safeguarding privacy, respecting ownership, and avoiding misuse. This module focuses on the principles and practices needed to share data ethically and effectively.

9.1 Ethical Use of Open Datasets

In the digital age, the accessibility of data has grown tremendously. Among the most widely shared forms of information are **open datasets**—collections of structured or unstructured data that are freely available for anyone to use, share, or modify. These datasets are often published by public institutions, research organizations, non-governmental groups, or even private companies with the intention of fostering transparency, promoting innovation, or supporting academic inquiry.

However, the benefits of open data come with ethical responsibilities. When data is used without careful consideration of privacy, context, or fairness, the results can lead to serious unintended consequences. Issues such as privacy breaches, data misrepresentation, amplification of social biases, and lack of informed consent must be addressed to ensure the **ethical application of open data**.

What Are Open Datasets?

Open datasets are publicly accessible collections of data that users can view, download, use, and often redistribute without paying fees or needing special permission. They are typically released under open licenses that allow free use, provided certain conditions—such as proper attribution—are met.

These datasets can vary widely in scope and content. Governments might publish statistics on public health, crime, or environmental quality; academic researchers could release experimental results or survey data; and corporations may open certain datasets to aid technological development. For example, tech companies might share image collections to support computer vision research or anonymized usage data to improve AI algorithms.

Although open datasets are intended to encourage knowledge sharing and progress, their widespread availability can pose risks when ethical guidelines are not followed.

Ethical Challenges Associated with Open Datasets

1. Risks to Personal Privacy

Even if datasets are stripped of obvious identifiers such as names or contact details, it's often possible to link them with other sources and reveal personal information. This risk grows when datasets are large, detailed, or include location and demographic variables.

Example: In a well-known case involving Netflix, the company shared user movie ratings in a bid to improve its recommendation system. Although personal names were removed, researchers were able to match anonymous Netflix users to public profiles on IMDb using rating patterns and timestamps. This demonstrated how seemingly "safe" data can still pose privacy risks.

This example highlights a major issue with open data: anonymization techniques are not always foolproof, especially when datasets are cross-referenced.

2. Misuse and Misinterpretation of Data

Another ethical concern is the misuse of data outside its original context. Without proper documentation or an understanding of how the data was collected, users might draw incorrect or misleading conclusions.

Example: When law enforcement agencies release crime statistics, the data may reflect **arrest patterns** rather than actual crime levels. Over-policed neighborhoods might appear to have higher crime rates, not because more crime occurs there, but because of targeted policing. If such data is used to build predictive policing tools without context, it may unfairly target certain communities.

Thus, taking data out of context or interpreting it without understanding its limitations can reinforce harmful narratives or flawed decision-making.

3. Bias and Inequity in Datasets

Open data can contain **inherent biases**, especially when it reflects historical or systemic inequities. Using such biased data in automated systems can perpetuate or even magnify social inequalities.

Example: The COMPAS algorithm, designed to assess the likelihood of criminal reoffending, was trained on justice system data that already reflected racial disparities. As a result, it unfairly labeled Black defendants as higher risk compared to white defendants with similar histories.

This illustrates how even open data that appears neutral can encode deep-seated biases, which become problematic when used to inform critical decisions like sentencing or bail.

4. Lack of Informed Consent

Many open datasets include information about individuals who may not have been aware that their data was being collected or made public. This raises concerns about autonomy and the ethical use of personal data.

Example: During the COVID-19 pandemic, governments and private firms released anonymized mobility data to study people's movement patterns and enforce lockdowns. In many cases, however, individuals were not clearly informed or asked for permission regarding the use of their location data.

Even when intentions are good—such as protecting public health—ignoring consent can undermine public trust and compromise ethical standards.

Core Principles for Ethical Use of Open Datasets

To reduce the risks outlined above, data practitioners, researchers, and organizations should follow a set of guiding principles that promote responsible and fair use of open data.

1. Transparency and Clear Intent

Anyone working with open datasets should be upfront about how they intend to use the data. This includes:

- Explaining the goals and scope of their analysis.
- Describing the methods and tools applied.
- Acknowledging the data's limitations, assumptions, or uncertainties.

Transparency builds trust with stakeholders and enables others to understand or critique the work effectively.

Best Practice: Researchers can publish "data documentation" or "model cards" that detail how the data was collected, what it represents, and what its intended applications are. These materials provide critical context for future users and prevent misunderstandings.

2. Protecting Privacy

Even if a dataset is labeled "open," it's essential to take extra steps to prevent identification of individuals. This includes:

- Avoiding unnecessary combination of datasets that could expose sensitive information.
- Applying advanced anonymization techniques like differential privacy.
- Using only the data truly needed for the task (data minimization).

Best Practice: For datasets involving personal or sensitive information, developers should consider conducting a **privacy impact assessment** before publication or use.

3. Fairness and Representation

Fair use of data means considering whether the dataset accurately represents the populations affected by the outcomes of its use. Datasets used for algorithmic decision-making should include diverse and inclusive data points to prevent skewed results.

Example: Many facial recognition systems perform poorly on people with darker skin tones because they were trained on datasets dominated by lighter-skinned individuals. This can result in false positives or exclusions in identity verification systems.

To address this, organizations should ensure **balanced representation** and perform **bias testing** throughout the development lifecycle.

4. Accountability and Responsibility

Anyone who uses or shares open data should be accountable for how it is applied. This involves:

- Ensuring the data is interpreted correctly.
- Being open to critique or correction.
- Keeping records of how the data was sourced, processed, and used.

Best Practice: Developers can include a "data lineage" log, which tracks the origins, transformations, and outputs related to a dataset, similar to version control in software development. This makes it easier to trace errors or unintended consequences.

Case Study: COVID-19 Data and Ethical Dilemmas

During the global COVID-19 crisis, governments and researchers rapidly shared health-related datasets to support decision-making and scientific collaboration. This unprecedented sharing of data allowed for real-time tracking of infections, hospitalizations, and mobility trends.

Positive Outcomes:

- Enabled public health officials to make data-informed decisions.
- Empowered researchers to model the virus's spread and develop responses.
- Allowed citizens and journalists to monitor government actions and transparency.

Emerging Ethical Issues:

- **Privacy Risks**: In small towns or rural regions, publishing case numbers by postal code risked identifying individuals who tested positive.
- **Data Misuse**: Publicly released movement data from phone apps led to speculation about compliance with lockdowns, often without considering social or economic constraints on people's ability to isolate.
- **Consent Gaps**: Many people were unaware that their location or health data might be shared, even in anonymized form, especially in contexts where contact tracing apps were installed without user approval.

This case illustrates that even when data is critical for saving lives, it must be handled with care, oversight, and respect for individual rights.

Best Practices for Ethical Use of Open Data

To guide ethical practices in using open datasets, the following strategies are recommended:

1. **Document the Dataset**
   Include information about data origin, collection methods, updates, and limitations. This helps avoid misuse and aids reproducibility.
2. **Conduct Risk Assessments**
   Regularly evaluate privacy risks, bias, and potential social impact before publishing or applying datasets.
3. **Ensure Diversity in Data and Teams**
   Having interdisciplinary and inclusive teams can help identify risks that might be missed by homogenous groups.
4. **Foster Data Literacy**
   Educate data users—especially students, journalists, and junior researchers—about ethical issues in data usage and interpretation.
5. **Establish Redress Mechanisms**
   Provide ways for individuals or groups to raise concerns if they believe they've been harmed by data usage, and be prepared to correct or retract misuse.

Open datasets offer immense value for innovation, transparency, and collaboration. However, they are not ethically neutral. Without proper safeguards, their use can compromise privacy, perpetuate bias, and lead to misinformed conclusions. Ethical data usage requires more than technical proficiency—it demands empathy, social awareness, and a commitment to justice.

By adopting clear principles of transparency, fairness, privacy protection, and accountability, we can ensure that the power of open data is used not just to accelerate progress, but also to **uphold the rights and dignity of individuals and communities**.

9.2 Respecting Ownership and Original Context

In a world where data fuels decision-making, drives technological innovation, and shapes public discourse, the concept of **data ownership and context** has gained new ethical significance. Whether personal, organizational, or governmental, data is not merely a technical resource—it's deeply connected to its origins, creators, and the people it represents. Failing to acknowledge this can lead to serious misuses, including privacy violations, misinformation, and exploitation of vulnerable communities.

This chapter explores the complex landscape of data ownership, the critical importance of understanding the original context of datasets, and ethical best practices for responsible data reuse.

Who Owns Data?

Determining who owns data is not always straightforward. Ownership can vary depending on how and why the data was generated and the agreements under which it was shared.

1. Individuals as Data Owners

Personal data—such as names, health records, browsing histories, and biometric identifiers—typically originates from individuals. In many legal systems, individuals have rights over how their personal data is collected, stored, and used. This includes rights to access, correct, and even delete their data.

However, in practice, these rights are often difficult to enforce due to lengthy terms of service, consent fatigue, or lack of transparency about data practices.

2. Organizational Ownership

Businesses and institutions often collect data during regular operations. This includes customer transactions, employee records, and usage logs. In such cases, the organization may claim ownership of the dataset while individuals retain rights to their personal information under data protection laws like GDPR or CCPA.

3. Government Ownership

Governments collect and maintain vast datasets, including census data, economic indicators, transportation records, and public health statistics. These datasets are often made available as open data to promote transparency, accountability, and innovation.

However, even public sector data can carry restrictions—especially if it includes sensitive or classified information.

Blurring Lines of Ownership

In the digital era, where data is easily copied, shared, and repurposed, **clear ownership becomes difficult to define**. For example, if a fitness app collects your health data and then sells anonymized insights to a pharmaceutical company, who truly "owns" that data—the individual, the app, or the buyer?

Beyond legality, **respecting ownership** means acknowledging the contributions, rights, and expectations of all parties involved in data creation and usage.

Understanding the Original Context

One of the most critical ethical concerns when using shared data is the **loss of context**. Data is never created in a vacuum—it reflects specific environments, intentions, cultural values, and social dynamics.

Risks of Context Loss

Using data outside its original purpose or setting can lead to:

a. Incorrect Conclusions

Data collected for one purpose may not be suitable for other applications without adjustments. Misapplying it can produce flawed results.

Example: Using survey data from urban populations to make policy decisions for rural areas may ignore critical differences in infrastructure, culture, and needs—leading to ineffective or even harmful outcomes.

b. Ethical Missteps

When data subjects share their information under specific assumptions, reusing it without transparency or consent can violate their trust.

Example: If people provide health data for local public health planning and it is later used by private companies for targeted advertising, this would likely breach their expectations and ethical norms.

c. Cultural Insensitivity

Indigenous data or community-specific information often holds cultural significance that outsiders may not fully understand. Using such data without permission or understanding can result in exploitation and offense.

Example: Publishing genealogical or linguistic data of indigenous communities without appropriate consent can undermine community autonomy and sacred knowledge systems.

Best Practices to Respect Ownership and Context

Respecting data's origin and its creators isn't just ethically sound—it also enhances the reliability and legitimacy of research and innovation. Here are some widely recognized best practices:

1. Comprehensive Metadata and Documentation

Metadata is crucial in conveying a dataset's **source, structure, purpose, and limitations**. Without it, data becomes detached from its meaning and risks misinterpretation.

Good metadata should include:

- The identity and role of the data collector.
- The purpose for which the data was gathered.
- Methodologies used (sampling techniques, data cleaning, etc.).
- Known limitations or biases in the dataset.
- Recommendations for suitable and unsuitable uses.

Example: A dataset on agricultural productivity should specify whether it reflects rain-fed or irrigated land, the time period it covers, and how yield was measured. Without this, researchers may incorrectly apply it in regions or models where the data is irrelevant.

2. Attribution and Citation

Data, like literature or code, deserves proper citation. Acknowledging the creators of a dataset not only gives credit where it's due but also allows users to trace the source and evaluate its reliability.

Citation should include:

- Dataset title and creator(s).
- Date of publication or last update.
- Version number (if applicable).
- DOI or permanent web link.
- Licensing terms.

Best Practice: Follow standard formats like those suggested by DataCite or individual academic disciplines. Including citations in reports, dashboards, and models promotes transparency and academic integrity.

3. Respect for Indigenous Data Sovereignty

Indigenous communities have long advocated for **control over data about their lands, resources, and people**. The principle of Indigenous Data Sovereignty emphasizes that communities should decide how their data is collected, stored, and shared.

The CARE Principles offer a framework for engaging with Indigenous data:

- **Collective Benefit**: Data should support the well-being of the community.
- **Authority to Control**: Communities must have a say in how their data is used.
- **Responsibility**: Data collectors should act in ways that reflect community values and interests.

- **Ethics**: Use of data must respect the dignity, rights, and cultural sensitivities of Indigenous peoples.

Example: When researchers analyze biodiversity data from sacred Indigenous lands, they should consult with community leaders, acknowledge spiritual connections to the land, and possibly restrict public sharing of sensitive information.

Ignoring these principles can lead to data colonialism—where external parties exploit local knowledge without consent or benefit-sharing.

4. Preserving Integrity and Avoiding Distortion

Ethical use of data also means **maintaining its authenticity**. Modifying or manipulating datasets to fit new narratives without transparency can mislead others and erode trust.

Users should avoid:

- Editing values or categories without recording the changes.
- Omitting metadata or documentation to simplify reuse.
- Cherry-picking data to support biased arguments.
- Aggregating or transforming data in ways that hide disparities or outliers.

Example: A dataset on income distribution that is averaged without noting extreme inequalities can give the false impression of fairness. Always include notes about any transformations or preprocessing steps applied.

Example: Ethical Considerations in Climate Data Reuse

Climate change research relies heavily on the use of shared datasets. These may come from local weather stations, satellite data, ecological surveys, or community monitoring programs.

Benefits of Open Climate Data:

- Enables global collaboration and model improvement.
- Helps predict natural disasters and plan mitigation strategies.

- Informs climate policy at national and international levels.

Ethical Concerns When Reusing This Data:

- **Lack of Acknowledgement**: Often, local institutions or citizen scientists who collected the data are not credited in global reports.
- **Misuse of Local Context**: Applying data from temperate zones to tropical regions without adjustment can distort projections.
- **Ignoring Indigenous Knowledge**: Environmental datasets often overlook traditional ecological knowledge held by Indigenous communities who have managed these ecosystems for generations.

Ethical climate research should include **attribution, local validation, and respect for data sovereignty**.

Emerging Ethical Guidelines and Frameworks

To guide ethical data use, various organizations and communities have developed principles and codes of conduct:

FAIR Principles (for Data Reusability)

- **Findable**: Data should have clear identifiers and be easily located.
- **Accessible**: Users should know how to retrieve the data.
- **Interoperable**: Data should work with other systems and tools.
- **Reusable**: Metadata and licensing should make data easy to reuse responsibly.

CARE Principles (for Indigenous Data Ethics)

As discussed, these emphasize community control, responsibility, and cultural sensitivity when using data that involves Indigenous peoples.

These principles should be **applied together**: FAIR ensures openness and usability; CARE ensures equity and justice.

In our increasingly data-driven world, recognizing who owns data and respecting its original context are not optional considerations—they are **ethical imperatives**. Whether the data originates from individuals, institutions, or communities, responsible use demands attention to consent, attribution, cultural sensitivity, and transparency.

By embedding best practices into every stage of data use—from documentation and attribution to interpretation and sharing—we foster **trust, inclusion, and integrity** in the global data ecosystem. Ethical data reuse not only honors the contributions of data creators but also strengthens the reliability and impact of research, innovation, and policy-making.

As we look to the future, the key challenge will be balancing the openness of data with the **rights and voices of those it represents**—ensuring that data is not just free, but also fair.

9.3 Encouraging Collaboration Without Exploitation

In the age of data-driven discovery, collaboration has become an essential component of progress. Whether in scientific research, public policy, healthcare, or technology development, working together across disciplines and borders often unlocks more insights than working in silos. **Data sharing**, especially through open access platforms, has become a foundation for many collaborative efforts.

However, alongside these benefits comes the risk of **exploitation**—where certain participants disproportionately benefit from shared data while others, often those who contributed the most or are most vulnerable, receive little recognition, compensation, or lasting value. Ethical collaboration requires intentionality, fairness, and respect. This chapter explores how to promote collaborative relationships that are equitable, inclusive, and respectful of all stakeholders involved.

Why Ethical Collaboration Matters in Data Sharing

Ethical collaboration ensures that partnerships are based not only on mutual interest but also on mutual **respect and reciprocity**. When handled responsibly, data collaboration can lead to:

- Empowerment of local and marginalized communities.
- More accurate and diverse insights due to inclusive data sources.

- Trust between data contributors and users.
- Innovations that reflect the needs of all stakeholders—not just a privileged few.

Without these safeguards, data collaborations risk reinforcing **power imbalances** and perpetuating historical injustices, such as extractive research practices or "data colonialism."

Common Forms of Exploitation in Data Collaborations

Despite the noble intent of many collaborations, exploitation can manifest in subtle or overt ways:

1. Data Extraction Without Benefit

In many instances, organizations collect data from underrepresented groups, underfunded researchers, or vulnerable communities with promises of future impact. However, the benefits—whether financial, academic, or policy-related—often flow to more powerful institutions or individuals.

Example: A tech company gathers health data from remote clinics in low-income countries to train diagnostic AI models. The resulting product is sold globally, but the clinics receive no direct benefit or access to the technology.

2. Lack of Attribution

The omission of proper credit is a widespread issue. Local data collectors, citizen scientists, or grassroots organizations often contribute significantly to data gathering but are excluded from academic publications, media recognition, or product development credits.

Example: A university publishes a paper using community-gathered environmental data but fails to name the community group or local volunteers in the authorship or acknowledgments.

3. Imbalanced Power Dynamics

Larger institutions, such as universities, NGOs, or corporations, often lead data initiatives. This allows them to define the project's direction, terms, and usage rules—leaving smaller partners with limited influence over outcomes.

Example: A development agency partners with a local NGO to gather social data. However, the analysis and conclusions are drafted entirely by the agency, with little input from the local organization.

4. Commercial Exploitation of Open Data

Even when data is open, ethical concerns arise if companies profit from community or government datasets without giving back or contributing to the ecosystem they benefit from.

Example: A transportation app uses publicly available traffic data to improve its services, but contributes nothing toward infrastructure improvement or community engagement.

Principles for Ethical and Equitable Collaboration

To address these concerns, partnerships must be built on clear principles that promote fairness, equity, and shared success.

1. Transparency

Clear communication is foundational to ethical collaboration. All parties should fully understand:

- The purpose and scope of the project.
- How the data will be used, stored, and potentially commercialized.
- Who stands to benefit—and in what ways.
- What roles and responsibilities each collaborator holds.

Best Practice: Develop a memorandum of understanding (MoU) or a data use agreement (DUA) at the start of the project outlining all of the above.

2. Mutual Benefit

Collaboration should be designed so that **everyone involved gains something meaningful**—whether in the form of resources, skills, recognition, or impact.

Examples of mutual benefits include:

- Sharing data insights or tools with contributors.
- Offering co-authorship or co-patents.
- Providing funding, training, or equipment to data collectors.

Example: An academic institution working with Indigenous communities on climate data co-publishes findings with community leaders and invests in local education initiatives.

3. Inclusive Participation

Genuine collaboration involves diverse voices **throughout the project lifecycle**—from planning and data collection to interpretation and dissemination.

This means:

- Consulting local stakeholders during project design.
- Involving non-technical participants in decision-making.
- Validating findings with data contributors before publishing results.

Example: In a health data project, community members serve on the advisory board, ensuring that research questions reflect local concerns and interpretations align with lived experiences.

4. Clear Data Governance

Well-defined data governance ensures that data ownership, access rights, and responsibilities are established and respected.

Key governance questions include:

- Who owns the data?
- Who has the right to modify or redistribute it?
- What licensing terms are in place?
- Are there restrictions on commercial or third-party use?

Best Practice: Use licensing mechanisms like Creative Commons to articulate usage rights clearly. When working with Indigenous data, respect local governance systems and apply the **CARE Principles** (Collective benefit, Authority to control, Responsibility, Ethics).

5. Capacity Building

One of the most ethical investments collaborators can make is building the **skills and infrastructure** of their partners, especially in under-resourced contexts.

This includes:

- Offering training in data collection, analysis, and visualization.
- Sharing tools and resources.
- Supporting internet or hardware access in remote regions.

Example: A global health organization training local health workers to manage, analyze, and publish their own data creates lasting empowerment rather than dependence.

Collaborative Tools and Frameworks

Several tools and platforms can help formalize and support ethical data collaboration:

1. Data Use Agreements (DUAs)

Legal or semi-formal documents that define terms of data access, usage, attribution, and security.

2. Open Science Framework (OSF)

An online platform that promotes transparent and collaborative research. It allows teams to manage data, share workflows, and track contributions.

3. Creative Commons Licenses

Provide standardized ways to communicate how data can be used, whether for commercial, academic, or public use.

4. Research Ethics Committees

Institutional review boards or ethics committees ensure that collaborative projects align with ethical standards and protect human subjects.

Case Example: Community Mapping in Crisis Zones

During humanitarian crises, local volunteers often play a crucial role in mapping terrain, buildings, and resources using platforms like OpenStreetMap (OSM). These maps help aid agencies coordinate responses, deliver resources, and save lives.

Ethical Concern: Despite the importance of local contributions, many international agencies fail to recognize or compensate local mappers. Moreover, decisions based on these maps are often made without community input.

Best Practices:

- Acknowledge contributors publicly (e.g., in dashboards, reports, and publications).
- Provide stipends or capacity-building support to mapping communities.
- Include local experts in decision-making processes and strategy planning.

This example illustrates how collaboration can be both life-saving and empowering—if done respectfully and ethically.

Respecting Culture and Sensitivity

Data reflects not just facts but **the cultures and identities of people and places**. When collaborators overlook this, they risk cultural insensitivity or even harm.

Key Guidelines:

- **Avoid data colonialism**: Don't extract data from the Global South solely for the benefit of the Global North.
- **Consult ethical review boards with local representation**: These groups understand the context better than external actors.
- **Respect protocols around sacred, communal, or sensitive information**: Some data may not be appropriate for public dissemination.

Example: Genealogical data from an Indigenous community might contain information that, while scientifically interesting, is spiritually significant and should remain private.

Avoiding Exploitation in Academia and Industry

In Academic Settings:

- Offer **co-authorship** to those who contribute meaningfully to data or analysis.
- Disclose **funding sources** and any potential conflicts of interest.
- Avoid "helicopter research," where external researchers collect data and leave without engaging or giving back.

In Industry Contexts:

- Be transparent about how data will be monetized.
- Share profits, royalties, or technology access with data providers.
- Avoid **"data-washing"**—presenting partnerships as ethical or community-driven without meaningful collaboration.

Indicators of Ethical Collaboration

A project is more likely to be ethical if it includes:

- Written agreements outlining rights and responsibilities.
- Clear, consistent attribution of all contributors.
- Shared access to tools, outputs, and findings.
- Opportunities for contributors to provide feedback or opt out.
- Tangible benefits for communities that extend beyond the duration of the project.

Building a Culture of Responsible Collaboration

True change comes not just from individual efforts but from **institutional culture and systemic commitment**.

Steps to Promote Ethical Collaboration:

1. **Include ethics training** in data science curricula and professional development.
2. **Establish internal review boards** for collaborative projects, especially those involving vulnerable communities.
3. **Reward ethical practices** in hiring, funding, and publishing—not just technical accomplishments.

Ethical behavior should not be an afterthought or a checkbox—it must be **a core value embedded in the DNA of every data project**.

Collaboration in data sharing has immense potential to solve complex problems, empower communities, and create shared value. But without a strong ethical foundation, these collaborations risk perpetuating the very inequalities they aim to address.

Encouraging collaboration without exploitation requires:

- Transparency,
- Mutual benefit,

- Inclusion,
- Strong governance, and
- Cultural respect.

By embedding these principles into our data practices, we can create collaborations that are not only productive but **transformative**—for everyone involved.

The ethical use of data, particularly in the context of open access and collaboration, is crucial in today's data-driven world. Sections 9.1 through 9.3 address key concerns related to privacy, ownership, and equitable partnerships in data use.

9.4 Ethical Use of Open Datasets

Open datasets are valuable resources that promote innovation, research, and transparency. However, they also pose significant ethical challenges. Even anonymized data can risk individual privacy when cross-referenced with other datasets. Data can also be misrepresented or taken out of context, leading to misleading conclusions. Additionally, datasets may contain biases that reinforce existing inequalities, and there are often issues of consent where individuals are unaware their data is being used.

To use open data ethically, it is important to ensure transparency in how and why the data is used. Respecting privacy through anonymization techniques and limiting data to what is necessary is vital. Users should strive for fairness by preventing discrimination in analysis and ensuring diverse data representation. Above all, accountability must be upheld, with clear responsibility taken for any harms caused by data misuse.

A practical example is the use of COVID-19 tracking data. While this data helped monitor the spread of the virus, it also raised concerns about patient privacy and the use of location data without explicit consent. This case underscores the importance of applying ethical standards, even in times of crisis.

9.5 Respecting Ownership and Original Context

Data ownership can belong to individuals, organizations, or governments, but the lines are often blurred, especially in the digital age where data is easily copied and reused. Ethical data use goes beyond legal compliance; it includes acknowledging those who generated the data and understanding the context in which it was collected.

Using data outside of its original context can result in incorrect interpretations and ethical violations. For example, repurposing data without knowing its intended use may violate the expectations of the people it represents. Cultural insensitivity can also occur if data from Indigenous or local communities is used without permission or awareness of its significance.

To avoid these issues, datasets should include detailed metadata, describing how and why the data was collected, as well as its limitations and intended use. Proper attribution must be given to the original creators, and cultural data should be handled with special care. The CARE Principles—Collective benefit, Authority to control, Responsibility, and Ethics—provide guidelines for working with Indigenous data respectfully.

An example of this is the use of local climate data by international researchers. While this data is helpful for global climate studies, failing to credit local data collectors and account for environmental context can undermine trust and result in ethical oversights.

9.6 Encouraging Collaboration Without Exploitation

Collaboration is essential for data-driven innovation, but it must be conducted ethically to avoid exploitation. Unethical practices in data collaborations include collecting data from under-resourced communities without offering benefits in return, failing to credit contributors, and allowing powerful institutions to dominate partnerships. In some cases, businesses profit from open government or community datasets without reinvesting in the data sources or sharing outcomes.

Ethical collaboration is based on transparency, mutual benefit, inclusive participation, and clear data governance. All collaborators should understand how data will be used, who will benefit, and what roles each party plays. The project should provide shared value, whether through co-authorship, skills training, or financial support. Inclusive participation means involving affected communities and smaller partners in all stages of the project, not just using them for data collection.

Clear governance structures should define who owns the data, who can use it, and under what terms. Capacity building is also crucial; smaller contributors should receive training, tools, or funding to ensure they can fully participate and benefit.

Several tools can support ethical collaboration, such as data use agreements (DUAs), the Open Science Framework (OSF) for managing research, and Creative Commons licenses that define acceptable use of shared data.

A notable example is community mapping in disaster-prone regions. Local volunteers use platforms like OpenStreetMap to map infrastructure for humanitarian efforts. Yet, these contributors are often excluded from recognition or decision-making. Ethical best practices in such cases include citing and compensating local mappers, involving them in planning, and providing training to support long-term resilience.

Cultural sensitivity is also essential. Data is often rooted in community values and practices, so collaborators must avoid "data colonialism," where information from the Global South is used for the benefit of the Global North. Ethical review boards should include local representation, and cultural protocols regarding sacred or communal data must be respected.

In both academic and corporate settings, ethical issues also arise. Academic institutions should offer co-authorship and disclose funding sources transparently. In corporate environments, transparency about data usage and equitable profit-sharing is necessary. Companies must avoid "data-washing," where partnerships are presented as ethical while exploiting contributors behind the scenes.

Indicators of ethical collaboration include documented agreements, fair credit in publications or products, clear feedback mechanisms, and lasting benefits for all involved. Institutions should actively promote a culture of responsible collaboration through ethics training, internal review processes, and rewards for ethical behavior—not just technical achievements.

Across these sections, the common theme is clear: ethical data use and collaboration depend on **respect, transparency, fairness, and shared responsibility**. Whether working with open datasets or forming data partnerships, it is essential to protect privacy, acknowledge contributors, understand context, and ensure that the benefits of data innovation are **equitably distributed**. By upholding these principles, we can build a data ecosystem that promotes trust, empowerment, and long-term social good—without exploitation or harm.

Responsible data sharing goes far beyond having access to datasets. It's about creating systems, relationships, and behaviors that ensure data is used fairly, ethically, and transparently. Whether navigating open data licenses, respecting data ownership, or collaborating across disciplines and cultures, the focus must remain on **people and purpose**, not just technology.

By embedding ethical practices into every layer of data sharing—from planning to publishing—organizations and individuals can help create a digital ecosystem that values integrity, trust, and mutual benefit.

Summary

Collaboration in data sharing holds immense potential to solve complex problems, empower communities, and generate shared value. But without a strong ethical foundation, these efforts risk reinforcing the very inequalities they aim to dismantle.

Encouraging collaboration without exploitation requires five key principles:

- **Transparency**
- **Mutual benefit**
- **Inclusion**
- **Strong governance**
- **Cultural respect**

By embedding these principles into our data practices, we can foster collaborations that are not only productive but also transformative—for everyone involved.

The ethical use of data, particularly in the context of open access and cross-sector collaboration, is essential in our data-driven world. Sections 9.1 through 9.3 have highlighted critical concerns around privacy, ownership, and equitable partnerships. Building on this, Sections 9.4 through 9.6 provide further guidance.

Open datasets offer significant value for innovation, transparency, and research. However, ethical challenges persist—even anonymized data can pose privacy risks when combined with other datasets. Misuse or misinterpretation can reinforce biases or lead to harmful decisions. Respecting privacy, maintaining context, ensuring diverse representation, and accepting accountability are all essential for ethical use. The example of COVID-19 tracking data reminds us that even in emergencies, ethical safeguards must not be overlooked.

Data ownership is often ambiguous, especially in digital spaces where reuse is common. Ethical use goes beyond legal compliance—it involves acknowledging data creators, preserving context, and applying cultural sensitivity. Using data outside its intended scope can lead to misinterpretation or disrespect. Including detailed metadata, proper attribution, and adherence to frameworks like the CARE Principles is key, particularly when working with Indigenous or community-generated data.

Ethical collaboration is more than data exchange—it's about building equitable relationships. Exploitative practices, such as extracting data from under-resourced communities without benefit-sharing, undermine trust and integrity. Ethical collaboration involves clarity around use, roles, and ownership; mutual benefits like co-authorship or capacity building; and inclusive governance structures. Tools like data use agreements, the Open Science Framework, and Creative Commons licenses can support this work. Community-led initiatives, such as local disaster mapping, show how ethical practices can amplify impact while respecting contributors.

Institutions—academic, corporate, governmental—must foster a culture of ethical collaboration through internal review, transparency, and rewards for responsible behavior. Avoiding "data colonialism," practicing cultural humility, and including local voices in decision-making are all critical to this shift.

Take Aways

Across all these dimensions, the common thread is clear: ethical data use and collaboration rely on respect, fairness, and shared responsibility. Whether using open datasets or forming international partnerships, it's essential to protect privacy, honor contributors, and ensure that the benefits of data innovation are equitably distributed.

Responsible data sharing is not just about access—it's about building systems, relationships, and behaviors that prioritize people over platforms, and purpose over profit. By embedding ethics at every stage—from planning to publishing—we can build a digital ecosystem rooted in integrity, trust, and mutual benefit.

Check your Understanding

Fill in the Blanks

1. Open datasets are publicly available for use, reuse, and __________.
2. Ethical data use requires transparency, privacy, and __________.
3. Combining datasets can lead to the __________ of personal information.
4. Reusing data without understanding context can lead to __________ conclusions.
5. The CARE principles are specifically designed to guide __________ data use.
6. An important step in ethical reuse is providing proper __________ to data creators.
7. Metadata includes information about the data's origin, structure, and __________.
8. Informed __________ is essential when collecting personal data.
9. Misuse of data can result in ethical and legal __________.
10. Attribution ensures that data contributors are properly __________.
11. Data sovereignty refers to the rights communities have over their __________.
12. Without proper documentation, datasets can be easily __________.
13. Exploiting open datasets without credit is a violation of data __________.
14. __________ is the practice of minimizing the amount of data collected.
15. De-identified data can still be at risk of __________.
16. Ethical sharing encourages __________ without causing harm.
17. Open data initiatives often come from __________ or research institutions.
18. The original __________ of data must be respected in any new analysis.
19. Cultural sensitivity is essential when working with __________ datasets.
20. Responsible sharing balances access with __________ protections.

Short Answer Questions

1. What is an open dataset?
2. Define the term "informed consent" in the context of data sharing.
3. Why is metadata important in data reuse?
4. List two ethical risks of using open datasets.
5. What is meant by data minimization?
6. What does the CARE principle stand for?

7. Why is attribution important when reusing shared data?
8. How can bias be introduced through open data reuse?
9. Name one way to protect individual privacy in open data sharing.
10. What does respecting data sovereignty mean?

Long Answer Questions

1. Explain how a lack of context in an open dataset can lead to misinterpretation. Use an example.
2. Analyze the role of metadata in preserving ethical standards in open data reuse.
3. Describe the ethical challenges of combining multiple open datasets and suggest ways to mitigate them.
4. Apply the CARE principles to a case where indigenous data is being used for academic research.
5. Discuss the importance of collaboration in data science and how to prevent exploitation of contributors.
6. Evaluate the impact of failing to attribute data sources in academic or commercial settings.
7. Analyze how open data in healthcare can both benefit and harm patients.
8. Propose a data sharing policy for a non-profit organization that deals with sensitive personal data.
9. Explain how informed consent can be obtained in large-scale open data collection projects.
10. Discuss how technology can support ethical data sharing (e.g., through licensing tools, access controls, or blockchain).

Answers

1. distribution
2. accountability
3. re-identification
4. misleading
5. indigenous
6. attribution

7. usage
8. consent
9. consequences
10. credited
11. data
12. misinterpreted
13. ethics
14. Data minimization
15. re-identification
16. collaboration
17. governments
18. context
19. cultural
20. privacy

Short Answer Keys

1. An open dataset is data that is freely available for anyone to access, use, modify, and share, usually under an open license.
2. Informed consent means individuals agree to share their data with full knowledge of how it will be used, stored, and potentially shared with others.
3. Metadata provides context about the data, including source, structure, collection methods, and limitations, helping ensure proper interpretation.
4. Risk of re-identifying individuals from anonymized data; Misinterpreting data without understanding its original context.
5. Data minimization is the principle of collecting only the data that is necessary for a specific purpose.
6. CARE stands for Collective Benefit, Authority to Control, Responsibility, and Ethics.
7. Attribution ensures original data contributors receive proper credit, recognition, and possibly continued collaboration.
8. Bias can be introduced by using data out of context or failing to account for sampling bias or structural inequalities.

9. De-identifying or anonymizing personal data before sharing.
10. Respecting data sovereignty means acknowledging and protecting the rights of communities or nations to control how their data is accessed and used.

Long Answer Keys

1. Without context, data can be misinterpreted. For example, crime statistics may seem higher in certain areas without considering population density or policing practices, leading to biased policy decisions.
2. Metadata provides essential background such as data origin, collection method, and structure. It ensures transparency and ethical reuse by allowing users to interpret data correctly and responsibly.
3. Ethical issues in combining datasets include re-identification risks and conflicting contexts. Mitigation includes anonymization, transparency, ethical review, and consistent documentation.
4. CARE principles guide respectful research with Indigenous data by ensuring community benefit, control over data, responsibility from users, and adherence to ethical practices.
5. Collaboration is vital in data science to pool diverse expertise. Avoid exploitation by giving credit, ensuring mutual benefit, and having clear agreements on contributions and outcomes.
6. Lack of attribution can lead to mistrust and legal issues. It undermines credibility and discourages data sharing. Proper credit maintains integrity and supports future collaboration.
7. Open healthcare data helps research but may harm individuals through breaches of privacy or misuse. Protecting identities and setting clear ethical guidelines balances benefits and risks.
8. A nonprofit's policy should include data minimization, anonymization, clear consent processes, access restrictions, and periodic reviews for ethical compliance.
9. In large-scale data collection, digital platforms can provide transparent consent forms, clear purposes for data use, opt-out options, and contact support for participants.

Chapter 10: Practical Lessons from the Field

Learning Outcomes

1. Recall notable ethical failures in data science, like COMPAS and Cambridge Analytica.
2. Identify causes of ethical issues, such as biased data, lack transparency.
3. Explain importance of transparency, fairness, and privacy in ethical data systems.
4. Describe how incidents influenced ethical practices and regulations in data science.

10.1 Notable Ethical Failures in Data Science

Data science has rapidly evolved into a cornerstone of decision-making across various industries, including healthcare, finance, criminal justice, and education. The growing influence of data science means that data practitioners hold significant responsibility in ensuring that their algorithms and models are fair, transparent, and ethical. However, despite its potential for positive change, data science has encountered several ethical failures. These failures often arise from a lack of foresight, systemic biases in the data, and limited oversight during development and deployment. By examining these high-profile cases, we can learn valuable lessons that will help guide the ethical use of data science in the future.

1. The COMPAS Algorithm and Criminal Justice Bias

Issue:

The COMPAS (Correctional Offender Management Profiling for Alternative Sanctions) algorithm was designed to assess the likelihood that a defendant would reoffend, aiding judges in making sentencing decisions. However, an investigation by **ProPublica** in 2016 revealed a significant racial bias in the algorithm's predictions. The model assigned higher risk scores to Black defendants compared to white defendants with similar criminal histories, increasing the likelihood of unfair treatment.

Root Cause:

The root cause of the bias lay in the training data used to develop COMPAS, which reflected systemic issues in the U.S. criminal justice system, such as racial disparities in arrests and convictions. Since the training data was not adjusted to account for these biases, the algorithm learned and perpetuated these same inequities. Furthermore, the proprietary nature of COMPAS meant that the algorithm's inner workings were not transparent, making it difficult for stakeholders (including defendants and judges) to understand how decisions were made.

Impact:

This bias had severe implications for racial justice, reinforcing already-existing inequalities. Black defendants were disproportionately assigned higher risk scores, potentially leading to harsher sentences and a deepening of racial disparities in the justice system. The lack of transparency in the system also led to public mistrust in how AI tools were being used in sensitive legal matters.

Lessons Learned:

- **Data Transparency:** Open algorithms and access to training data are critical to ensure fairness and accountability.
- **Bias Mitigation:** It is crucial to address systemic biases in data before using it to train models that impact people's lives.

2. Amazon's Discriminatory Hiring Tool

Issue:

Amazon developed an AI-driven recruitment tool aimed at improving the efficiency of hiring software engineers. However, the tool showed a clear gender bias, systematically downgrading resumes that included the word "women" or referenced women's colleges or organizations. This led to the exclusion of qualified female candidates from the hiring process.

Root Cause:

The algorithm was trained on resumes collected over a 10-year period, a majority of which were submitted by male candidates. As a result, the model learned to associate male traits (e.g., technical skills or leadership experience) as signals of a candidate's success. The system inadvertently penalized resumes that suggested the candidate was female, reinforcing gender stereotypes in the hiring process.

Impact:

The discriminatory tool perpetuated gender bias in the technology industry, a sector already facing challenges with gender diversity. Although Amazon abandoned the tool in 2018, this episode highlighted the need for greater attention to bias in AI tools used for recruitment and hiring, where fair and equal opportunities are paramount.

Lessons Learned:

- **Training Data Awareness:** When training models on historical data, it is essential to recognize and address inherent biases that may exist within the data.
- **Bias in Hiring:** Using AI to assist in hiring decisions requires careful evaluation of the potential for bias that could exclude qualified candidates, especially from underrepresented groups.

3. Facebook-Cambridge Analytica Scandal

Issue:

The Facebook-Cambridge Analytica scandal erupted in 2018 when it was revealed that Cambridge Analytica, a political consulting firm, had harvested data from millions of Facebook users without their explicit consent. This data was then used to create psychographic profiles that influenced voter behavior during elections.

Root Cause:

Facebook's data-sharing policies allowed third-party developers to access user data, including information from users' friends, without sufficient oversight or user consent. Cambridge Analytica exploited this loophole to collect massive amounts of data, which was then used for targeted political advertisements and messaging during key electoral events.

Impact:

The scandal resulted in widespread public outrage and increased global scrutiny of Facebook's data privacy practices. It led to regulatory investigations, fines, and the eventual overhaul of Facebook's data-sharing policies. The scandal also sparked wider debates about the ethics of data privacy, informed consent, and the potential misuse of personal data in political campaigns.

Lessons Learned:

- **Data Privacy:** Data must be collected and used with full transparency, user consent, and respect for privacy.
- **Regulation and Oversight:** The lack of oversight in Facebook's data-sharing policies underscored the need for stronger regulatory frameworks to govern the collection and use of personal data, especially when it is used to influence public opinion.

4. Google Photos and Racial Labelling

Issue:

In 2015, Google Photos' image-recognition algorithm mistakenly labelled photos of Black individuals as "gorillas," a deeply offensive and harmful error. This resulted from the algorithm failing to accurately recognize and classify images of people of colour.

Root Cause:

The issue stemmed from the algorithm's training data, which lacked sufficient diversity. Google's image-recognition system was predominantly trained on images of lighter-skinned individuals, leading to poor performance when applied to darker-skinned individuals. Additionally, the testing processes did not adequately account for edge cases, such as the potential for offensive mislabelling.

Impact:

The incident sparked public outrage, particularly within communities of colour. It also highlighted the risks of deploying AI models without adequate testing on diverse populations. Google removed the offensive label but initially failed to fully address the underlying issue with their algorithm.

Lessons Learned:

- **Diversity in Training Data:** A key lesson is the importance of using diverse and representative datasets to train AI systems to ensure that they perform equitably across different demographic groups.
- **Testing for Edge Cases:** AI models must undergo rigorous testing, including on underrepresented groups, to prevent harmful mistakes from occurring in real-world applications.

5. Apple Card Credit Limit Controversy

Issue:

In 2019, several tech industry leaders, including Apple co-founder Steve Wozniak, publicly criticized the Apple Card credit limit algorithm for offering lower credit limits to women than to men, despite both individuals sharing finances. This sparked concerns about algorithmic bias in the financial sector.

Root Cause:

The bias was likely rooted in historical credit data, which reflected gender-based disparities in financial behavior and borrowing patterns. Additionally, the opaque nature of the decision-making process made it difficult to understand how the algorithm arrived at its conclusions, leading to allegations of unfair treatment.

Impact:

The controversy prompted investigations by regulatory bodies and significant reputational damage to Apple. It also contributed to calls for greater transparency in AI-driven financial tools and highlighted the need to ensure that algorithms in the financial sector are free from bias.

Lessons Learned:

- **Bias in Financial Data:** Historical data in sectors like banking can reflect entrenched social biases, and it is crucial to actively work to address these biases in algorithms.

- **Algorithmic Transparency:** Consumers and regulators must have access to clear explanations of how AI systems make decisions, especially when they impact significant financial outcomes.

The ethical failures in data science discussed above provide valuable lessons for practitioners, businesses, and policymakers. They emphasize the importance of transparency, fairness, and accountability in the development and deployment of AI and data-driven systems. By learning from these missteps, the data science community can work towards creating more ethical, responsible, and inclusive systems that prioritize the well-being of all individuals. These lessons also highlight the need for continuous reflection and improvement, as the field of data science continues to evolve and impact society at large.

10.2 Learning from High-Profile Incidents

Ethical failures in data science, while damaging, present significant learning opportunities. By examining the incidents where algorithms, human oversight, societal biases, and institutional practices have failed, we can gain essential insights into how to prevent similar issues from occurring in the future. These failures highlight systemic issues within data-driven systems, but they also provide a roadmap for how we can improve data science practices in ways that promote fairness, accountability, and transparency.

1. Transparency is Non-Negotiable

What We've Learned:

Opacity in data science systems can lead to significant mistrust, and when issues arise, it becomes difficult to diagnose or correct them. Transparency should go beyond merely publishing technical papers or reports; users, stakeholders, and auditors must be able to understand how algorithms work. This is especially important when algorithms have real-world implications for individuals, such as in healthcare, criminal justice, or finance.

Key Takeaways:

- **Explainable AI (XAI)** is crucial, especially in high-stakes areas where decisions directly impact people's lives. In healthcare, law, and finance, transparency in decision-making helps build trust and ensures accountability.
- **Open-sourcing models** or providing comprehensive documentation helps external reviewers assess fairness and identify issues that may have been overlooked internally.

Example in Action:

The **COMPAS** algorithm's lack of transparency led to public outcry and mistrust. In response to these issues, organizations like the **Partnership on AI** and events like the **Fairness, Accountability, and Transparency (FAT) conferences** have promoted algorithmic audits and the adoption of models that are explainable and interpretable. These initiatives aim to improve transparency and accountability across the field.

2. Bias is Inevitable—but Manageable

What We've Learned:

It's unrealistic to eliminate all biases from data since all data reflects real-world inequalities. However, understanding and mitigating these biases is within our control. The goal should be to detect and reduce bias in a way that doesn't compromise the performance of algorithms but ensures fairness for all groups.

Key Takeaways:

- **Diverse training datasets** are essential to avoid reinforcing existing biases, such as racial or gender biases. A diverse dataset helps ensure that models perform equitably across all demographic groups.
- **Regular audits** using fairness metrics (such as demographic parity and equalized odds) should be implemented to monitor algorithmic bias and identify unintended consequences.
- **Involvement of ethicists and social scientists** during the model development phase helps to identify potential blind spots that may otherwise go unnoticed by technical teams.

Example in Action:

Google and **Microsoft** have incorporated **fairness teams** into their product design processes to proactively address bias. These teams work to ensure that models are tested for fairness, and that solutions to address bias are considered before deployment.

3. **Consent and Privacy Must Be Respected**
What We've Learned:

The **Cambridge Analytica scandal** revealed a catastrophic failure in obtaining informed consent. Users' data was exploited without their explicit knowledge or understanding, raising questions about consent and privacy. This highlighted the importance of not only asking for consent but also ensuring that users understand how their data will be used and the implications of that use.

Key Takeaways:

- **Data minimization** is a key practice—only collect the data that is necessary for the task at hand. This reduces the potential for misuse and respects users' privacy.
- **Clear and accessible privacy policies** are essential. Legal jargon should not obfuscate the user's understanding of how their data will be used. Transparency in data collection is paramount.
- **Anonymization and differential privacy** techniques should be used where appropriate to protect user identities while still enabling data-driven insights.

Example in Action:

Regulations like the **General Data Protection Regulation (GDPR)** in the EU and the **California Consumer Privacy Act (CCPA)** have set benchmarks for privacy and consent. These laws give users more control over their data and impose strict guidelines on data collection, usage, and storage, ensuring that organizations must seek informed consent and provide transparency about data practices.

4. **Regulation is a Double-Edged Sword**
What We've Learned:

While some in the tech industry fear that regulations could stifle innovation, these rules are often necessary to ensure ethical practice. Regulatory frameworks provide essential guardrails to ensure that data science practices are responsible, fair, and respectful of human rights.

Key Takeaways:

- **Clear ethical standards** provided by regulations can foster public trust and facilitate broader adoption of AI technologies, especially when users and stakeholders feel that systems are accountable.
- Regulatory frameworks, such as **GDPR**, have influenced global practices by setting strict data privacy standards that have become global benchmarks, even for companies outside the EU.

Example in Action:

The **AI Act** proposed by the European Union categorizes AI applications by their risk level and stipulates stricter requirements for high-risk applications, such as those used in healthcare or criminal justice. These regulations aim to ensure that AI systems are deployed safely, ethically, and without bias, especially in high-stakes contexts where the consequences of errors can be severe.

5. Diversity in Teams Drives Better Outcomes

What We've Learned:

Homogeneous teams are more likely to overlook or fail to recognize biases in the data and systems they create. A diverse team—comprising varied perspectives across gender, race, culture, and academic background—helps to identify potential issues before they become problems and ensures that ethical considerations are embedded throughout the development process.

Key Takeaways:

- **Inclusion** isn't just about fulfilling diversity quotas; it's a technical necessity. Diverse teams bring different viewpoints and problem-solving approaches, which leads to more robust and ethical AI systems.

- **Varied perspectives** help identify potential blind spots in data and model design, improving the overall effectiveness and fairness of the technology.

Example in Action:

DeepMind has implemented **inclusion fellowships** to promote diversity in AI research, providing opportunities for individuals from underrepresented backgrounds. Similarly, **OpenAI** works with scholars from diverse backgrounds to ensure a range of perspectives in their research. These efforts help ensure that AI systems are designed with fairness and inclusivity in mind.

High-profile ethical failures in data science underscore the need for more robust, transparent, and inclusive practices. By reflecting on these incidents, we can distill several crucial lessons that will help shape the future of AI and data science. Transparency, bias mitigation, privacy, regulation, and diversity are not just ethical ideals—they are practical necessities for building systems that are fair, accountable, and trustworthy. These lessons will guide the next generation of data scientists and policymakers in creating responsible, ethical AI systems that benefit all of society.

10.3 Building Better Systems Through Reflection

As the field of data science and AI continues to evolve, one of the key realizations is that creating better systems requires continuous reflection—not just post-mortem analysis after failures occur. Reflection should be an integral part of the development and deployment process, ensuring that ethical considerations are embedded in every stage of a system's lifecycle. Practitioners must be proactive in considering potential ethical pitfalls and work actively to mitigate them. The following strategies illustrate how organizations and individuals can integrate ethical reflection into their everyday work to build more responsible, fair, and accountable data systems.

1. Ethical Design Reviews

Best Practice:

Just as technical designs undergo architecture reviews to assess their feasibility, scalability, and performance, ethical implications should be formally reviewed during development. By incorporating ethical design reviews, teams can proactively identify and address potential harms or biases before they make their way into the final product.

- **Establish Ethics Review Boards:** Create dedicated groups within the organization that specialize in reviewing and addressing ethical concerns. These boards can act as decision-making bodies for identifying risks and ensuring that systems align with ethical standards.
- **Integrate Checklists:** Develop ethical review checklists that prompt teams to consider how their work might impact vulnerable groups, including marginalized communities or those affected by historical biases.
- **Use Ethical Development Tools:** Leverage tools designed to assist in identifying and mitigating ethical issues. For example, **IBM's AI Fairness 360** and **Google's What-If Tool** are platforms that allow teams to audit and assess the fairness of AI models and datasets during development.

Example in Action:

The **AI Fairness 360** toolkit from IBM allows data scientists to assess and reduce bias in machine learning models, offering various fairness metrics and bias mitigation techniques. This integration of fairness checks throughout the development process helps to ensure that systems are built with fairness in mind, not just as an afterthought.

2. Post-Deployment Monitoring

Best Practice:

Ethical reflection doesn't end once a system has been deployed. In fact, post-deployment is when ethical challenges may become more apparent, especially as systems interact with the real world and evolve in ways that weren't anticipated during development. Continuous monitoring ensures that systems remain ethical throughout their lifecycle.

- **Implement Feedback Loops:** Establish systems for collecting feedback from users and other stakeholders to identify any unintended consequences or emerging ethical issues. This can help catch biases, errors, or harmful impacts that weren't apparent during the development phase.

- **Provide Reporting Avenues for Users:** Allow users to easily report problems, harms, or inaccuracies they encounter while using the system. This creates a channel for real-time ethical reflection and rapid response to issues.
- **Schedule Regular Audits:** Conduct ongoing audits of deployed systems to check for "model drift" (i.e., when a model's predictions or decisions begin to deviate from its intended behavior) and to reassess the fairness and accuracy of the model as new data becomes available.

Example in Action:

Post-deployment monitoring was a key focus in the aftermath of the **COMPAS algorithm** controversy. ProPublica's investigation into racial bias in the COMPAS risk scores sparked ongoing efforts to monitor and audit algorithms used in the criminal justice system. Continuous feedback and transparency are now considered essential to ensure these systems don't perpetuate harmful patterns over time.

3. Documentation and Datasheets for Datasets

Best Practice:

Clear documentation is essential for ensuring transparency, accountability, and proper understanding of how data was collected, its intended use, and any inherent limitations. This also helps future developers better understand the ethical considerations of the data they are working with.

- **Datasheets for Datasets:** Following the work of **Timnit Gebru** and colleagues at Google, creating "datasheets" for datasets can promote greater transparency in data collection and usage. These datasheets should describe the dataset's origins, any potential biases, intended use cases, and caveats.
- **Model Cards:** Similar to datasheets for datasets, **model cards** provide comprehensive documentation about how a model was trained, the data it was trained on, and its limitations. These tools help developers understand the potential risks associated with using the model and provide transparency to users.

- **Integrate Documentation into the Development Pipeline:** Documentation should be considered part of the development process, not an afterthought. By integrating this practice into the pipeline, organizations ensure that ethical considerations are well-documented and easily accessible for future review or adjustments.

Example in Action:

The **Datasheets for Datasets** initiative, introduced by Timnit Gebru and colleagues, has gained widespread adoption in the AI community. It encourages transparency in how datasets are collected, highlighting potential risks and biases. By making such documentation standard practice, developers can better understand and mitigate issues before they arise.

4. Foster Ethical Culture, Not Just Compliance

Best Practice:

Building a truly ethical system requires more than just following legal requirements or ticking off compliance checkboxes. Organizations should cultivate an ethical culture that prioritizes moral responsibility in decision-making at all levels. This culture can drive better practices, leading to systems that are not only compliant but also just and fair.

- **Host Regular Ethics Workshops:** Provide opportunities for employees to engage in ongoing discussions about ethics in AI and data science. These workshops can help practitioners stay informed about new ethical challenges and foster a shared sense of responsibility.
- **Recognize and Reward Ethical Decision-Making:** Encourage and reward ethical decision-making by recognizing individuals and teams who take a proactive approach to solving ethical challenges. This could involve offering incentives for teams that prioritize fairness and transparency in their work.
- **Encourage Whistleblowing:** Create an environment where employees feel comfortable speaking up when they see ethical concerns or potential harms arising from data-driven systems. This can be facilitated through anonymous reporting channels or dedicated ethics officers who are empowered to address concerns.

Example in Action:

Organizations like **Microsoft** and **Google** have implemented ethics workshops and training sessions to promote ethical awareness and ensure their teams are prepared to tackle complex ethical dilemmas. By fostering a culture of ethical awareness, these companies aim to ensure that ethics are an integral part of their operational fabric.

5. Scenario Planning and Red Teaming

Best Practice:

Borrowing from cybersecurity practices, data science teams can use **scenario planning** and **red teaming** to test systems for potential vulnerabilities, both technical and ethical. These practices involve imagining the worst-case scenarios, including how systems might be misused, exploited, or cause harm to individuals or society.

- **Simulate Edge Cases:** Test systems against edge cases or rare, but possible, scenarios where the system could perform poorly or cause unintended harm. For example, in facial recognition systems, teams should consider cases where the system might misidentify individuals from marginalized communities.
- **Adversarial Attacks:** Conduct "red teaming" exercises where internal teams adopt adversarial roles to intentionally exploit weaknesses in the system. This can include testing how the system could be gamed for malicious purposes or identifying ways in which it might be biased in specific contexts.

Example in Action:

OpenAI used red teaming before releasing their GPT-based models, testing for outputs that could lead to harmful or biased content. By simulating adversarial interactions and potential harmful uses, OpenAI was able to identify vulnerabilities and improve safeguards before launching the model to the public.

Building ethical data systems requires a commitment to continuous reflection and improvement. By embedding practices such as ethical design reviews, post-deployment monitoring, thorough documentation, fostering an ethical culture, and using scenario planning or red teaming, data practitioners can ensure that their systems are not only technically sound but also socially responsible. These practices, when integrated into the everyday workflow, promote fairness, accountability, and trust in AI and data science technologies. The ultimate goal is to build systems that don't just work well—they work ethically, benefiting individuals and society as a whole.

Summary

As data science and AI continue to shape various industries, it is critical to ensure that ethical considerations are integral to the development and deployment of systems. Learning from past failures in the field helps shape better practices and guidelines that can lead to more responsible, fair, and accountable systems.

Notable Ethical Failures in Data Science

Several high-profile ethical failures highlight the challenges and risks associated with data-driven systems:

1. **COMPAS Algorithm**: Found to be biased against Black defendants in the criminal justice system, showcasing the dangers of biased training data and lack of transparency.
2. **Amazon's Hiring Tool**: Discriminated against women by downgrading resumes with gendered terms, revealing biases in training data and model assumptions.
3. **Facebook-Cambridge Analytica**: Exploited user data without informed consent, underscoring the importance of respecting privacy and user control.
4. **Google Photos Racial Labeling**: Mistakenly labeled Black individuals as "gorillas," highlighting the need for diverse datasets and thorough testing.
5. **Apple Card Credit Limit Bias**: Showed gender-based disparities in credit limits, raising concerns about algorithmic bias in financial systems.

Learning from High-Profile Incidents

Ethical failures offer valuable lessons for building better systems:

1. **Transparency**: Open, understandable models and processes are critical to building trust and accountability, particularly in high-stakes fields like healthcare and law.
2. **Bias Management**: Bias is inevitable, but diverse training data and regular fairness audits can help detect and mitigate its effects.
3. **Respect for Consent and Privacy**: Clear, accessible privacy policies and minimal data collection ensure respect for user rights.
4. **Regulation**: Ethical standards, like GDPR, help foster public trust and ensure safe and fair practices, even if regulation may seem burdensome at first.
5. **Diversity in Teams**: Diverse teams lead to better, more ethical problem-solving and identification of potential risks, improving the quality of AI systems.

Building Better Systems Through Reflection

Ethical reflection must be continuous, not just an afterthought after failures. Some key strategies include:

1. **Ethical Design Reviews**: Establish ethics review boards, integrate ethical checklists, and use tools like IBM's AI Fairness 360 to evaluate potential harms early in the development process.
2. **Post-Deployment Monitoring**: Systems must be monitored post-launch to identify drift, biases, and unintended consequences. Feedback loops and regular audits are essential.
3. **Documentation and Datasheets**: Comprehensive documentation, such as datasheets for datasets and model cards, promotes transparency and helps future developers understand limitations and biases in the system.
4. **Foster Ethical Culture**: Organizations should make ethics a core cultural value by hosting workshops, rewarding ethical decision-making, and encouraging employees to raise concerns.
5. **Scenario Planning and Red Teaming**: Simulating edge cases and conducting adversarial tests (red teaming) can identify potential ethical vulnerabilities before deployment.

The future of data science lies in proactive, continuous reflection on the ethical implications of AI and data systems. By embedding ethical practices such as transparency, bias management, privacy respect, regulation, diversity, and ongoing monitoring, we can create systems that are not only effective but also fair, accountable, and trustworthy. These steps ensure that data science serves the broader public good while minimizing harm and maximizing societal benefits.

Ethical maturity in data science doesn't come from avoiding failure—it comes from learning, adapting, and proactively anticipating risks. The notable ethical lapses of the past have spurred a movement toward responsible AI, fairness audits.

Check your understanding

Fill in the Blanks

1. The _______ algorithm in the criminal justice system was found to be biased against Black defendants.
2. In 2018, the _______ scandal involved the unauthorized harvesting of Facebook user data.
3. The _______ recruitment tool developed by Amazon discriminated against female applicants.
4. Google's image recognition algorithm mistakenly labeled Black people as _______.
5. The _______ Act is a regulation aimed at ensuring fairness and transparency in AI within the European Union.
6. Data science ethics can often be impacted by _______ biases in training datasets.
7. The _______ company developed an AI tool to predict the risk of reoffending for criminals.
8. _______ is the practice of only collecting data that is strictly necessary for a project.
9. The Cambridge Analytica scandal raised questions about _______ consent and privacy in data collection.
10. One of the major ethical failures in data science involved Amazon's biased algorithm for _______.
11. The lack of _______ in AI tools is a key factor in ethical failures.
12. The _______ team at Microsoft works on addressing fairness and diversity in AI research.
13. Apple's credit limit controversy in 2019 was linked to _______ bias in financial algorithms.
14. In order to avoid ethical problems, data scientists should incorporate _______ audits into the development process.

15. AI systems should be regularly monitored to ensure they do not _______ over time.
16. Data-driven systems can amplify societal _______ if not carefully monitored for fairness.
17. In 2015, Google Photos labeled Black people as _______ due to algorithmic flaws.
18. The _______ policy enforces data privacy and aims to give users control over their information.
19. In 2016, ProPublica found that the COMPAS algorithm disproportionately flagged _______ defendants as high-risk.
20. The ethical failure of the _______ hiring tool at Amazon was caused by gender bias in the dataset.

Short Answer Questions

1. What was the main issue with the COMPAS algorithm in criminal justice?
2. How did Amazon's AI recruitment tool discriminate against female applicants?
3. What was the main problem with Facebook's data-sharing practices during the Cambridge Analytica scandal?
4. Describe one key reason why Google Photos' image recognition system misclassified Black people.
5. What does "data minimization" mean in the context of ethical data science?
6. How did the Apple Card controversy highlight gender bias in financial algorithms?
7. Explain how biased data can influence the fairness of machine learning models.
8. What role does transparency play in mitigating ethical risks in data science?
9. Name one regulatory framework aimed at protecting users' privacy in data science.
10. How can diverse teams help mitigate algorithmic biases in data science?

Long Answer Questions

1. Analyze the ethical implications of using the COMPAS algorithm in the criminal justice system. What are the broader social consequences of such biased predictions?
2. Discuss the ethical issues surrounding Amazon's recruitment tool. How can organizations address these biases to create a fairer hiring process?

3. Evaluate the long-term impact of the Cambridge Analytica scandal on public trust in data science. How can companies avoid similar privacy violations?
4. Assess how Google could have avoided the racial bias in its image recognition system. What steps could be taken to improve AI accuracy and fairness?
5. Critically examine the role of explainable AI in reducing ethical risks in data science. Why is transparency crucial in building trust with users?
6. Explain how data scientists can identify and mitigate bias in machine learning models. What steps should be taken to ensure fairness in AI algorithms?
7. Discuss the ethical challenges of using AI for predictive policing. How can data scientists ensure such systems do not perpetuate racial or socioeconomic biases?
8. Analyze how regulatory frameworks like GDPR or CCPA impact the way data science is conducted. What challenges do these regulations pose for companies?
9. Reflect on the potential dangers of relying on AI for financial decision-making. How should data scientists balance automation with human oversight in financial algorithms?
10. Propose strategies for ensuring diversity and inclusion in data science teams. How can diverse perspectives contribute to more ethical and fair data systems?

Answers

Fill in the Blanks

1. COMPAS
2. Cambridge Analytica
3. Amazon
4. gorillas
5. AI
6. societal
7. COMPAS
8. Data minimization
9. informed
10. hiring
11. transparency
12. Fairness

13. gender
14. regular
15. drift
16. inequalities
17. gorillas
18. GDPR
19. Black
20. Amazon

Short Answer Questions (Answer Keys)

1. The COMPAS algorithm was found to be biased, disproportionately flagging Black defendants as high-risk for reoffending, even when their criminal history was similar to white defendants.
2. Amazon's AI tool was trained on resumes primarily submitted by men, leading the algorithm to favor male candidates and penalize resumes that referenced women's colleges or organizations.
3. Facebook allowed third-party developers to access and misuse user data without proper consent or oversight, leading to the unauthorized harvesting of data for political profiling.
4. The misclassification occurred because the training data for Google Photos lacked sufficient diversity, causing the algorithm to make inaccurate and offensive assumptions about the people in photos.
5. Data minimization refers to the principle of only collecting and storing the minimum amount of data necessary for a particular project or task, to reduce privacy risks.
6. The Apple Card algorithm provided lower credit limits to women, even when they shared joint finances with their husbands, which led to claims of discrimination based on gender.
7. Biased data reflects historical inequalities or prejudices and can cause machine learning models to replicate and perpetuate these biases, leading to unfair and discriminatory outcomes.
8. Transparency allows stakeholders to understand how algorithms work, ensuring that models can be audited for fairness and that their decision-making processes are clear and justifiable.

9. The **General Data Protection Regulation (GDPR)** is a regulatory framework that ensures data privacy and gives users more control over their personal information.
10. Diverse teams bring a variety of perspectives, which helps identify potential biases and ethical issues early, ensuring that AI systems are fairer and more inclusive.

Long Answer Questions (Answer Keys)

1. The COMPAS algorithm's bias against Black defendants raises serious ethical concerns about fairness, equality, and racial justice. The algorithm, which is used to predict the likelihood of reoffending, can perpetuate existing racial disparities in the justice system. A biased algorithm can lead to wrongful sentencing, with innocent individuals potentially receiving harsher punishments. The broader social consequence is the erosion of trust in both the criminal justice system and the technologies used to make critical decisions, as it disproportionately affects marginalized communities and deepens societal inequalities.
2. Amazon's AI recruitment tool was flawed due to its reliance on historical hiring data, which was overwhelmingly male-dominated. As a result, it developed a bias against female candidates, penalizing resumes with terms related to women's colleges or female-oriented experiences. Ethical issues include gender discrimination and the perpetuation of existing inequalities in the workplace. To address these biases, organizations must ensure that AI systems are trained on diverse and representative datasets, incorporate fairness checks during model development, and promote transparency in how decisions are made. Additionally, human oversight should be integrated into the recruitment process to validate AI outcomes.
3. The Cambridge Analytica scandal severely damaged public trust in how personal data is handled, especially regarding privacy and consent. People became more cautious about sharing their data with companies and were more skeptical of data-driven services. In the long term, this can slow innovation in data science and lead to stricter regulations. To avoid similar violations, companies must prioritize informed consent, provide transparent data policies, and ensure that users have control over their information. Ethical data handling practices, regular audits, and compliance with privacy laws like GDPR can also help restore trust.

4. Google could have avoided the racial bias in its image recognition system by ensuring that its training data was diverse and representative of all racial and ethnic groups. In particular, data science teams must incorporate a wide range of images that reflect the real-world diversity of human populations. To improve AI accuracy and fairness, companies should implement fairness audits, regularly test for biases, and integrate ethical design reviews during development. Additionally, algorithms should be designed to be transparent and interpretable, so users and developers can understand and address potential issues.
5. Explainable AI (XAI) refers to the ability to understand and interpret how AI systems arrive at decisions. This is critical for reducing ethical risks because it helps identify and correct biases, errors, or unfair outcomes in models. Transparency in AI decision-making fosters trust with users, as they can see how and why decisions are made, ensuring that algorithms are not acting in ways that are opaque or unjust. Moreover, it allows for accountability in case of errors or harmful outcomes, making it easier to rectify issues and ensure fairness.
6. Data scientists can identify bias by performing regular audits and fairness assessments on their models. This involves analyzing the model's performance across different demographic groups to ensure that it is not disproportionately favoring one group over others. Steps to mitigate bias include diversifying the training data, applying fairness constraints during model training, using techniques such as re-weighting or re-sampling data, and incorporating fairness metrics into the model evaluation process. Ensuring fairness also involves promoting transparency in model design and encouraging collaboration with ethicists and social scientists to assess the broader societal impact of AI systems.
7. Predictive policing uses historical crime data to predict where future crimes are likely to occur. However, these systems often reflect and perpetuate historical biases, such as racial profiling and socioeconomic inequalities, because they rely on biased data sources, like arrest records that may disproportionately affect marginalized communities. Data scientists can ensure fairness by auditing the data to identify and remove biased inputs, using fairness-enhancing algorithms, and ensuring transparency in model decisions. They should also work with community stakeholders to ensure the system's predictions are used responsibly and do not reinforce harmful stereotypes or discriminatory practices.

8. The GDPR (General Data Protection Regulation) and CCPA (California Consumer Privacy Act) enforce strict guidelines on how personal data is collected, stored, and processed. These frameworks prioritize user privacy and data protection, which has significant implications for data science practices. Companies must ensure compliance by adopting data minimization practices, allowing users to access or delete their data, and being transparent about data usage. The challenges these regulations pose include the need for significant changes to data collection methods, increased operational costs to maintain compliance, and potential delays in deploying data-driven systems.
9. AI systems used for financial decision-making can optimize processes, but they also pose risks, including the potential to reinforce biases, make incorrect predictions based on flawed data, or lead to market instability. Data scientists must balance automation with human oversight by ensuring that key financial decisions are reviewed by experienced professionals who can interpret the AI's results and make context-sensitive adjustments. Incorporating ethical reviews, using transparent and explainable models, and building fail-safes to catch potential errors are essential to minimizing the risks of automation in finance.
10. Strategies for ensuring diversity in data science teams include implementing inclusive hiring practices, offering mentorship programs for underrepresented groups, and fostering a culture of collaboration that values different viewpoints. Diverse teams are better equipped to identify and address biases in data models, as team members bring unique perspectives and lived experiences to the table. Additionally, diverse teams are more likely to consider the broader social impacts of AI systems, ensuring that data science solutions are fairer, more inclusive, and better reflect the needs of all communities.

Chapter 11: Laws, Standards, and Ethical Alignment

Learning Outcomes

1. **Recall** the key principles of data privacy regulations, such as GDPR and CCPA.
2. **Define** the concept of algorithmic bias and explain its potential impact on decision-making.
3. **Identify** the primary roles and responsibilities of a Data Protection Officer (DPO) within an organization.
4. **Explain** the importance of transparency and accountability in AI systems and their ethical implications.

Introduction

Data science has become a powerful force in reshaping industries such as healthcare, finance, retail, and public services. From predictive analytics in hospitals to personalized recommendations in e-commerce, the reach of data-driven technologies is immense. However, as data science becomes increasingly embedded in everyday decision-making, the consequences of its misuse—whether intentional or not—grow more significant. This has sparked global discussions around ethics, privacy, fairness, and accountability.

While legal regulations provide a formal structure to govern data use, ethical data science must go beyond mere compliance. Ethical alignment requires data scientists and organizations to consider societal norms, human rights, and the broader consequences of their technologies. In this section, we delve into the evolving legal landscape, explore international standards, and discuss the gap between what is legal and what is ethical in data science.

11.1 Overview of Data Ethics Regulations

As data science increasingly influences core aspects of society—from personalized services to public decision-making—the need to ethically govern its use has never been more critical. Data ethics regulations are responses to rising public concern over privacy violations, algorithmic bias, opaque AI systems, and unfair treatment stemming from automated decisions. These regulations aim to ensure that data technologies are used in ways that respect individual rights and uphold societal values such as fairness, accountability, and transparency.

Key Data Ethics Regulations

1. General Data Protection Regulation (GDPR) – *European Union*

The **GDPR**, enacted in 2018, stands as one of the most comprehensive data protection frameworks in the world. Its core purpose is to safeguard the personal data and privacy of individuals within the European Union and the European Economic Area.

Key Features:

- Requires clear and informed **consent** before collecting personal data.
- Grants individuals the **right to access**, **correct**, and **erase** their data ("right to be forgotten").
- Promotes **data protection by design and by default**, embedding privacy into the system architecture.
- Mandates **data breach notifications** within 72 hours of discovery.

Example: A fitness app operating in the EU cannot start tracking user location or sharing data with third parties unless users have explicitly opted in. If it later wants to use that data for marketing, new consent must be obtained.

2. California Consumer Privacy Act (CCPA) – United States (California)

The **CCPA**, effective from January 2020, offers California residents strong data rights similar in spirit to GDPR, though with a slightly different scope and structure.

Key Features:

- Consumers have the right to know **what data** is being collected about them and **why**.
- Right to **request deletion** of personal data.
- Right to **opt-out** of the sale of personal data to third parties.

- Businesses must disclose data collection practices in **clear, non-technical language**.

Example: A California-based user can demand an e-commerce company disclose the complete profile it has built based on their browsing and shopping habits. The user may also choose to stop the company from selling that profile to advertisers.

3. Health Insurance Portability and Accountability Act (HIPAA) – United States

HIPAA, enacted in 1996, specifically governs how health-related data is handled in the U.S. It primarily applies to healthcare providers, insurers, and their business associates.

Key Features:

- Defines **Protected Health Information (PHI)** and requires that it be kept confidential and secure.
- Ensures that **access to patient data is restricted** to authorized personnel.
- Patients must provide **informed consent** before their health data is used beyond clinical purposes.
- Organizations must implement **technical and administrative safeguards**, such as encryption and audit trails.

Example: If a hospital wants to use patient data for an AI-driven clinical trial, they must first anonymize the data or obtain patient consent. A failure to do this could result in legal penalties and loss of trust.

4. The Artificial Intelligence Act (AI Act) – *European Union (Proposed)*

The **AI Act**, introduced by the European Commission in 2021, is the world's first major legislative proposal aimed at regulating AI systems comprehensively based on their **potential risk**.

Key Features:

- **Risk-based classification**: AI systems are categorized as minimal-risk, limited-risk, high-risk, or unacceptable-risk.
- **High-risk systems** (e.g., facial recognition, biometric ID, and credit scoring) must meet stringent requirements related to:
  - **Bias mitigation**
  - **Transparency and explainability**
  - **Human oversight**
  - **Robustness and security**
- Systems deemed **unacceptable risk** (e.g., social scoring) may be banned outright.

Example: A firm offering AI-driven hiring platforms in the EU must prove that its algorithm does not discriminate based on race, gender, or nationality and that candidates can understand how decisions were made.

Challenges in Regulation

Despite the development of these comprehensive laws, several challenges persist in regulating data ethics effectively:

1. Rapid Technological Advancement

Technology often outpaces lawmaking. AI tools evolve faster than legal systems can adapt, leaving **regulatory gaps** around novel applications like:

- Generative AI
- Autonomous decision-making
- Real-time biometric tracking

These gaps can allow unethical uses of data to go unchallenged, at least temporarily.

2. Global Inconsistencies

Data ethics laws differ widely across regions, making it difficult for international companies to maintain uniform compliance.

Example:

- A U.S.-based tech firm may legally process consumer data under U.S. laws but violate GDPR standards if it serves European customers.
- China's **Personal Information Protection Law (PIPL)** has stricter rules on cross-border data transfer, conflicting with U.S. practices.

This **regulatory patchwork** creates legal ambiguity and increases compliance costs, while sometimes leaving ethical considerations fragmented or secondary.

3. Enforcement and Accountability

Even where laws exist, enforcement can be inconsistent. Smaller organizations may lack resources to comply, and regulators may struggle to audit complex AI systems.

Example: Algorithms used in predictive policing or hiring may pass compliance checks on paper but still reproduce bias in practice if oversight is weak or audits are infrequent.

The rise of data science has led to the implementation of important legal frameworks aimed at protecting personal rights and promoting ethical practices. Regulations like GDPR, CCPA, HIPAA, and the upcoming EU AI Act are shaping how organizations build and manage data-driven systems. However, the **true challenge lies not only in compliance** but in developing **globally coherent, forward-looking, and enforceable ethical standards**.

To meet this challenge, organizations must take proactive steps—going beyond what the law mandates—to ensure fairness, transparency, accountability, and respect for human dignity in their data practices. By aligning legal compliance with ethical intent, the data science community can build trust and drive innovation responsibly.

11.2 Aligning Practice with Local and Global Norms

Aligning data science practices with both local and global norms is crucial for building ethical, responsible, and legally compliant systems. While legal regulations such as the **General Data Protection Regulation (GDPR)** and **California Consumer Privacy Act (CCPA)** provide concrete frameworks, effective ethical alignment requires going a step further. Organizations must consider **regional legal systems, cultural expectations**, and **international ethical standards** to ensure they operate responsibly across borders.

Local Norms and Legal Systems

In different parts of the world, the perception of data ethics—especially around privacy, consent, and control—varies widely. These differences are often shaped by history, governance models, and cultural values. For a data science practice to be ethical, it must **respect and reflect local laws and cultural sensitivities**.

1. Cultural Sensitivity

Cultural norms significantly influence what is considered ethical or acceptable in data usage. Privacy, for example, may be viewed as a basic human right in some regions and as a matter of national interest in others.

- **Western Countries (e.g., U.S., EU):**
  These countries tend to prioritize individual privacy. Laws such as GDPR and CCPA stem from a deep-seated belief in personal autonomy and data sovereignty.
  - *Example:* In the U.S., companies must inform users about the collection of personal data and provide opt-out options, especially in sectors like advertising.
- **Asian Countries (e.g., China, Singapore):**
  Governments may take a more **state-centric** approach to data, emphasizing control and surveillance for reasons like national security, economic planning, or social stability.
  - *Example:* In China, real-name registration and state surveillance programs are legally supported, reflecting a different balance between personal privacy and national interests.

Key Consideration for Practitioners:
Data scientists must **understand and adapt to the expectations of the users they serve**.

This might involve adjusting consent mechanisms, transparency efforts, or data sharing policies based on cultural norms.

2. Data Localization Laws

Some countries enforce **data localization**, which requires companies to store and process specific types of data within the country's borders. These laws are driven by concerns around **national security**, **economic control**, and **digital sovereignty**.

- **Example – Russia:**
  The Russian government requires that data about Russian citizens be stored on servers located in Russia. This has prompted compliance issues for global tech companies like LinkedIn, which was banned after failing to comply.
- **Example – China:**
  China's **Cybersecurity Law** mandates that "critical information infrastructure" operators must store personal and important data within the country. Cross-border data transfer is allowed only after passing government security assessments.

Implication:
Companies operating in multiple countries face **technical and legal challenges**, such as:

- Maintaining separate data infrastructures.
- Navigating compliance with conflicting legal regimes.
- Dealing with regulatory uncertainty and enforcement variability.

Global Norms and International Collaboration

While local norms govern domestic operations, **global ethical principles** help promote consistency, trust, and fairness in the international landscape. Several international efforts have emerged to bridge regulatory gaps and **establish common ground for ethical AI and data practices**.

1. OECD AI Guidelines

The **OECD's Principles on Artificial Intelligence** provide globally recognized standards for trustworthy AI. They are designed to be flexible enough to accommodate local laws while encouraging shared values.

Key Principles:

- AI should benefit people and the planet.
- AI systems must respect the rule of law, human rights, and democratic values.
- Transparency, explainability, and accountability are essential.
- Robust safety and security standards should be in place.
- AI actors should be held responsible for proper functioning throughout the AI lifecycle.

Example:
An AI system used for loan approvals must be **explainable** so regulators and users can understand how decisions are made, especially if the applicant is denied credit.

2. United Nations' Ethical Guidelines for Digital Cooperation

The **UN High-Level Panel on Digital Cooperation** emphasizes the importance of inclusivity, equity, and sustainable development in the digital age.

Key Focus Areas:

- Bridging the digital divide and promoting data equity.
- Ensuring responsible data governance, particularly in vulnerable or underdeveloped regions.
- Promoting the ethical use of data and AI to uphold human dignity.

Example:
A tech company collecting data from users in sub-Saharan Africa should ensure the **benefits of data use are shared**, and that data isn't exploited without consent or value return to the community.

3. APEC Cross-Border Privacy Rules (CBPR)

The **Asia-Pacific Economic Cooperation (APEC)** developed the **CBPR system** to address the challenge of maintaining **data privacy in international commerce**.

Purpose:

- Allow cross-border data flows while ensuring a baseline of privacy protection.
- Create a system of mutual recognition between member countries.

Example:
A U.S. company certified under CBPR can transfer user data to Japan without facing complex compliance challenges, provided privacy standards are upheld consistently in both countries.

Challenges in Aligning with Multiple Norms

1. **Conflicting Legal Requirements**
   For instance, GDPR may prohibit certain types of surveillance, while local laws in another country may mandate them. Navigating such conflicts requires **careful legal planning and ethical judgment**.
2. **Ethical Trade-offs**
   What is ethical in one context may be considered unethical elsewhere. For example, using AI to analyze student performance may be seen as helpful in one country and as an invasion of privacy in another.
3. **Resource Inequality**
   Low-income countries may lack the infrastructure to implement strict data governance, putting them at risk of **digital exploitation** by powerful multinational firms.

To practice ethically in a globalized world, data scientists and organizations must understand and respect **both local customs and international principles**. Aligning with local norms ensures **cultural and legal relevance**, while aligning with global norms promotes **trust, fairness, and consistency** across borders.

Ethical data science requires:

- **Cultural intelligence**
- **Legal awareness**
- **Commitment to global values** like transparency, equity, and accountability

By navigating these complexities thoughtfully, organizations can foster responsible innovation that respects human rights and earns societal trust, no matter where they operate.

11.3 Bridging Legal Requirements and Moral Responsibility

In the field of data science, **legal compliance** and **moral responsibility** often intersect—but they are not the same. Laws provide the **minimum standard** of acceptable behavior, while ethics invite professionals to consider what is **right and just**, even in the absence of regulation. As data-driven technologies affect more aspects of daily life—from hiring to healthcare, credit scoring to criminal justice—**bridging the gap between what is legal and what is ethical** becomes increasingly important.

Legal vs. Moral Responsibility

1. Minimum Legal Standards: The Compliance Baseline

Laws like the **GDPR**, **CCPA**, and **HIPAA** set important foundations:

- Mandating user consent.
- Ensuring data transparency.
- Protecting personal data from misuse.

However, legal compliance doesn't necessarily equate to **ethical behavior**. Companies may still exploit **gray areas** to act in ways that technically follow the law but go against user interests or public good.

Example: Dark Patterns

- A company may **legally obtain user consent** for data collection under GDPR.

- But they might use **dark patterns**—manipulative interface designs—to pressure or trick users into consenting.
- While legal, this undermines **informed consent**, violating ethical norms of autonomy and respect.

2. Ethical Considerations Beyond the Law

Ethical responsibility means **going beyond what the law requires**—adopting practices that prioritize **fairness, human dignity, and long-term societal benefit**.

Example: Fairness in AI

- No law may *require* you to mitigate algorithmic bias—especially if the model is legally compliant and technically sound.
- But an ethically responsible company may choose to:
    - Test for disparate impact.
    - Apply fairness constraints.
    - Retrain models using more inclusive datasets.
- This helps ensure that **marginalized or vulnerable groups are not unfairly impacted**, even in legally compliant systems.

Accountability and Transparency

Both law and ethics emphasize the need for **clear oversight**, **traceability**, and **responsibility** in data science operations. Accountability is not just about being punished when something goes wrong—it's about ensuring that **those responsible for data-driven decisions can explain and justify them**.

1. Ethical Audits

An **ethical audit** is a proactive process in which organizations examine their systems—especially AI and machine learning models—for potential risks related to:

- Bias

- Lack of explainability
- Discriminatory outcomes
- Violations of user autonomy

Unlike legal audits (which check for regulatory violations), ethical audits assess a system's **alignment with moral values and social equity**.

Example: AI in Financial Services

- A bank using machine learning to approve loans may find that its algorithm, though legally compliant, disproportionately rejects applicants from low-income neighborhoods.
- An ethical audit might:
    - Investigate the **training data** for historical bias.
    - Adjust decision thresholds to promote **equal opportunity**.
    - Provide transparent reasoning for each decision (model explainability).

This process demonstrates a **commitment to fairness and equity**, not just legality.

Why the Gap Matters

Bridging the legal-ethical gap is essential because:

1. **Laws Lag Behind Technology**
    - Rapid advancements in AI and big data mean that laws often **don't catch up in time** to address new ethical dilemmas (e.g., generative AI, deepfakes, biometric surveillance).
    - By the time a legal framework exists, **harm may already be done**.
2. **Ethical Lapses Damage Trust**
    - Even if a company follows all regulations, unethical practices (e.g., exploiting user data for manipulation) can lead to **public backlash**, brand damage, and loss of user trust.
    - Trust is a **competitive advantage** in data science.
3. **Global Operation Requires Broader Vision**

- Laws vary widely by region, but ethical standards—like fairness, respect, transparency—can serve as **unifying principles** for global teams and systems.

Toward a Culture of Ethical Responsibility

To move beyond checkbox compliance, organizations must foster a **culture of ethics** that permeates technical development, business strategy, and day-to-day decision-making.

Best Practices:

- **Integrate ethics into design reviews** and development workflows.
- **Provide training** for data scientists and developers on fairness, transparency, and accountability.
- **Create internal reporting systems** where employees can flag ethical concerns without fear.
- **Publish ethical impact assessments** to remain transparent with users and regulators.

In the realm of data science, doing what is **legal** is not always the same as doing what is **right**. While laws are vital to set clear rules and boundaries, ethical responsibility demands that organizations think **proactively** and **holistically** about the consequences of their data use.

True ethical leadership in data science means:

- **Anticipating harm**, not just reacting to it.
- **Taking accountability**, even when no law demands it.
- **Designing systems that serve people first**, not just profits or performance metrics.

By aligning legal compliance with **moral integrity**, data science practitioners and organizations can build technologies that are not only **innovative** but also **trustworthy, just, and socially responsible**.

Summary

As data science increasingly influences critical decisions across industries, there is a growing need to balance legal compliance with ethical responsibility. Laws provide the foundational rules, but ethical considerations demand a deeper commitment to fairness, privacy, accountability, and social good.

Overview of Data Ethics Regulations

Governments and organizations worldwide have introduced laws to protect individuals from the misuse of data. Key regulations include:

- **GDPR (EU)**: Ensures user consent, data minimization, and the right to be forgotten. Promotes transparency and accountability.
- **CCPA (California)**: Grants users rights to access, delete, and opt out of personal data sharing.
- **HIPAA (U.S.)**: Protects the privacy and security of healthcare data, requiring strict access control and encryption.
- **EU AI Act**: Classifies AI systems by risk level and imposes rigorous transparency and safety standards on high-risk applications.

Challenges:

- Technology evolves faster than regulations.
- Global inconsistencies create complexity for international companies.
- Laws may not address all ethical dimensions of AI and data usage.

Aligning Practice with Local and Global Norms

To ensure ethical data use, organizations must respect both **local cultural expectations** and **universal ethical principles**:

- **Local Norms**: Vary by region; for example, Western countries often emphasize individual privacy, while others prioritize national security.

- **Data Localization**: Some countries (e.g., Russia, China) require personal data to be stored within national borders, challenging global companies.
- **Global Norms**:
    - **OECD Guidelines** promote transparency, fairness, and accountability in AI.
    - **UN Ethical Principles** stress data equity, inclusion, and protection of human rights.
    - **APEC Privacy Framework** supports cross-border data transfers with privacy safeguards.

Bridging Legal Requirements and Moral Responsibility

Legal compliance sets the **minimum standard**, while **moral responsibility** calls for organizations to proactively prevent harm, ensure fairness, and build public trust.

1. **Legal ≠ Ethical**
    - Meeting legal standards doesn't guarantee ethical behavior. Ethical design requires going beyond what is legally required.
2. **Moral Responsibility**
    - Involves implementing fairness, inclusivity, and transparency, even if not mandated by law.
3. **Ethical Audits**
    - Assess AI systems for bias, fairness, and societal impact, complementing legal reviews.
4. **Laws Lag Behind Tech**
    - New technologies often emerge faster than regulation, creating ethical gray areas.
5. **Public Trust is at Risk**
    - Ethical failures—even if legal—can damage reputation and credibility (e.g., Facebook-Cambridge Analytica).
6. **Consistency Across Borders**
    - A global ethical approach ensures fair practices even in countries with weak or conflicting laws.
7. **Culture of Ethics**

- Embedding ethics into team culture, rewarding responsible behavior, and encouraging whistleblowing strengthen organizational integrity.

Final Takeaway

To responsibly navigate the fast-paced world of data science and AI:

- **Legal compliance is essential**—but **not enough**.
- Ethical leadership ensures that data systems are designed and deployed with **human dignity, fairness, and trust** in mind.
- Organizations that embed **both legal and moral frameworks** will lead the way in building a just, equitable digital future.

As data science continues to evolve, it is increasingly crucial to balance legal compliance with moral responsibility. Laws like the GDPR, CCPA, and AI regulations provide necessary frameworks for data protection, but ethical considerations demand that organizations go beyond these legal boundaries to protect individuals' rights, foster inclusivity, and promote fairness. Aligning practices with both local and global norms ensures that data science contributes to societal progress while minimizing harm. By bridging the gap between legal requirements and moral responsibility, data scientists and organizations can contribute to a more equitable and just digital world.

Check your Understanding

1. The ______ stands for ______, a regulation in the European Union focused on data privacy.
2. The ______ is the ______, a law designed to protect the privacy rights of California residents.
3. ______ refers to systematic errors in algorithms that can result in unfair treatment of certain groups.
4. A ______ is responsible for ensuring compliance with data protection laws within an organization.
5. ______ is the process of obtaining permission from individuals before collecting or using their personal data.
6. The ______ proposed by the ______ aims to regulate artificial intelligence based on its risk levels.
7. ______ laws require that certain types of data be stored and processed within the jurisdiction of a specific country.
8. ______ refers to the movement of personal data between countries or regions.
9. ______ in AI systems refers to making the functioning of algorithms understandable and accessible to users.
10. ______ is a principle that mandates the inclusion of privacy considerations from the very beginning of system design.
11. The ______ is part of the ______, allowing individuals to request the deletion of their personal data.
12. ______ is the process of removing identifiable information from datasets to protect user privacy.
13. The ______ for Artificial Intelligence emphasize principles like ______, ______, and ______.
14. ______ are design strategies that manipulate users into making decisions they did not intend.
15. The ______ is a U.S. regulation that governs the privacy of ______ data.
16. ______ help ensure that AI systems operate in a ______ and ______ manner.

17. ______ responsibility in data science goes beyond legal compliance and ensures data practices do not cause harm to individuals.
18. ______ (AI) is a field that aims to create machines capable of performing tasks that normally require human intelligence.
19. ______ mandates that companies must inform individuals about the ______ of collecting their personal data.
20. ______ in data can occur if the dataset used for training an algorithm is not representative of all relevant ______ groups.

Short Answer Questions

1. What is the primary purpose of the GDPR?
2. Define "informed consent" in the context of data privacy.
3. What does "algorithmic bias" mean, and why is it problematic?
4. List two main responsibilities of a Data Protection Officer (DPO).
5. What is the significance of transparency in AI systems?
6. How does privacy by design differ from privacy by default?
7. What are "dark patterns" in user interface design, and why should they be avoided?
8. Explain the concept of data localization.
9. What is the role of the OECD in AI regulation?
10. What does the right to be forgotten entail under GDPR?

Long Answer Questions

1. Discuss the key features of the GDPR and how it influences the way organizations handle personal data. What challenges do businesses face when ensuring compliance with this regulation?
2. Compare and contrast the CCPA and GDPR in terms of their scope, enforcement, and consumer rights. How do these two laws shape the way companies approach data protection?

3. Explain what algorithmic bias is and provide real-world examples where algorithmic bias has led to unfair outcomes. What steps can organizations take to address these biases in AI systems?
4. Analyze the ethical implications of dark patterns in user interface design. How do dark patterns manipulate users, and what should organizations do to ensure ethical user interface practices?
5. Evaluate the role of a Data Protection Officer (DPO) within an organization. What skills and qualifications are necessary for a DPO to effectively oversee compliance with data protection laws?
6. Explore the ethical challenges that arise from cross-border data transfers. How can organizations balance the need for global data flow with the protection of user privacy?
7. Discuss the concept of privacy by design and privacy by default. How can organizations incorporate these principles into the development of their data handling practices?
8. Evaluate the potential impact of the AI Act proposed by the EU. How would such regulations influence the development and deployment of AI technologies, and what are the potential challenges and benefits?
9. Discuss the importance of conducting ethical audits for AI systems. How can organizations ensure that their AI systems are fair, transparent, and accountable through these audits?
10. Describe the relationship between legal compliance and ethical responsibility in data science. How can organizations go beyond meeting legal requirements to ensure they act responsibly in the collection and use of data?

Answers

Fill in the Blanks

1. GDPR, General Data Protection Regulation
2. CCPA, California Consumer Privacy Act
3. Algorithmic bias
4. Data Protection Officer (DPO)
5. Informed consent
6. AI Act, European Union
7. Data localization

8. Cross-border data transfer
9. Transparency
10. Privacy by design
11. Right to be forgotten, GDPR
12. Data anonymization
13. OECD Guidelines, fairness, accountability, transparency
14. Dark patterns
15. HIPAA, healthcare
16. Ethical audits, fair, transparent
17. Ethical responsibility
18. Artificial Intelligence (AI)
19. GDPR, purpose
20. Bias in data, demographic

Short Answer – Answers Only

1. The GDPR is designed to protect the personal data and privacy of individuals in the EU and gives them control over how their data is collected, stored, and used.
2. Informed consent means users are clearly informed about what data is being collected, how it will be used, and have the freedom to agree or decline.
3. Algorithmic bias is a systemic issue where an algorithm produces unfair results due to biased training data or flawed assumptions, often harming marginalized groups.
4. A DPO ensures that the organization complies with data protection laws and advises on privacy strategies and assessments to minimize data risks.
5. Transparency ensures that users can understand how AI systems make decisions, which increases accountability and trust.
6. Privacy by design means embedding privacy into the system architecture from the start, while privacy by default means settings are pre-configured to protect user data automatically.
7. Dark patterns are misleading design tactics that trick users into actions they might not want to take, such as sharing data or buying services, and they are unethical.

8. Data localization requires data to be stored and processed within a specific country's borders to ensure privacy and national security.
9. The OECD provides ethical AI guidelines focusing on fairness, accountability, transparency, and the promotion of beneficial outcomes for society.
10. The right to be forgotten allows individuals to request deletion of their personal data from a company's system when it's no longer necessary or relevant.

Long Answer – Answers Only

1. GDPR introduces rights like consent, data access, and erasure, ensuring user control and data transparency. It applies to all organizations handling EU citizens' data. Compliance challenges include resource costs, legal complexities, managing data subject rights, and ensuring international data transfer compliance.
2. GDPR is broader in scope and emphasizes consent, while CCPA focuses on consumer rights like access and opt-out from data selling. Both require businesses to improve transparency and control, but GDPR imposes heavier penalties. These laws push global organizations toward better data practices.
3. Algorithmic bias can lead to unfair treatment in hiring, policing, or credit scoring. Examples include biased facial recognition or resume screening tools. Mitigation includes diverse datasets, regular audits, fairness-aware algorithms, and inclusion of ethical oversight during development.
4. Dark patterns exploit users by hiding choices or misleading them, such as automatically opting them into data sharing. Ethical UI design should prioritize honesty, clarity, and autonomy. Organizations should avoid manipulative designs and prioritize user welfare and informed decision-making.
5. A DPO manages data protection compliance and advises on risks and assessments. Required skills include legal expertise, IT understanding, and strong communication. Certifications like CIPP/E enhance credibility. DPOs bridge gaps between technical, legal, and organizational privacy responsibilities.
6. Cross-border data transfer risks include lower protection standards and legal conflicts. Ethical handling requires encryption, legal contracts like SCCs, and compliance with

global laws. Companies must assess third-party vendors and secure consent for international data sharing.

7. Privacy by design embeds protection early in system creation, while privacy by default enforces strong settings without user action. Examples include limiting data collection, offering opt-in features, and encrypting data. These principles ensure compliance and user respect.
8. The AI Act introduces rules based on AI risk levels. Benefits include increased trust, legal clarity, and reduced harm. Challenges include regulatory burden, cost of compliance, and slower innovation. Businesses must prepare for risk classification and documentation.
9. Ethical audits review AI for bias, transparency, and compliance. They involve testing outputs, reviewing training data, involving stakeholders, and adjusting models as needed. Fairness can be ensured by ongoing monitoring, documenting processes, and involving third-party reviewers.
10. Legal compliance is the baseline, while ethical responsibility addresses fairness, dignity, and long-term social impact. Going beyond the law involves prioritizing user rights, avoiding harmful practices, and fostering an internal culture focused on ethics and accountability.

Chapter 12: Fostering Ethical Awareness in Organizations

Learning outcomes

1. Define the concept of ethical data use and its importance within an organization.
2. Identify key components required to establish a culture of ethical awareness in data practices.
3. Describe the role and significance of ethics training for data professionals.
4. Explain the accountability mechanisms that contribute to ethical behavior at all organizational levels

Introduction

In today's data-driven world, ethical data use is no longer a nice-to-have—it is a strategic imperative. As organizations increasingly rely on data to power decision-making, innovation, and customer engagement, the ethical implications of how data is collected, processed, and shared have become more critical than ever. Beyond complying with regulations, companies must build a culture where ethical principles are embedded in every layer of their operations. This chapter explores how organizations can create such a culture by focusing on three key pillars: cultivating ethical awareness, providing targeted ethics training for data professionals, and establishing clear systems of accountability. Through practical strategies and real-world examples, we'll examine how ethical data practices not only safeguard individual rights and build public trust, but also drive long-term business success and resilience.

12.1 Creating a Culture of Ethical Data Use

Establishing a culture where **ethical data use** is prioritized is essential for organizations aiming to foster **public trust**, achieve **regulatory compliance**, and encourage **sustainable innovation**. A culture rooted in ethics goes beyond rule-following—it builds a shared organizational mindset that anticipates and addresses the moral implications of data-driven decisions.

🔍 Key Components of an Ethical Data Culture

1. **Leadership Commitment**

Strong ethical cultures begin at the top. Leadership must actively **champion ethical data use** by setting expectations, modeling integrity, and reinforcing data governance as a strategic priority.

- Executives and managers should make ethics a standing agenda item in decision-making.
- Leaders must allocate resources to ethics training, risk assessments, and oversight mechanisms.

Impact: When ethical values are visibly upheld by leadership, they cascade throughout the organization, fostering a sense of shared responsibility.

2. Clear Ethical Guidelines

An organization-wide **code of ethics** should clearly define what constitutes acceptable and unacceptable behavior when collecting, using, and sharing data.

- These guidelines should cover principles such as **data privacy**, **informed consent**, **non-discrimination**, **accountability**, and **transparency**.
- Guidelines must be accessible and easily understandable to all employees, not just technical staff or legal teams.

Tip: Periodically update the code of ethics to reflect new risks, technologies, and societal expectations.

3. Open Communication Channels

Creating an environment where employees feel safe to raise concerns, ask questions, or report ethical dilemmas is crucial.

- Regular **ethics forums**, **team check-ins**, and **internal newsletters** can support open dialogue.
- Establish anonymous reporting systems or designated ethics officers who can handle concerns confidentially and professionally.

Benefit: Encouraging candid conversations fosters early identification of risks and enables collaborative problem-solving.

4. **Integration into Daily Operations**

Ethics shouldn't be treated as an afterthought or separate function—it must be **embedded into daily workflows**.

- Integrate ethical reviews into **project planning**, **model development**, and **user experience design**.
- Encourage teams to apply tools like **ethical impact assessments**, **bias detection models**, and **data usage checklists** throughout the product lifecycle.

Result: Ethical awareness becomes routine, not reactive, helping teams spot potential issues before they escalate.

5. Continuous Evaluation and Improvement

Ethical practices must evolve alongside technology. Organizations should implement regular **audits**, collect **employee and user feedback**, and stay updated on global ethical frameworks and legal standards.

- Use third-party assessments or internal review boards to evaluate systems for fairness and privacy.
- Encourage a **feedback culture** where lessons learned from failures or near misses are used to strengthen future practices.

Outcome: Continuous improvement ensures relevance, resilience, and long-term ethical integrity.

Real-World Example: Olay's "Decode the Bias" Campaign

In 2021, skincare brand **Olay** partnered with the **Algorithmic Justice League** and **O'Neil Risk Consulting & Algorithmic Auditing** to assess its AI-powered **Skin Advisor System** for algorithmic bias.

- The audit revealed the system performed better for lighter skin tones and younger users, indicating a lack of diverse training data.
- In response, Olay:
  - Adjusted its algorithm to better serve users of all skin types and ages.
  - Launched initiatives to promote **diversity in AI and STEM**, especially among women and people of color.

Why it matters: Olay's proactive response highlights how companies can take **constructive action** when faced with ethical challenges. It also reinforces the value of transparency and community engagement in restoring trust.

Building a culture of ethical data use isn't a one-time project—it's an ongoing commitment that touches every part of an organization. By aligning leadership, guidelines, communication, operations, and evaluation, companies can create systems that not only meet legal requirements but also **earn public trust and contribute to societal well-being**.

12.2 Ethics Training for Data Professionals

As data science becomes more deeply embedded in decision-making, it's essential that professionals are not only technically skilled but also ethically aware. An effective ethics training program helps data practitioners **identify risks**, **navigate ethical dilemmas**, and **make responsible decisions** that align with both legal and societal expectations.

Key Components of an Effective Ethics Training Program

1. Role-Based Training

Training should be customized to fit different job functions within the organization.

- **Why it matters**: Each role encounters unique ethical challenges.
- **Examples**:
  - **Data Scientists**: Focus on fairness, bias detection, and model explainability.
  - **Marketing Teams**: Concentrate on privacy, consent, and user trust.
  - **Product Managers**: Learn to balance ethical impact with business goals.

2. Real-World Scenarios

Use practical case studies and historical incidents to illustrate the consequences of ethical decisions—both good and bad.

- **Benefits**:
  - Encourages critical thinking.
  - Highlights the real impact on users, society, and business.
- **Examples**:
  - Facebook–Cambridge Analytica for privacy misuse.
  - Amazon's biased hiring algorithm for AI fairness failure.

3. Interactive Learning

Moving beyond lectures, effective ethics training includes active participation.

- **Methods**:
  - Simulations of ethical dilemmas.
  - Scenario-based quizzes.
  - Role-playing and group discussions.
- **Why it works**: Engaging formats improve retention and participation.

4. Continuous Education

Ethical norms and regulatory frameworks evolve quickly.

- **Approach**:
  - Provide refresher training annually or bi-annually.

- Share updates via newsletters or ethics briefings.
    - Organize periodic ethics "lunch & learns."
- **Result**: Professionals stay current with best practices and changing laws (like GDPR, CCPA, or the AI Act).

5. ☑ **Evaluation and Feedback**

Review the effectiveness of the training programs to continuously improve them.

- **Tactics**:
    - Collect participant feedback post-training.
    - Use short assessments to test learning.
    - Measure outcomes through behavior or compliance metrics.

☆ Best Practices in Ethics Training

- **Ongoing, Bite-Sized Learning**
  – Regular, shorter sessions (e.g., monthly 1-hour discussions) are more effective than one-off long seminars.
- **Applied, Realistic Activities**
  – Let employees work through challenges the organization could realistically face.
- **Executive Involvement**
  – Senior leadership should be part of the training process to:
    - Set an example
    - Show commitment
    - Address questions and concerns openly

Real-World Example: University of Melbourne's Ethics Education

The **University of Melbourne** offers professional development courses focused on topics like:

- **AI ethics**
- **Responsible innovation**

- **Inclusive leadership**

These courses help leaders apply ethical frameworks in practical situations, reinforcing governance and data responsibility across sectors such as healthcare, education, and government.

Ethics training for data professionals is no longer optional—it's a **core part of modern digital literacy**. By tailoring programs to roles, using engaging formats, and involving leadership, organizations can develop teams that **not only comply with the law but also uphold public trust and do the right thing.**

12.3 Encouraging Accountability at Every Level

Accountability is crucial in ensuring that all individuals and teams uphold ethical standards and remain responsible for their actions and decisions. This fosters a culture of trust, integrity, and ethical responsibility within organizations.

Strategies to Promote Accountability:

1. Clear Expectations

- **Establish and Communicate Ethical Standards:** Clearly define the ethical responsibilities and expectations for all individuals within the organization. This ensures everyone understands their role in maintaining ethical practices.
- **Actionable Example:** Create a detailed code of ethics that is regularly communicated to all employees.

2. Transparent Processes

- **Implement Transparent Decision-Making:** Make decision-making processes clear and accessible to all stakeholders. Transparency allows individuals to understand the rationale behind decisions and ensures actions are justified.
- **Actionable Example:** Publicly share how key decisions, such as data collection methods or algorithmic models, are made and the ethical considerations involved.

3. Regular Audits

- **Conduct Periodic Audits of Data Practices:** Regular audits help identify potential ethical or compliance issues. They also ensure that data practices align with legal and organizational standards.
- **Actionable Example:** Schedule regular audits to assess data usage and decision-making processes, ensuring compliance with ethical standards.

4. Whistleblower Protections

- **Provide Mechanisms for Reporting Unethical Behavior:** Establish safe, confidential channels for employees to report unethical actions or violations. Protecting whistleblowers ensures that individuals can uphold ethical standards without fear of retaliation.
- **Actionable Example:** Create an anonymous reporting system or hotline to report unethical behavior, ensuring employees feel safe in doing so.

5. Recognition and Consequences

- **Recognize Ethical Behavior and Address Unethical Actions:** Reinforce the importance of accountability by acknowledging individuals or teams who demonstrate ethical conduct. Conversely, ensure that unethical actions are addressed promptly and fairly.
- **Actionable Example:** Implement a reward system for teams that uphold ethical practices and ensure that there are clear consequences for violations.

Real-World Example: Data Governance at a Financial Institution

- A **financial institution** implemented a **comprehensive data governance framework**, setting clear roles and responsibilities for data handling.
- The framework included **regular audits** and ensured that decision-making was transparent.
- Employees were encouraged to report data issues anonymously, and those following data policies were recognized and rewarded.

- This approach fostered a **culture of accountability**, improving overall data management practices and ensuring compliance with ethical standards.

more **detailed suggestions** and **real-world examples** to further explore how to implement these accountability strategies effectively within an organization:

1. Clear Expectations

- **Detailed Implementation:**
    - **Develop a Code of Ethics**: Write a comprehensive and accessible code of ethics that includes specific data-related ethical standards (e.g., data privacy, algorithmic fairness). This should be a living document, regularly reviewed and updated.
    - **Onboarding and Ongoing Training**: Integrate the code of ethics into new employee onboarding and provide periodic ethics training sessions.
    - **Regular Communication**: Keep ethical standards top of mind through newsletters, town halls, and internal communication platforms to ensure they are always a focus.
- **Real-World Example:**
  Salesforce: Salesforce has built its ethical framework around the concept of trust, with a strong emphasis on transparency. They regularly hold "Trust" meetings where data governance and ethical behavior are emphasized, and they clearly communicate ethical expectations to their employees.

2. Transparent Processes

- **Detailed Implementation:**
    - **Open Decision-Making Frameworks**: Publish the decision-making criteria for important data-related processes. For instance, if you're developing an AI model, ensure that stakeholders are aware of the criteria used to select the data and algorithms.

- **Documented Processes**: Develop documentation for data handling procedures, including consent processes, data usage, and data sharing practices. This allows teams to review and understand the rationale behind each action.
- **Stakeholder Engagement**: Invite feedback from external stakeholders, such as customers or third-party auditors, to review processes and ensure transparency.

- **Real-World Example:**
  IBM: IBM is known for its commitment to transparency, especially in the field of AI. IBM publishes detailed whitepapers on its AI models, explaining how they are developed, tested, and deployed. Their **AI Fairness 360 toolkit** is an example of how they ensure that AI algorithms are transparent and auditable.

3. Regular Audits

- **Detailed Implementation:**
  - **Scheduled Internal Audits**: Set up a regular schedule for auditing data practices, from data collection to processing and storage. This can involve checking for algorithmic biases, data accuracy, and compliance with privacy regulations like GDPR.
  - **External Audits**: Periodically engage third-party auditors to assess data practices, ensuring that your internal audits are objective and transparent.
  - **Audit Trail**: Maintain a detailed log of all data handling activities, so auditors and stakeholders can track how data has been used, who accessed it, and for what purpose.
- **Real-World Example:**
  Facebook (Meta): In response to previous data privacy scandals, Facebook implemented a robust auditing system where third-party auditors periodically assess their data privacy and security practices. They also conduct internal audits to ensure compliance with evolving privacy laws like the GDPR.

4. Whistleblower Protections

- **Detailed Implementation:**

- **Anonymous Reporting Systems**: Set up anonymous digital platforms or hotlines where employees can report ethical violations without fear of retaliation.
- **Clear Anti-Retaliation Policies**: Ensure that the company has clear anti-retaliation policies in place. Employees should feel confident that reporting unethical behavior will not lead to negative consequences.
- **Whistleblower Support**: Provide counseling or support for whistleblowers to ensure that they feel safe and empowered to come forward.

- **Real-World Example:**

  Google: Google offers an internal whistleblower program through which employees can report concerns related to unethical activities or breaches of company policy. The company also emphasizes the importance of non-retaliation, and employees are protected from adverse actions when reporting ethical violations.

5. Recognition and Consequences

- **Detailed Implementation:**
    - **Reward Ethical Behavior**: Create a system where employees or teams who demonstrate exemplary ethical behavior are publicly recognized, either through awards, bonuses, or career advancement.
    - **Document Consequences for Violations**: Have a clear, documented set of consequences for employees who violate ethical guidelines. This could range from re-training to disciplinary action, depending on the severity of the infraction.
    - **Publicize Success Stories**: Celebrate and share success stories where ethical behavior led to positive outcomes for the company or customers. This sets a positive example for others to follow.
- **Real-World Example:**

  Patagonia: Patagonia is known for prioritizing environmental and social responsibility. Employees who embody these values are often recognized in front of their peers, and ethical actions are rewarded. The company also holds employees accountable for any actions that may harm their sustainability goals.

Further Suggestions for Encouraging Accountability:

- **Encourage Cross-Functional Accountability:**
  Ensure that different teams—data scientists, marketing, IT, legal, and leadership—work together on ethical initiatives. This encourages a broader understanding and collective responsibility for ethical data use.
- **Leverage Technology to Track Accountability:**
  Use tools like audit logs, machine learning fairness tools (e.g., IBM's AI Fairness 360 or Google's What-If Tool), and compliance management software to automate tracking and accountability. These tools can help ensure that actions are easily traceable and auditable.
- **Empower Employees with Ethical Decision-Making Tools:**
  Provide employees with tools and resources that allow them to make informed ethical decisions. For example, developing a simple checklist or ethical decision-making framework can help guide them when faced with difficult choices.

Final Thoughts on Building a Culture of Accountability:

Promoting accountability within an organization is not just about enforcing compliance but also about fostering an environment where ethical behavior is valued, recognized, and supported at all levels. When employees at all levels are empowered to act ethically and held accountable for their actions, the organization as a whole benefit from increased trust, improved data practices, and a stronger reputation in the marketplace.

Summary

Building accountability in data practices within an organization fosters a culture of integrity, transparency, and trust. By setting clear expectations, encouraging transparency, conducting regular audits, protecting whistleblowers, and recognizing ethical behavior, organizations can ensure responsible data handling and decision-making. Here's a summary of the strategies discussed:

1. **Clear Expectations**:
    - Establish and communicate ethical standards through a code of ethics.
    - Integrate ethical guidelines into employee onboarding, training, and ongoing communication.
2. **Transparent Processes**:
    - Implement open decision-making frameworks to allow stakeholders to understand the rationale behind data-related choices.
    - Maintain thorough documentation of data handling procedures for clarity and review.
3. **Regular Audits**:
    - Conduct periodic audits of data practices to ensure compliance with ethical standards and detect potential issues.
    - Use internal and external auditors to maintain objectivity and transparency.
4. **Whistleblower Protections**:
    - Set up anonymous reporting mechanisms for employees to report unethical behavior without fear of retaliation.
    - Reinforce anti-retaliation policies to protect whistleblowers and ensure safe reporting.
5. **Recognition and Consequences**:
    - Reward employees who demonstrate ethical behavior to promote a culture of accountability.
    - Implement clear, documented consequences for ethical violations to reinforce the importance of adhering to guidelines.

Real-World Examples:

- **Salesforce** emphasizes transparency and trust through regular "Trust" meetings and strong communication of ethical standards.
- **IBM** publishes detailed AI-related whitepapers, ensuring transparency and accountability in their AI practices.
- **Facebook** (Meta) regularly engages third-party auditors to assess their data privacy and security practices.
- **Google** offers whistleblower protection programs to encourage employees to report ethical violations without fear of retaliation.
- **Patagonia** rewards employees who uphold environmental and social responsibility values, emphasizing a culture of ethical behavior.

Promoting accountability ensures that organizations adhere to ethical data practices, avoid legal pitfalls, and maintain customer trust. By encouraging cross-functional collaboration, using technology to track accountability, and providing employees with ethical decision-making tools, organizations can create a culture where ethical data use is prioritized at every level. This ultimately contributes to better data governance and more responsible innovation.

By focusing on these areas, organizations can foster an environment where ethical data use is the norm, data professionals are well-trained in ethical practices, and accountability is upheld at all levels. This holistic approach not only ensures compliance but also builds trust with stakeholders and drives sustainable success.

Check your Understanding

Fill-in-the-Blanks Questions

1. Ethical data use involves respecting individual __________ and ensuring transparency.
2. A culture of __________ data use helps build trust with stakeholders.
3. Leadership plays a key role in setting the __________ for ethical practices.
4. A code of __________ outlines acceptable data handling behaviors.
5. __________ communication enables employees to report ethical concerns.
6. Ethical training should include __________-based learning for different roles.
7. Accountability means taking __________ for one's decisions and actions.
8. Regular __________ help monitor compliance with ethical standards.
9. Whistleblower protection ensures employees can report misconduct without __________.
10. Ethical behavior in data practices supports organizational __________ and sustainability.
11. __________ fairness is a critical topic in data ethics training.
12. __________ by design integrates privacy measures from the beginning.
13. A strong ethical culture reduces legal and reputational __________.
14. Ongoing training ensures professionals are up to date with __________ standards.
15. Open __________ fosters a climate of ethical awareness.
16. Transparent processes build __________ in how decisions are made.
17. Ethics training should include __________ case studies.
18. Data governance frameworks promote ethical data __________.
19. Recognition of ethical behavior reinforces positive __________.
20. Organizations should align their ethical efforts with global __________ and standards.

Short Answer Questions

1. What is meant by ethical data use?
2. List two benefits of creating a culture of ethical awareness.
3. What is the purpose of a code of ethics in an organization?
4. Mention two topics that ethics training for data professionals should cover.
5. Define the term "accountability" in an ethical context.

6. How can leadership influence ethical behavior in organizations?
7. What is the role of audits in maintaining ethical standards?
8. Why is it important to tailor ethics training based on employee roles?
9. What are whistleblower protections, and why are they essential?
10. How do recognition and rewards influence ethical behavior?

Long Answer Questions

1. Discuss how an organization can establish a culture of ethical data use, providing examples.
2. Explain the importance of leadership in modeling and promoting ethical practices across departments.
3. Describe the structure of an effective ethics training program for data professionals.
4. Evaluate how role-specific ethics training helps reduce ethical violations in data handling.
5. Analyze the challenges organizations face when trying to enforce accountability.
6. Propose strategies to ensure transparent communication of ethical concerns within teams.
7. Explain how periodic audits and evaluations contribute to long-term ethical compliance.
8. Assess the impact of ethics training on decision-making in data-intensive roles.
9. Compare reactive versus proactive approaches to ethical data governance.
10. Design a framework that integrates ethical awareness, training, and accountability in an organization.

Answers

Fill in the Blanks

1. privacy
2. ethical
3. tone
4. ethics
5. open
6. role
7. responsibility
8. audits

9. retaliation
10. integrity
11. algorithmic
12. privacy
13. risks
14. ethical
15. dialogue
16. trust
17. real-world
18. management
19. behavior
20. norms

Answer Keys – Short Answer Questions

1. **Ethical data use** means managing data in a way that respects individuals' privacy, ensures fairness, and complies with legal and moral standards.
2. It builds stakeholder trust and minimizes legal and reputational risks.
3. A **code of ethics** provides a framework for employees to understand and follow acceptable behavior when handling data.
4. Topics may include **data privacy**, **algorithmic fairness**, or **responsible AI use**.
5. **Accountability** is the obligation of individuals to answer for their decisions, actions, and the outcomes, especially in ethical matters.
6. Leadership sets the tone for ethical culture by **modeling integrity** and integrating ethics into strategic decisions.
7. Audits help identify unethical practices, ensure compliance, and demonstrate **commitment to accountability**.
8. Different roles handle data differently; tailoring training ensures that each employee understands **specific ethical implications** of their work.
9. **Whistleblower protections** allow employees to safely report unethical behavior without fear of punishment or retaliation.

10. Recognizing and rewarding ethical behavior encourages continued integrity and **reinforces positive organizational norms**.

Answer Keys – Long Answer Questions

1. **Establishing a culture of ethical data use** involves leadership commitment, clear guidelines, regular training, open dialogue, and integrating ethics into all processes. Example: Google's AI Principles guide development to avoid harm and bias.
2. Leaders model behavior, set policy direction, allocate resources for ethics training, and build a culture of transparency. Ethical tone from the top influences team-level practices.
3. Effective ethics training includes modules on privacy, fairness, case studies, interactive activities, and role-specific instruction. It helps employees recognize and handle ethical dilemmas effectively.
4. Role-specific training ensures that employees are equipped with relevant ethical tools. For example, marketing staff focus on consent while engineers address algorithmic bias.
5. Challenges include lack of clarity in roles, weak enforcement, and cultural resistance. Clear guidelines, support systems, and performance metrics can improve accountability.
6. Transparent communication requires safe channels (like anonymous hotlines), open discussion forums, and active encouragement from leadership to report issues.
7. Periodic audits detect unethical behavior, improve data practices, and maintain compliance. They provide insights into gaps and help in continuous improvement.
8. Ethics training helps employees evaluate decisions beyond legality—considering fairness, transparency, and user impact. It strengthens moral reasoning in ambiguous scenarios.
9. **Reactive governance** addresses problems after they occur; **proactive governance** anticipates risks, implements safeguards, and integrates ethics early in development.
10. A strong framework includes leadership advocacy, mandatory ethics training, regular audits, clear reporting channels, and a reward system for ethical behavior.

Chapter 13: The Path Forward: Challenges and Innovations

Learning Objectives

1. Define the key ethical issues related to emerging technologies, such as AI, ML, and blockchain.
2. Identify strategies for proactively addressing future risks associated with technological advancements.
3. Describe the role of continuous monitoring and audits in maintaining ethical standards in new technologies.
4. Explain the importance of sustaining ethical integrity during periods of rapid technological change.

Introduction

As the technological landscape continues to evolve, organizations face new challenges and opportunities in maintaining ethical standards. Emerging technologies bring a host of potential benefits but also introduce complex ethical dilemmas. This section explores the ethical issues surrounding emerging technologies, how to proactively address future risks, and how to sustain ethical integrity in times of rapid change.

Ethics in Emerging Technologies

Emerging technologies such as **Artificial Intelligence (AI)**, **Machine Learning (ML)**, **Blockchain**, and **Quantum Computing** are transforming industries and reshaping how societies function. While these technologies hold immense promise for innovation and solving complex problems, they also introduce new ethical challenges. Addressing these challenges is crucial to ensuring these technologies are used responsibly and equitably.

1. Bias and Fairness in AI and Machine Learning

AI and ML algorithms are only as good as the data they are trained on. If the data contains biases—whether intentional or unintentional—the resulting models can perpetuate or amplify these biases, leading to unfair or discriminatory outcomes.

- **Example**: In 2018, **Amazon** discontinued an AI recruitment tool after discovering it was biased against female candidates. The tool had been trained on resumes submitted over a ten-year period, which were predominantly from male applicants, leading to an algorithm that favored male candidates for technical roles. This is an example of how biased historical data can lead to biased AI decisions, exacerbating gender disparities in hiring.
- **Ethical Challenge**: The risk of reinforcing existing societal biases and unfair practices in hiring, criminal justice, lending, and other critical areas. It is vital to ensure that AI systems are designed to detect, understand, and mitigate biases. Regular audits and fairness metrics can be employed to assess and correct these biases in AI models.

2. Transparency and Accountability

One of the biggest ethical concerns with AI and machine learning, particularly deep learning, is the **lack of transparency** in how decisions are made. Many AI systems are seen as "black boxes" because their decision-making processes are often not easily understood or explained, which raises accountability concerns, especially when things go wrong.

- **Example**: In **2018**, an **autonomous Uber vehicle** struck and killed a pedestrian in Arizona. The vehicle's AI system failed to recognize the pedestrian in time, but the lack of transparency in the decision-making process made it difficult to understand why the AI failed. This lack of clarity raised significant ethical concerns about accountability: who should be held responsible when an autonomous system causes harm?
- **Ethical Challenge**: Ensuring that AI systems are transparent and their decision-making processes can be understood by humans is critical. There needs to be a way

to explain AI decisions, especially in high-stakes environments like healthcare, transportation, and law enforcement. AI companies and developers must create more interpretable models and ensure that systems have built-in accountability mechanisms.

3. Data Privacy and Security

Emerging technologies, particularly AI and the **Internet of Things (IoT)**, collect massive amounts of personal and sensitive data. The way this data is used, stored, and shared introduces significant **privacy concerns**. As technology evolves, so do the risks of **data breaches**, **unauthorized surveillance**, and the **erosion of personal privacy**.

- **Example**: The use of **facial recognition technology** has sparked significant privacy debates. In cities like **San Francisco**, local governments have banned the use of facial recognition by law enforcement due to concerns over surveillance and the potential violation of citizens' privacy. The technology can be used to track individuals without their consent, raising fears of mass surveillance and the infringement of personal rights.
- **Ethical Challenge**: How can we balance the benefits of data collection with the need to protect individual privacy? Ensuring that data is collected and processed with explicit consent, stored securely, and used only for its intended purposes is crucial. Additionally, implementing robust encryption methods and safeguarding against data breaches is essential for maintaining trust in emerging technologies.

4. Autonomy and Human Control

Emerging technologies like **self-driving cars**, **drones**, and **autonomous weapons** raise significant ethical questions about the balance between human control and machine autonomy. The degree to which these systems should be allowed to make independent decisions without human intervention is an ongoing debate.

- **Example**: The ethical debate surrounding **autonomous weapons**—such as drones or AI systems used in military operations—raises serious concerns. In scenarios where these systems make decisions about the use of force, such as targeting and striking individuals, questions arise about accountability and control. Should AI systems be allowed to make life-or-death decisions, or should humans retain the ultimate decision-making power, especially in warfare?

- **Ethical Challenge**: Determining the level of human control necessary for critical decisions in high-risk areas like military warfare, healthcare, and autonomous vehicles. For example, self-driving cars may make decisions about braking or avoiding accidents without human input. However, in life-or-death situations, should humans still have the final say in these decisions? Establishing ethical guidelines and boundaries for autonomous systems is essential to avoid harmful consequences and ensure human oversight.

Emerging technologies offer profound opportunities but also present new ethical dilemmas that must be addressed. The challenges of **bias and fairness**, **transparency and accountability**, **data privacy**, and the balance between **human control and autonomy** require careful consideration and proactive solutions. Companies, governments, and organizations must work together to develop frameworks, guidelines, and regulations that ensure these technologies are used responsibly and ethically. This is vital not only for preventing harm but also for fostering public trust and maximizing the potential benefits of emerging technologies in a fair and just manner.

13.1 Addressing Future Risks Proactively

As technology continues to evolve at a rapid pace, organizations must anticipate and manage potential future risks. To address these risks effectively, companies need a combination of strategic planning, ethical foresight, and collaboration across various sectors. This proactive approach ensures that emerging technologies are not only innovative but also aligned with societal values and ethical standards.

Proactive Strategies for Managing Future Risks

1. Developing Ethical Frameworks for Emerging Technologies

To guide the development and deployment of new technologies, organizations should create or adopt comprehensive ethical frameworks. These frameworks provide clear guidelines on issues such as fairness, transparency, privacy, and accountability, helping organizations navigate the ethical complexities associated with technological innovation.

- **Example**: The **European Union** has proposed ethical guidelines for AI development, emphasizing the need for AI systems to be transparent, accountable, and fair. These guidelines encourage organizations to assess and mitigate risks related to bias, privacy violations, and the misuse of AI technologies.

2. Engaging in Cross-Disciplinary Collaboration

The ethical challenges posed by emerging technologies span multiple fields such as law, economics, sociology, and philosophy. To address these challenges effectively, organizations must collaborate across disciplines. Engaging experts from different sectors ensures that the technology is developed in a way that respects societal values and ethical standards.

- **Example**: In the development of **autonomous vehicles**, collaboration between **engineers**, **ethicists**, **lawmakers**, and **sociologists** is essential to create a safe, fair, and socially acceptable technology. Engineers ensure the vehicle is technically sound, ethicists address concerns like fairness and decision-making in critical situations, lawmakers ensure regulatory compliance, and sociologists consider the societal impacts and public concerns regarding the technology.

3. Implementing Continuous Monitoring and Auditing

Since technologies like **AI** and **blockchain** evolve rapidly, it is crucial to continuously monitor and audit these systems after deployment. Regular audits can help identify risks, biases, and vulnerabilities that may not have been apparent during development. This ongoing evaluation ensures that systems remain aligned with ethical standards and can be updated when new risks emerge.

- **Example**: In **2019**, experts conducted an audit of popular **facial recognition systems** and found that many were less accurate at identifying people with darker skin tones. This bias could lead to discriminatory outcomes, such as misidentifying individuals and disproportionately affecting marginalized communities. Regular audits of such systems are crucial to prevent such biases from perpetuating.

4. Incorporating Ethics in Education and Training

To ensure that future technologies are developed and used responsibly, it is essential to incorporate ethics into the education and training of professionals in fields like **data science**, **engineering**, and **AI**. Equipping technologists with the tools and knowledge to address ethical challenges ensures that innovation is aligned with societal well-being.

- **Example**: The **Massachusetts Institute of Technology (MIT)** offers courses focusing on **AI ethics**, emphasizing the societal impact of AI technologies. These courses equip future technologists with the skills to address ethical issues such as fairness, transparency, and accountability when developing AI systems, ensuring that these technologies are used responsibly.

As emerging technologies continue to reshape the world, addressing future risks proactively is essential. By developing ethical frameworks, fostering cross-disciplinary collaboration, implementing continuous monitoring, and integrating ethics into education and training, organizations can help mitigate potential risks. This approach not only ensures responsible innovation but also promotes the development of technologies that align with societal values, enhancing trust and accountability in the process.

13.2 Sustaining Ethical Integrity in Rapid Change

The rapid pace of technological advancement creates significant challenges for maintaining ethical integrity in organizations. As new technologies emerge, companies must quickly adapt while ensuring their operations and products continue to align with ethical principles. This requires organizations to commit to continuous learning, accountability, and governance. To successfully sustain ethical integrity amid rapid change, organizations must implement strategies that balance innovation with strong ethical considerations.

Strategies for Sustaining Ethical Integrity in Rapid Change

1. Agile Governance Structures

Organizations need flexible governance structures that can adapt swiftly to technological advances. Agile governance ensures that ethical considerations are integrated into every phase of technology development—from initial concept to final deployment. This adaptability helps organizations remain responsive to emerging ethical issues as technologies evolve.

- **Example**: **Microsoft's AI and Ethics committee** reviews all AI projects to ensure they meet ethical guidelines, and it remains flexible enough to adjust these guidelines as technology advances. This ensures that ethical concerns are addressed in real time as new AI technologies are developed.

2. Ethics-Driven Innovation

Ethics-driven innovation involves ensuring that ethical considerations are embedded from the very beginning of the product development process. Organizations must prioritize ethics when designing and developing new technologies, making sure that ethical decision-making is integral to the innovation process.

- **Example**: **IBM's Watson Health division** adopts ethical guidelines to ensure that AI-driven healthcare innovations are transparent, unbiased, and promote fairness. These guidelines help steer the division toward developing health technologies that respect privacy and do not perpetuate inequality.

3. Incorporating Stakeholder Feedback

To maintain ethical integrity, organizations must engage with diverse stakeholders, including consumers, employees, regulatory bodies, and advocacy groups. By gathering feedback from these groups, organizations can identify ethical concerns they may not have anticipated and make adjustments as needed.

- **Example**: **Facebook** has faced significant ethical scrutiny over issues like privacy and content moderation. In response, the company established an **independent oversight board** to address concerns raised by users, experts, and advocacy groups. This approach ensures that ethical concerns are addressed by multiple perspectives, helping improve the platform's ethical standards.

4. Building a Culture of Ethical Leadership

Ethical leadership is crucial for guiding organizations through periods of rapid change. Leaders must set the tone for the organization by demonstrating a commitment to ethics. They should be transparent about challenges, take accountability for mistakes, and prioritize long-term ethical considerations over short-term business gains.

- **Example**: In **2020**, **Patagonia's CEO, Rose Marcario**, publicly committed to sustainability and ethical sourcing despite global supply chain disruptions. Her leadership demonstrated a strong ethical stance, highlighting how the company prioritized ethical values like environmental responsibility, even in challenging times.

Sustaining ethical integrity in the face of rapid technological change requires proactive strategies that incorporate agile governance, ethics-driven innovation, stakeholder engagement, and ethical leadership. Organizations that implement these strategies are better equipped to navigate the challenges posed by new technologies while maintaining a strong ethical foundation. By doing so, they can innovate responsibly, build trust with stakeholders, and contribute to the development of technologies that align with societal values and ethical standards.

Summary

The discussion focussed on the importance of maintaining ethical practices in data science and emerging technologies, addressing both the challenges and strategies for ethical decision-making, accountability, and responsible innovation in rapidly evolving environments.

1. **Creating a Culture of Ethical Data Use**:
   - Ethical data practices must be championed by leadership, with clear guidelines, open communication, and continuous evaluation. It's essential to embed ethical considerations in everyday operations.
   - **Example**: Olay's initiative to address bias in its Skin Advisor System is a proactive example of integrating ethics into data use.
2. **Ethics Training for Data Professionals**:
   - An effective training program tailored to different roles, incorporating real-world scenarios and continuous education, helps data professionals make informed ethical decisions.
   - **Example**: The University of Melbourne's tailored courses in AI ethics equip professionals to implement ethical practices.
3. **Encouraging Accountability at Every Level**:
   - Clear expectations, transparent processes, regular audits, and whistleblower protections are vital to fostering accountability within an organization.
   - **Example**: A financial institution that implemented robust data governance and accountability mechanisms illustrates this strategy's success.
4. **Ethics in Emerging Technologies**:
   - Emerging technologies like AI, ML, and blockchain present ethical challenges related to bias, transparency, privacy, autonomy, and human control.
   - **Examples**: Amazon's AI recruitment tool scrapped for bias, Uber's autonomous vehicle incident, and facial recognition technology raising privacy concerns.
5. **Addressing Future Risks Proactively**:
   - Ethical frameworks, cross-disciplinary collaboration, continuous monitoring, and integrating ethics in education can help manage the risks of emerging technologies.

- **Example**: The European Union's proposed ethical guidelines for AI and MIT's courses in AI ethics.

6. **Sustaining Ethical Integrity in Rapid Change**:
    - Agile governance, ethics-driven innovation, stakeholder engagement, and strong ethical leadership are essential to maintaining ethical integrity during rapid technological change.
    - **Example**: Microsoft's adaptable AI ethics committee, IBM's ethics-driven health innovations, and Patagonia's ethical commitment in sustainability demonstrate how organizations can balance innovation with ethical responsibility.

In conclusion, organizations must adopt a proactive, integrated approach to ethics, aligning their technological advancements with societal values, ensuring that ethical practices are sustained even amidst rapid technological changes.

The path forward for ethical data use in emerging technologies requires organizations to be proactive, adaptable, and committed to continuous improvement. As technology continues to evolve, addressing ethical concerns with foresight, collaboration, and innovation will be crucial to ensuring that new technologies benefit society as a whole while minimizing potential risks. By embedding ethics into every stage of technological development, organizations can build a foundation of trust, accountability, and integrity that will guide them through the rapid changes ahead.

Check your Understanding

Fill-in-the-Blanks Questions

1. Emerging technologies like AI and blockchain raise ethical concerns about __________ and fairness.
2. AI algorithms can perpetuate __________ if they are trained on biased data.
3. The process of ensuring transparency in AI systems is referred to as __________.
4. Autonomous vehicles need to be programmed to prioritize __________ in case of unavoidable accidents.
5. Ethical concerns in blockchain include data __________ and the risk of misuse in illegal activities.
6. Continuous __________ is essential for identifying biases and vulnerabilities in emerging technologies.
7. AI models are often criticized for being __________, meaning their decision-making process is not easily understood.
8. One of the biggest ethical concerns surrounding facial recognition is the violation of __________.
9. To maintain ethical standards, companies should establish __________ to guide the development of new technologies.
10. The implementation of __________ policies ensures that organizations are prepared for the ethical challenges posed by emerging technologies.
11. Data collected by IoT devices can pose risks to __________ if not properly managed.
12. Ethical frameworks for AI include principles such as fairness, __________, and accountability.
13. The rise of __________ technologies challenges traditional legal and regulatory frameworks.
14. Ensuring that new technologies do not harm vulnerable populations is an important aspect of __________ ethics.
15. In autonomous systems, the challenge of maintaining __________ control is a critical ethical issue.
16. Ethical considerations in AI should include the protection of individual __________.

17. Companies can avoid ethical pitfalls by conducting __________ to identify risks in their systems.
18. __________ in ethical decision-making helps organizations address issues proactively rather than reactively.
19. A culture of __________ within organizations encourages adherence to ethical guidelines during technological development.
20. In cases of rapid technological change, organizations must focus on __________ integrity to maintain public trust.

Short Answer Questions

1. What is one ethical concern associated with the use of AI in decision-making?
2. How can blockchain technology be misused from an ethical standpoint?
3. What does "algorithmic fairness" refer to in the context of AI?
4. Why is data privacy a critical concern in emerging technologies?
5. How does transparency in AI systems help build trust with users?
6. What role do audits play in addressing ethical issues in emerging technologies?
7. Define "autonomous systems" and provide one example.
8. What is meant by "bias" in AI, and how can it affect outcomes?
9. Why is continuous monitoring essential for maintaining ethical integrity in new technologies?
10. What is the importance of cross-disciplinary collaboration in addressing ethical concerns in technology?

Long Answer Questions

1. Analyze the ethical implications of using facial recognition technology in public spaces. Consider both security benefits and privacy concerns.
2. Discuss the role of leadership in ensuring that emerging technologies are developed and used ethically. Provide examples of companies that have set ethical standards for their technologies.

3. Evaluate the risks of bias in machine learning algorithms and propose strategies to mitigate these biases in AI systems.
4. Propose a set of ethical guidelines for the development of autonomous vehicles. How can these guidelines ensure safety and fairness?
5. Examine the ethical challenges associated with data privacy in the context of the Internet of Things (IoT). What steps can organizations take to safeguard user data?
6. Discuss the concept of "algorithmic transparency" and explain how it can be achieved in AI systems. How does transparency enhance accountability?
7. Evaluate the need for a global regulatory framework for emerging technologies like AI and blockchain. What challenges would such a framework face in terms of enforcement?
8. Explore the ethical concerns surrounding AI in healthcare. How can healthcare providers ensure that AI technologies are used to enhance patient care while protecting patient rights?
9. Assess the role of ethics in AI and machine learning research. How can researchers be held accountable for the ethical implications of their work?
10. Discuss the importance of maintaining ethical integrity during rapid technological changes. How can organizations balance innovation with ethical considerations?

Answers

Fill-in-the-Blanks

1. bias
2. bias
3. transparency
4. human life
5. security
6. monitoring
7. black-boxed
8. privacy
9. ethical frameworks
10. risk management
11. privacy
12. transparency

13. disruptive
14. social
15. human
16. rights
17. audits
18. proactivity
19. accountability
20. ethical

Answer Keys – Short Answer Questions

1. **Ethical concern in AI decision-making**: One major ethical concern is **bias**, where AI systems can inadvertently perpetuate or amplify biases present in the data they are trained on, leading to unfair decisions.
2. **Misuse of blockchain technology**: Blockchain could be misused for **illegal activities** such as money laundering or trading illicit goods due to its pseudonymous nature and decentralized structure.
3. **Algorithmic fairness in AI**: **Algorithmic fairness** refers to ensuring that AI systems make decisions without bias and treat all individuals or groups equitably, regardless of their characteristics like race, gender, or ethnicity.
4. **Data privacy concern in emerging technologies**: Emerging technologies, especially **IoT** devices, collect sensitive personal data, raising significant concerns about the security of this data and potential breaches that can violate individuals' privacy.
5. **Importance of transparency in AI systems**: **Transparency** in AI helps users understand how decisions are made, building trust in the system and ensuring that the algorithm's decision-making process can be scrutinized for fairness and accountability.
6. **Role of audits in emerging technologies**: Audits in emerging technologies are essential for identifying **risks, biases, and vulnerabilities** in systems, ensuring compliance with ethical standards, and improving the technology's accountability.
7. **Definition and example of autonomous systems**: **Autonomous systems** are machines or technologies capable of performing tasks without human intervention. Example: **self-driving cars**.

8. **Bias in AI**: **Bias** in AI refers to the tendency of an AI model to make unjust or unequal decisions based on skewed or non-representative data. It can affect the **accuracy and fairness** of the AI system.
9. **Continuous monitoring in emerging technologies**: Continuous monitoring ensures that technology systems are **up to date** and remain compliant with ethical standards, identifying issues such as bias or privacy violations in real-time.
10. **Importance of cross-disciplinary collaboration in ethics**: Cross-disciplinary collaboration ensures that emerging technologies are developed and evaluated from diverse perspectives, including **law, sociology, engineering**, and **ethics**, to address all possible ethical concerns comprehensively.

Answer Keys – Long Answer Questions

1. **Ethical implications of facial recognition technology**: The use of facial recognition technology in public spaces raises concerns about **privacy** as it enables constant surveillance without individual consent. While it provides **security benefits**, such as helping law enforcement identify criminals, it can lead to **abuses of power** if used without proper regulation. Additionally, the **accuracy** of these systems can be questioned, especially with **racial and gender bias**, leading to the potential for discriminatory practices. Thus, ethical guidelines must be established to prevent misuse and ensure **accountability**.
2. **Role of leadership in ethical technology development**: Leadership plays a critical role in setting the **ethical tone** of an organization. Leaders must ensure that ethical standards are **integrated into product design**, implementation, and deployment. They must take a proactive approach by establishing clear **ethical frameworks** and encouraging transparency. For example, companies like **Google** and **Microsoft** have adopted ethical AI guidelines that promote fairness, transparency, and accountability, demonstrating how leadership can guide the responsible use of emerging technologies.
3. **Bias in machine learning algorithms and strategies to mitigate it**: Bias in machine learning algorithms arises when training data is **non-representative** or contains inherent biases. This can result in unfair or discriminatory outcomes, particularly when it comes to **gender, race, or socio-economic status**. To mitigate these biases, companies can **diversify**

datasets, ensure **continuous evaluation and auditing**, and implement **bias detection tools**. For instance, **IBM** developed tools that allow developers to monitor and correct biases in AI systems. Addressing bias requires a combination of technological solutions and ethical oversight.

4. **Ethical guidelines for autonomous vehicles**: Autonomous vehicles must adhere to ethical guidelines that prioritize **human life**, safety, and fairness. One key ethical issue is how self-driving cars should make decisions in unavoidable accidents (e.g., should the car prioritize the safety of the driver over pedestrians?). The **ethical guidelines** should include transparency in decision-making, accountability for mistakes, and a clear **commitment to minimizing harm**. Additionally, the deployment of autonomous vehicles should be accompanied by robust **regulations** to ensure their ethical use in real-world scenarios.
5. **Ethical challenges of data privacy in IoT**: The **Internet of Things (IoT)** involves the collection and transmission of vast amounts of personal data through interconnected devices. Ethical challenges related to IoT include **data breaches**, unauthorized data sharing, and the **lack of user consent**. To address these concerns, organizations must implement **strong data protection policies**, ensure that data is **anonymized** where possible, and obtain **explicit consent** from users before collecting personal information. Regulations such as **GDPR** can help enforce strict privacy standards in the IoT sector.
6. **Achieving algorithmic transparency in AI systems**: **Algorithmic transparency** refers to the ability to understand and trace the decision-making processes of AI systems. Achieving transparency can be done by developing **explainable AI** models, where AI decisions are made understandable to humans. This can be done by providing **justifications** for decisions and ensuring that the models are **auditable**. For instance, **Google's AI ethics guidelines** emphasize transparency, ensuring that their AI systems are explainable and accountable to users.
7. **Global regulatory framework for emerging technologies**: A global regulatory framework for emerging technologies, like **AI and blockchain**, could ensure consistent standards across countries, facilitating **ethical development** and reducing misuse. However, this framework would face challenges such as **differences in legal systems**, political will, and enforcement capabilities. Moreover, balancing **innovation** with **ethical**

guidelines can be difficult, as regulatory bodies must ensure that they do not stifle technological progress while still enforcing necessary safeguards.

8. **Ethical concerns in AI for healthcare**: AI in healthcare offers the potential for improved **diagnosis**, **personalized medicine**, and **efficiency**. However, ethical issues such as **patient privacy**, **data security**, and the **fairness** of algorithmic decisions must be addressed. AI models must be trained on **diverse datasets** to avoid biases in diagnosis or treatment recommendations. Healthcare providers should ensure **transparency** in AI decision-making and maintain strong **data protection protocols** to safeguard patient confidentiality and trust.
9. **Ethics in AI and machine learning research**: Researchers in AI and machine learning must be mindful of the ethical implications of their work. They should adhere to **ethical research guidelines**, **promote fairness**, and prioritize **transparency**. Researchers can be held accountable by participating in **peer reviews**, adhering to ethical codes of conduct, and ensuring that their algorithms do not perpetuate bias or inequality. Collaboration with **ethicists** is essential to assess the potential social impact of AI innovations and ensure responsible development.
10. **Sustaining ethical integrity in rapid technological changes**: To sustain ethical integrity in the face of rapid technological advancements, organizations must embed ethics into their **organizational culture** and ensure that **decision-making** processes account for the potential social consequences of new technologies. Leaders should encourage **open discussions** about ethical concerns and create structures for ongoing **evaluation and accountability**. Additionally, ethics-driven innovation can be maintained by adopting **agile governance** frameworks that adapt quickly to new challenges while ensuring that ethical principles remain at the core of technological progress.

Glossary of Ethical and Technical Terms

Adversarial Debiasing

A technique used during model training that employs adversarial networks to reduce the model's ability to learn biased patterns by penalizing it for predictions that rely on sensitive attributes.

Algorithmic Bias

Systematic and repeatable errors in a computer system that create unfair outcomes, often privileging one group over others due to the influence of biased data or model design.

Bias Audit

A formal process used to evaluate datasets and predictive models for potential biases, including unfair treatment across demographic groups or unintended discriminatory patterns.

Calibration by Group

A post-processing method that adjusts predicted probabilities so that predictions are accurate and fair across different demographic groups.

Demographic Parity

A fairness metric requiring that the outcome (e.g., positive classification) is equally distributed across groups, regardless of their actual outcomes or attributes.

Equalized Odds

A fairness criterion that requires equal false positive and false negative rates for different groups, ensuring similar model performance across demographics.

Ethical AI

A framework for developing artificial intelligence systems that prioritize fairness, accountability, transparency, and respect for human rights.

Exclusion Bias

A type of bias that arises when certain relevant data points or groups are omitted from a dataset, resulting in incomplete or skewed model performance.

Exploratory Data Analysis (EDA)

A data analysis approach used to summarize and visualize the main characteristics of a dataset, often as a first step to uncover patterns, trends, or potential biases.

Fairness Constraints

Rules or parameters introduced during model training to ensure that fairness metrics are considered in the model's optimization process.

Fairness Metrics

Quantitative measures used to assess how equitably a machine learning model treats different groups. Common metrics include demographic parity, equalized odds, and predictive parity.

Historical Bias

Bias embedded in historical data due to past inequalities or discriminatory practices, which can be perpetuated by models trained on such data.

In-processing Techniques

Fairness interventions applied during model training, including modifying the learning algorithm to reduce bias or add fairness objectives.

Individual Fairness

A fairness concept that ensures individuals who are similar in relevant aspects receive similar outcomes from a model.

Label Bias

Bias introduced during the labeling process, often due to subjective or prejudiced decisions made by human annotators.

Measurement Bias

Bias caused by inaccuracies or inconsistencies in the tools or methods used to collect data, leading to unreliable or distorted inputs.

Predictive Parity

A fairness metric requiring that different groups have equal predictive performance, such as precision or positive predictive value.

Post-processing Techniques

Adjustments made after a model has been trained to correct or mitigate biased outcomes in its predictions.

Pre-processing Techniques

Methods applied to data before model training to reduce bias, such as re-sampling, re-weighting, or data augmentation to ensure representativeness.

Sampling Bias

Occurs when the sample used to train a model is not representative of the population, leading to skewed or unfair predictions.

Sensitive Attributes

Characteristics such as race, gender, age, or disability status that are protected by law or considered ethically important to monitor for fairness.

Transparency

The practice of making model design, data sources, decision-making logic, and potential impacts visible and understandable to stakeholders.

Unfair Discrimination

Occurs when individuals or groups are treated unequally by a model due to biased data or design, without a justifiable reason related to performance or relevance.

www.ingramcontent.com/pod-product-compliance
Ingram Content Group UK Ltd.
Pitfield, Milton Keynes, MK11 3LW, UK
UKHW062007290726
14090UKWH00022B/1439